"I'm just a guy who makes movies."

CLINT

A RETROSPECTIVE
BY RICHARD SCHICKEL

PALAZZO

This edition published in Great Britain in 2014 by

PALAZZO EDITIONS LTD
2 Wood Street
Bath, BA1 2JQ
United Kingdom

www.palazzoeditions.com

Design and layout © 2012, 2014 Palazzo Editions Ltd
Text © 2011, 2012, 2014 Richard Schickel
Please see picture credits on page 296 for image
copyright information

Publishing Director: Colin Webb
Art Director: Terry Jeavons
Managing Editor: Sonya Newland

A CIP catalogue record for this book is available from
the British Library

ISBN 978-0-9571483-6-9

Printed and bound in China by Imago

OPENING PAGE The apprentice actor ready for action.
TITLE PAGE The compelling poster art for *Dirty Harry*, 1971.
CONTENTS PAGE Clint on set for *Dirty Harry*.

CONTENTS

Introduction

"Don't look back. Something might be gaining on you." Satchel Paige, the great Negro Leagues baseball pitcher, once offered this as some sage advice. It's a bit of wisdom I've followed most of my life. I've left the retrospectives to other people, who may or may not have a better perspective on what I've done or left undone.

I was lucky in that film didn't claim my undivided attention until I'd had the chance to do a little bit of living; I was twenty-five years old before playing my first big part, twenty-eight when I got steady work on the television western, Rawhide, *which kept "rollin', rollin', rollin'" for seven years. Those long apprentice years were a great learning experience; learning about the nuts and bolts of moviemaking and, more importantly, I began to discover what I wanted to do and not do.*

Mostly, I learned to trust my own instincts. How else can you explain the decision to go off to Italy and Spain to make a spaghetti western called A Fistful of Dollars, *the surprise success of which established the possibility of my making more feature films? At the time, I wasn't thinking about that. I just thought it would be a fun way to spend my summer hiatus from* Rawhide. *Besides, I'd never been to Europe. I thought I might learn something about how they make movies in foreign countries.*

I don't want to pretend that I lacked ambition or that I allowed myself in those days to be blown this way or that by what people were offering me. In particular, I was eager to direct. I saw that the director was at the center of the filmmaking process, not just one of the components in it, as an actor is, and that appealed to me. Which does not mean that I imagined someday I would be making Unforgiven, Mystic River, Million Dollar Baby, *or any of the other pictures that the critics and the public have responded*

7

to favorably in recent years. I'm obviously an American director. Which means that, like my colleagues, my roots are in genre moviemaking. For me, genre conventions add a certain strength to the movies. At the same time, they offer the possibility of creating variations on their basic themes, a chance to refresh the film in question, making it new for the audience and for me.

Don Siegel, my directorial mentor, always used to say that analysis leads to paralysis, and I agree with him one hundred percent. On the other hand, Don always tried to make the process of creating a film very rational. He left nothing to chance; he planned his shoots and his shots, carefully, sensibly, and efficiently. And that's what I've always tried to do, too. I just don't believe in wasting other people's time and money. I certainly don't believe in ratcheting up everybody's anxiety when the goal is simply to make the best movie possible. We try to make an atmosphere that is relaxed, good-humored, and anxiety-free.

Looking back, I suppose I've made a few pictures I probably shouldn't have. But you don't know that going in. I've always said that I have no idea whether a movie is going to be a success. My criteria when committing to a picture are simple: is it something I'd like to work on or I'd like to see? So far, that's worked out very well. I've been able to work a very long time at something I love doing and see no reason to stop. I've seen more of the world than I ever imagined. I've worked with people it has been a joy and a privilege to know. And done at least a few films that I'm very proud of and hope will have some life beyond my own. Finally, I hope this "retrospective" will be out of date almost as soon as it's published. I can't say now, any more than I could have at the beginning, that the best is yet to come. But I hope that's true. And I mean to keep working toward that end.

Clint Eastwood

OPPOSITE A portrait taken for *Parade* in 1992 by Eddie Adams, the acclaimed Vietnam War photographer.

8

The Whole Ride

1. **I like seeing Clint enter a restaurant. Or wait—let me refine that statement—I like *not* seeing him enter a restaurant. He takes a certain pride in the fact that he knows the back way into every banquet room in Los Angeles—you know, enter the service door, proceed through the kitchen, mount the back stairs, find your way to the green room, there to amiably await presentation of whatever award is about to be bestowed on you. It's the same way with eateries; he seems to know all the side doors in town.**

So here he is—smiling pleasantly—ready to settle down to his fish, pasta, or chicken, with maybe a beer or a glass of white wine, and an agreeable, often lengthy, always agenda-free conversation. The reason for these coolly evasive tactics is simple—to avoid the paparazzi and the shoal of fans who generally gather with them. It seems slightly to puzzle him that, as he approaches eighty, he remains the object of their attention. Haven't they had enough of him by this time?

I've been with him when, despite his best efforts, they surround him. Generally, he's pleasant with them—he knows most of them by sight—signing autographs, politely rejecting their gifts (things like old *Rawhide* comic books, in which he has no interest), staying on the move until he breaks free. On the other hand, I've occasionally seen him get angry with them: "Listen, you sonovabitch, this is the third time I've seen you today. Enough."

Sometimes he becomes proactive. One time we were doing a Q&A at UCLA and they caught him in the parking lot after our appearance. He edged toward his old, impeccably maintained Mercedes, gave me a nod (we were going to join a friend for lunch), and took off, the photographers in hot pursuit. That's something he sometimes enjoys, speeding through the streets, up alleys, through parking lots, losing the tailing mob. He arrived at lunch with an amused account of his shrewdly improvised evasive tactics.

Clint's taste for just sort of popping up, unannounced and unexplained, has occasionally been reflected in movies like *High Plains Drifter* and *Pale Rider*, in which he played apparitional figures, very likely ghosts (although he has always avoided a forthright admission of that identification). But no matter what the film, he has never been a big fan of back stories, especially for his own character. He also says audiences like movies that are open-ended. A mystery solved is a mystery forgotten; a mystery not fully resolved has the potential to haunt you for a long time.

His air of good-natured mystery is, of course, a way of maintaining privacy, although, in Clint's case, it also helps if you're six feet three inches, widely (if erroneously) suspected of packing a .44 Magnum, and are armed with a lifetime's wiliness when it comes to dodging semi-psychotic admirers. But that's quintessential Clint. On any occasion short of the Oscars, he drives himself everywhere, *sans* security. And this may be why he has so many homes—six of them last time I counted—all (save Los Angeles) in communities that take a benignly protective interest in defending his right of free passage. In Carmel, his main residence, he goes to the movies with his wife and kids just like regular folks.

OPPOSITE Clint accepts the Lifetime Achievement Award from the Directors Guild of America in 2006.

The habit of restlessness was ingrained in him early. When he was a kid his family wandered up and down the West Coast as his father sought what work he could find in Depression America. It made for a tight-knit family, which is the source of his basic values, but it was also hard on Clint—a shy lad not entirely comfortable as the perpetual new kid in class—and it may be the source of his screen character's most basic element: from as far back as *A Fistful of Dollars*, his first spaghetti western, he has so often been the guy who just sort of drifts into town, encounters some ordinary people oppressed by some kind of evil, helps sets things to right, and then departs without explanation.

On the other hand, he is in his nature an orderly man, maintaining a pace and a demeanor that have remained unchanged in the thirty-three years I've known him. I suspect that's also a product of his childhood, when he probably wished for the more settled existence that the Eastwoods did not achieve until they finally rooted themselves in Oakland when Clint was a teenager. "Straight strands," is a phrase he uses when he talks about moviemaking—stories and characters moving along a fated path, even when that path is, for a time, hidden from the audience. He has a lot of faith in fate—in the way it quietly tugs people along.

Not that he has ever seemed to me to be an enigma to himself. He knows who he is, and he knows what he means to the ever-watching world. But still his habitual garb is a polo shirt, chinos, and sneakers, his usual pace an ambling one, his usual expression a shy and watchful smile. A friend of ours was once being questioned by the press about some non-issue and a couple of reporters called Clint for a comment. "How do you want me to play it?" he asked our pal, "Smart or dumb?" It seemed obvious to both of us that the latter option was the one Clint preferred. My guess is that quite a few Hollywood sharpsters have been lulled, if not gulled, by Clint's amiably questioning air. If nothing else, it amuses him.

It amuses me as well. We met at the home of mutual friends in the summer of 1976, not long after he released *The Outlaw Josey Wales*, a movie I liked a lot and had reviewed favorably. My first impression was of a composed, thoughtful man, with no interest in dominating the room. He listened, contributed comfortably to the conversation, and seemed interested in meeting a movie critic, in those days kind of an odd bird for him. Back then he was not good in his formal encounters with the press. He was shy and, I think, somewhat uncomfortable about his lack of formal education (a semester at a community college). But he's a man who works hard on what he perceives as his shortcomings and he's become, over the years, quite a good interview.

In the years that followed we would sometimes have lunch together when he was in New York or I was in Los Angeles. These visits were not always coincident with the release of a new movie by him—which rendered him unique among moviemakers, whom you always heard from when they had a new picture coming out and never in between. It seems significant to me that I can't remember a thing we talked about—that's how casual our encounters were. But, for the record, we became friends.

2. What I most remember about those early days were some lunches we shared in Los Angeles. Clint kept on the lot a junker car that had somehow escaped demolition in one of his pictures, and he liked sputtering around in it—to a hamburger joint in an insalubrious neighborhood in downtown LA that someone had recommended, to a chili parlor in the deeper reaches of the Valley (he was less choosy about his diet in those days). The countermen and customers recognized him, of course, but with no more than a widening of the eyes, maybe a nod of the head. There has always been, I think, a tacit acknowledgment among a substantial portion of his audience that he is one of them—a working-class guy with no need to elude that identity. Or make a big deal of it, either.

OPPOSITE A rare photograph as new romantic, taken by Jack Robinson for *Vogue*, 1969.

Offhand, I can only think of one movie, *White Hunter Black Heart*, where he played against that type, and I think the fact that he works so steadily is reassuring to this crowd. You have a job, you do a job—and lucky you for having one that's more interesting and rewarding than mine. "I'm just a guy who makes movies," he once said, and they like that idea, especially since he famously makes them frugally, efficiently, unpretentiously, and without a lot of tedious self-reflection.

Clint was at an interesting point in his career when he made *Josey Wales*. The apprentice years—mostly in small parts—were long gone. But not forgotten, especially by him. Looking back on them he has often reflected that tall, sandy-haired, and shy, he was the wrong physical type for stardom as it was then defined. Leading men in those days were darker and more authoritative in manner, more openly romantic. I've often thought that Clint came to his present eminence from further back in the pack than almost anyone else in the race; there was nothing overnight in his stardom. But he had persevered, digging many a swimming pool to support himself and his wife, Maggie, and had been rewarded with his long-running role as Rowdy Yates on *Rawhide*, which, in turn, had led to the spaghetti westerns that made him, if not quite a star, then star eligible, by transforming his native shyness into something a little more edgy and ironic.

As of 1976 it had been eight years since he played in the last of the spaghetti westerns and he had made fifteen American movies, mostly at Universal, where he was then headquartered. These films included his first directorial effort, the deliciously scary *Play Misty for Me*, as well as the underappreciated *The Beguiled* (directed by Don Siegel), both strange, dark studies in male sexual carelessness and female revenge against the casually questing cock. They had made him a force to be reckoned with in the industry.

But Clint was restive at Universal—he says because he hated the intrusion of the studio tour trams on his life, though I suspect the chilly factory-like atmosphere of the place was also a factor. So when his friend and lawyer, Frank Wells, became part of the management team at hard-pressed Warner Bros. (the others were the wildly funny and smart John Calley and the former agent, Ted Ashley) he was receptive to their overtures. He had worked on the lot a few times during his apprentice years and found it "homey." As a movie-going kid he'd loved James Cagney,—"a fearless kind of actor; he just seemed to dive in"—and Bogart, especially noticing his comically unflattering, character-driven haircuts in movies like *High Sierra* and *The Treasure of the Sierra Madre*.

But the main thing was that Warner Bros. had by now acquired a script he'd been tracking—*Dirty Harry*. Clint was by this time a star, no question about that, but *Dirty Harry* made him a superstar—no question about that either, even if Pauline Kael had launched her lifelong anti-Eastwood crusade by calling it "a fascist masterpiece." He's always said he didn't mind the controversy. What worried him was being stuck in a box. He might have thought, as he said to me recently, "Westerns were successful for me, so I'll just do westerns. Cop dramas were successful; I can just do cop dramas and call it a day. Have a nice little series somewhere and have the paycheck and a few beers and a nice life." Pause. "But that wasn't enough. Personally, it wasn't enough."

In particular, he was determined—long before *Play Misty for Me*—to be a director. An actor, in his word, was just a "component" in the picture-making process. And he saw in that profession the potential for boredom. A lot of actors, he says, "just get vacuumed into a certain genre and they just don't want to do it any more; they get tired of wearing Kleenex on their collars."

Implicit in Warner Bros.' wooing was the promise of taking greater responsibility for his own destiny as a director-producer. Not that it was put so bluntly. He just said, in effect, "No tours, right," and came over. "It was a one-day deal," he says about moving into the little Spanish

bungalow—forever known as "The Taco Bell"—which had once been Dolores Costello's dressing room, Harry Warner's and Steve McQueen's office. There he has abided these many years, with—a few coats of paint and a couple of new posters aside—the place fundamentally unchanged—the Hollywood habit of letting wives and girlfriends impressively redecorate the office firmly avoided.

Josey Wales was the first product of Clint's new Warner deal. Like almost all of his movies it is firmly rooted in genre tradition; it is self-evidently a western. And its title character is self-evidently an Eastwood character—a taciturn loner wandering a wilderness. Bitterly so, since Civil War border raiders have burned out his farm and killed his family. But, slowly—and this is what makes the film memorable—a surrogate family accretes around him—an Indian chief and a rather mysterious Indian woman, a waiflike woman (played by Sondra Locke, whose long relationship with Clint began here) and her grandmother, among others. There's even a stray hound. Whereupon, a recurring Eastwood trope takes over: they're a needy, disorganized bunch which, given his omnicompetence in the ways of the West, he organizes, in the process losing his surly ways, returning eventually to his former self as a peaceable father-figure.

Josey Wales is a spacious movie, rather calm in its development, though with enough gunplay to satisfy Clint's most loyal following. And his fondness for it is abiding. "I think it's as good as *Unforgiven*," he once said to me. "It's just that maybe the timing was wrong, some people weren't quite ready for it." By "those people" he means the critics (the film was a box-office success), who still saw his Leone movies as exercises in brutality, instead of what they were—witty rejuvenations of a weary genre—and still found Harry Callahan beyond their polite pale. They would, as we all know, eventually come around. In the meantime Clint would revert to the movie's main theme endlessly—in pictures as diverse as *Bronco Billy* and *Pale Rider*, as recent as *Million Dollar Baby* and *Gran Torino*.

3. Harry Callahan had been the negative take on his basic family-friendly spirit, a radical loner since the death of his wife, a workaholic with maybe a beer and a slice of stale pizza waiting in the fridge when he returns, late at night, to his soulless apartment. It was that aspect of his character, more than his views on the Miranda Decision (and other court cases that expanded the rights of criminals at the expense of their victims), that Clint insists drew him to the character. In a sense, he was every convenience-store clerk with no life outside his paltry job. Except, of course, Harry's job was not paltry. It has its plodding moments, but it was also intermittently exciting, and in his relationship with San Francisco's municipal bureaucracy, it gave him plenty of "take this job and shove it" moments, in which he enacted the most deeply satisfying fantasy of his stuck-in-grade audience.

I take *Dirty Harry*—superbly directed by Don Siegel, Clint's go-to director and always warmly acknowledged mentor in those days—and its second sequel, *The Enforcer*—the movie in which he briefly finds love with the chunky, earnest, and entirely adorable Tyne Daly—to be completely serious and rewarding movies in the best populist tradition, blending painfully human issues with a completely satisfying action format. "I probably made one or two more of those than I should have," Clint later admitted, but the films were always profitable and making them was a way of maintaining his comfortable relationship with his Warner Bros. bosses.

As we all know, that's a handshake deal—with each project set up on its own terms, though typically Clint foregoes substantial front money in return for heavy and immediate backend participation in the grosses. A recent unauthorized biography describes Clint in its title as an

"American Rebel," which is essentially nonsensical. Like many great movie careers (think Alfred Hitchcock or Howard Hawks), his is based on maintaining non-rebellious relationships with his studio.

He works so fast and frugally that it's almost impossible for the studio to lose money on his films. Nonetheless, he always tells the executives, as he puts it, "I can't guarantee you a big-selling movie. The only thing I can do is try to make a movie you'll be proud to have your shield on at the beginning of the picture."

That, though, is not quite the end of the matter. "If somebody is putting up money for you to make a movie, there's no reason to get disrespectful about it. You want to do the best you can for the scenes. That doesn't mean you cut out scenes just because they're too expensive," he muses. "But at least you don't waste stuff. You don't shoot a lot of stuff you're not going to use, or re-shoot the scenes because you did them wrong in the first place". In other words, know what you want to do, do it efficiently, and move on confidently.

This is a truly radical statement. Think back on the reams of reportage you've read over the decades, in which directors and studios have publicly fought over the production and presentation of films, the numbers of movies that have been ripped from their auteur hands and re-cut by the studio. Think, too, about all legendary, career-ending cost overruns on pictures ranging from *Cleopatra* to *Heaven's Gate*. Think also about a guy who has brought all his pictures in ahead of schedule and under budget. Then think about Clint's thirty-five years at Warner Bros.—the longest-standing actor-director relationship with a single studio in the history of the movies, one that encompasses one-third of the history of the medium itself—and you are truly thinking outside any of the narrow historical boxes into which we attempt to cram our understanding of the movie past.

4. In those first Warner Bros. years, "he was pretty much carrying us on his back," says John Calley, which led him to put a nearly blind trust in Clint's instincts. The word around town at the time was that Clint and the studio were operating on a "one for me, one for them" basis. But it was a little more complicated than that. Or maybe we should say that it was a lot less calculated. Setting aside most of the *Dirty Harry* sequels and a few other pictures, Clint has never been a developer of ideas. He's not one to spend a lot of time meeting with writers and going over draft after draft of a script. More-or-less finished screenplays have a way of drifting in his direction. He reads them and quickly makes up his mind—in the case of *Bronco Billy*, while it lay open on an assistant's desk. "I thought I'd give it four or five pages," he recalls, but "I finished the whole thing right there at the desk." I guess you could say that it was for "him," in that it did not make a lot of money for the studio, and that it explored, in a comical way, the *Josey Wales* family-building theme.

It has been said that the script for *Every Which Way But Loose* (that's the one about Clint's even dimmer Philo Beddoe playing opposite Clyde, the orangutan) came to Clint in the hope he would pass it on to his friend, Burt Reynolds, who had just had a $100 million success with *Smokey and the Bandit*. Clint, however, snaffled it for himself, much to the dismay of the studio and all his closest advisors. I think he sensed it was time to subject his macho image to some ribbing. Calley was almost alone in backing him. "If he wants to make a movie about a monkey, let him," he remembers thinking. "If he told me to date a monkey, I'd do it." There was a screening for the studio brass, at which the word "unreleasable" was murmured, with Calley dissenting. "Someone's going to make a lot of money on this picture," he said. And so they did. It became Clint's biggest grosser to date.

So a picture that in profitable retrospect looks like one "for them" was, in fact, one for "him." Indeed, what may be the best movie he made in the late 1970s and early 1980s, *Escape from Alcatraz*, was not made at Warner Bros. Director Don Siegel controlled Richard Tuggle's screenplay, and had fallen out with Warner Bros. and, to a degree, with Clint. It had something to do with Clint's rise in status since they had made the first of their five films together and Siegel's feeling that their relationship, in which he had been a mentoring figure, had shifted. That got patched up over a beer and a sandwich—Clint speaks often of Siegel, and always with great affection—but the film was made for Paramount.

In the eight years after *Josey Wales*, Clint made ten movies, almost all of them highly entertaining, many of them a little bit eccentric, and most of them commercially successful. Of the lot, only one, *Firefox*—which represented a reversion to the weightless, big-scale adventure mode of his old *Where Eagles Dare* manner—is entirely uninteresting. But one of them, *Honkytonk Man*, the least expensive and least profitable of the ten, deserves special attention. It's a Thirties period piece about an alcoholic and tubercular country-and-western singer named Red Stoval, who, after a lifetime of passing the hat in roadhouses, has an offer to audition for the Grand Ole Opry. With his fourteen-year-old nephew (played very well by Clint's son, Kyle) as driver and conscience, he hits the road for Nashville. They have many comic adventures before they arrive at their destination, where an onstage coughing fit spoils Red's chances for success (though he does record some songs that, the movie implies, may grant him a sliver of mortality).

The picture was largely ill-received—people were not ready for Clint to be quite so antiheroic—though I remain deeply fond of it. But that's not the point. One of the questions that tugs at Clint's mind is self-destructiveness—a matter he would return to in a more somber spirit in *Bird* six years later. Verna Bloom, who played Red's sister in *Honkytonk Man*, once said to me that she thought Red was what Clint might have been like had he been a failure—amiable, restless, capable of good work that goes largely unseen, and with a core of integrity visible only to a few. Clint wonders: are such men so afraid of failure that they unconsciously will it? Or is it the possibility of success that spooks them?

Whatever the case, he says, "I'd be shaking them and saying, 'Hey, you've got something great going here, don't wreck it.'" On the other hand, he's a fatalist. He believes—and not solely about fuck-up musicians—that irresistible and generally inexplicable forces control our lives, and that no amount of well-intentioned shaking can change the courses we choose. I think this may be why he doesn't usually develop films from scratch. Fate puts a script in his path, he senses its value and he goes with it. "I sort of like Bill Goldman's idea: 'nobody knows anything.'"

I asked him once if he had ever indulged in lengthy ratiocination before embracing a project. He groped through memory for a long moment and then said he'd hesitated over *In the Line of Fire*. He liked the script but, having just directed and starred in *Unforgiven*, didn't want to do double duty again. He proposed hiring another director (Wolfgang Petersen, as it turned out). So the deal was done. And how long did this delay extend? "Oh, a few days."

5. In the late 1970s and early 1980s Clint began to amass the mind-boggling grosses that are one crude measure of his achievements: $1.8 billion at the home box office, $2.3 billion worldwide, with close to a half billion more in video sales. These figures do not count the takings from non-Warner Bros. films or from ancillary rights, or the recent grosses on *Gran Torino* or *Invictus*, the former probably being, dollar-in, dollar-out, his most profitable production.

Not that we've ever discussed anything as vulgar as money. Once, more than a decade ago, he did allow that he probably had enough to "coast it on out," though coasting was not an activity that was then, or is now, high on his agenda. Indeed, he has expressed "great wonderment" as to why "Billy Wilder and Frank Capra and a lot of wonderful directors gave out in their sixties." Sure, he says, they had some "bad ones" in their later careers, "but, you know, they had bad ones along the way when they were in their heydays, too. But you go ahead, you continue on"—like John Huston, "making good pictures right up to the end, even from a wheelchair with an oxygen mask on."

Not that anyone ever expects to see Clint—who may be the fittest man of his age on the planet—in that condition. In part that's because he's not a *writer*-director. Writing, especially for the aging, is in some ways the hardest part of filmmaking because of its emotional, as opposed to physical, toll. More important by far is that he keeps his professional life radically stripped down, which enables him to focus his concentration on the step-by-step process of making a movie which, if you don't allow yourself egotistical distractions—deal-making, status-mongering, publicity-hungering—is, or should be, a comparatively straightforward one. It's the simple secret of his on-time, under-budget schedules. And, of course, it's the reason why he's been able to make so many movies in comparison to his peers.

It also relieves the pressure on individual films. If you make only one movie every three or four years, it quickly falls into the "long-awaited" category, raising studio, critical, and audience expectations to a sometimes unsatisfiable level. If you make one or more a year you can afford to say, "All right, that one didn't go over so well. Fine. How do you like the new one?"

He once challenged Joe Hyams, the shrewd and literate Warner Bros. vice-president, who subtly masterminded Clint's public relations for a couple of decades, to name ten Clark Gable movies, which, of course, he could not. Clint's point was that, in the movies' classic age, the idea was to remain an inescapable presence in the public's eye, which required a certain fecundity on the star's part. They would, he thought, tolerate the not-so-hot more patiently than they would long absences from their gaze.

So in the late Seventies and early Eighties he kept busy. As I've implied—and always excepting *Escape from Alcatraz*—I liked his unpretentious little films best—the orangutan movies, *Bronco Billy*, *Honkytonk Man*; they seemed to express the Clint I had come to know more clearly than his more muscular adventures. Then, in 1984, came *Tightrope*, at which point, as Hyams once said to me, "my job became much easier." Clint played a New Orleans detective named Wes Block, pursuing a sexually kinky killer—and discovering that, in milder form, he shared some of the criminal's *outré* tastes. It's explicable—Wes has endured a bitter divorce, has custody of his children (one of whom was played by Clint's daughter, Alison), and is full of unexpressed anger at womankind. That problem works itself out fairly easily when he meets a sympathetic social worker (Geneviève Bujold). But at least some critics picked up on the fact that, within the confines of a genre film, Clint was playing a rather curious character.

Usually, in the movies, a rogue (if eventually salvageable) cop's sin is more like Harry Callahan's; he's prone to deploying "excessive force" in his investigations, not to handcuffing hookers to the bedstead. Clint plays Wes as a man of considerable sweetness when the blackness is not upon him; we understand his aberration to be a temporary one. But still—when had a star actor even touched upon this kind of darkness? "It was fun to play," Clint says mildly, noting that by this time Dirty Harry had become a little bit boring to play. Hyams, however, was more enthused. He took out an ad in *The New York Review of Books*, quoting extensively from the film's excellent reviews.

In the eight years that followed, leading up to *Unforgiven*, the line between Clint's genre work and his more overtly aspiring films became more blurred. In *Pale Rider*, for instance, he was a gunfighter riding to the *Shane*-like rescue of the beleaguered families of a mining community. But he was also, so we were led to believe, a ghost, albeit one with a taste for whiskey and lonely women and, in his guise as an itinerant preacher, not what you would call a wildly enthusiastic Gospel spieler. In *Heartbreak Ridge* he's a marine drill sergeant, hilariously spouting obscenities at his troops, yet equally hilarious as a befuddled husband trying to woo back his ex-wife (Marsha Mason). To that end he puzzles over women's magazines that extol the virtues of the new, more sensitive male. "Did we mutually nurture one another?" he inquires of Mason. "Hell," she unimprovably replies, "I thought we were married."

6. These movies—along with *Bird* (1988) and *White Hunter Black Heart* (1990)—constitute the beginnings of Clint more or less consciously questioning most of the commonly held premises of American masculinity.

It was a topic that had been tugging at his mind for a long time. When he was a young actor he had been a member of a talent program at Universal, playing small roles and studying acting. The studio was not looking for character players; it was looking for potential stars. To that end he was constantly advised to play "ballsy." It was an expression Clint claims never to have heard, even during his army service. "Walk into the commissary like you own it," people would say to him, and he would think, "But I don't own it." Or they'd say, "Come in and kick the wall down," and he'd think that wasn't exactly what the script called for. "I've always felt you didn't have to take a pill for manhood," he says and relates an anecdote about meeting the retired, undefeated heavyweight champion, Rocky Marciano. "He didn't try to break my hand or anything. It was a very gentle handshake, almost like a woman's. He didn't have to show me anything; he knew who he was."

It's the way Clint was raised. His father was "a very gentle person, but he always taught respect for my mother and the family unit meant a lot to him. He was no pushover. He was quite the opposite. I grew up around men like that, who never had any particular doubts about themselves."

Is there a QED here? I think so. But, perhaps, with a footnote. There is something uncomplicated in the way the Eastwoods took care of one another. Yet in their peripatetic years, they were, economically at least, hard-pressed. And Clint has to have felt that insecurity. It is why, I think, Clint's characters so often ride to the rescue of impoverished but always decent families, people who are puzzled and damaged by the failures of their dreams. I think it's why his personal manner is so self-effacing. As we speak he fixes me with a sober glance. "We're not acting now," he says. "We're being in regular life. So be a regular guy."

This brings us to *Bird* and his attitude toward irregular guys like Charlie Parker, which is an ambiguous mix of love and impatience. He was clearly a hero of Clint's jazz-addled adolescence— Clint's family was musical, with his mother being his first piano teacher—a man doing amazing things with his alto saxophone, but also "a self-destruct." He adds: "The only time I have resentment is when somebody destroys their talent." He compares Bird to Art Tatum, who was ninety percent blind, and overcame his handicap to become "this fabulous genius on the piano." *Bird* offers no explanation for Parker's "crime." It just mournfully accepts it. If there's any joy in this very dark movie, it derives from its portrait of Bird's world. "They were playing for themselves. If you wanted to listen, fine, if you didn't that was fine, too. It wasn't a show-bizzy deal like pop music is now, where there are lights and costumes and a lot of things that are important to the act besides

the music. They just stood up and performed." It is, I can't resist saying, the attitude you find on an Eastwood set—good-humored, open to riffing, but moving quietly along. (Clint doesn't even say "Roll 'em" at the beginning of a take or "Cut" at the end of it; it's more likely "Whenever you're ready" at the beginning, "Okay" at the end.)

Bird was respectfully received, and as Clint had openly predicted to the studio, no big box-office winner. The same was true of *White Hunter Black Heart* in 1990. There was grumbling about Clint's attempt to imitate John Huston's accent, which was actually pretty decent, but off-putting to his fans, as "John Wilson" distractedly attempts to direct *The African Queen* when his mind is more set on killing an elephant. That's largely a fiction invented by Peter Viertel, the Huston pal who worked on the screenplay and wrote a novel about the experience. What really bugged people was Clint's playing against type, as the piss-elegant Huston, focusing on his Purdy shotguns, pussy, and fine dining; and, of course, bent on killing one of the noblest creatures on the planet.

As Wilson admits, it's more than a crime, it's a sin—and it's grand-scale sinning that primarily interests Wilson. He gets his shot—and funks it, causing the death of his native guide. He is last seen slumped in his director's chair, rolling his film's first shot. Was it simple cowardice that led to his downfall? Or was it an inability, in the end, to commit the acknowledged sin? The picture doesn't say. And Clint still doesn't say. He notes mildly that he's never shot at any living thing and doesn't quite understand the impulse to do so. "I just feel they're here, too, so what's the use of shooting something you don't need to survive?" (Clint is a fiscal conservative and subject to grumble fits about intrusive government, but on social issues ranging from gun control to abortion rights he is a liberal—or maybe I should say a libertarian of a non-intrusive kind. He equably tolerates my heavy smoking and once or twice I've even lured him into drinking a Martini.)

7. These movies were part of a mild downturn in Clint's career as he approached and entered his sixties (let us not discuss *Pink Cadillac*, *The Rookie*, or the last *Dirty Harry* sequel, *The Dead Pool*, here). He blames this, in part, on the unavailability of good, open-market scripts, and I once asked him if he was worried about his career during this passage. "No," came the reply. "I figured there are always people willing to take a chance on you if you were fairly well established. Look at Brando in his later years."

But he knew he had an ace in the hole. Or as he once put it to me, "A nice little gold watch in my pocket. I'd take it out sometimes and kind of look at it and rub it a little bit." We're talking, of course, about *Unforgiven*. The story is by now well known: how the script, at the time under option to Francis Coppola, had been submitted to him as a sample of David Webb Peoples' work, how Clint acquired it after Coppola's option ran out, how he decided to sit on it for years, he said because he needed to be a little older to play William Munny, the tormented hero, and I think also, perhaps, because it offered him a hedge against adversity. Some of his intimates knew about the property and occasionally wondered impatiently when Clint was going to get to it. The moment arrived in 1991—not without a small hiccup.

Clint thought perhaps some rewrites might be in order, and Peoples said fine. "He was just anxious to have it made because it had been sitting around for many years. So, I started writing and writing, fooling with things, changing things. And all of a sudden I realized I was wrecking it. So I called him up and I said, 'Forget what I said. I'm just going to shoot it the way it is. I'm killing it with improvements.'" It was the first Eastwood script I read before the picture was made and I remember saying, "Well, if you don't screw it up, it's going to be your masterpiece."

By this time I was living in LA and Clint had narrated a television documentary I made, and we had taken to seeing each other more frequently. I hinted to Joe Hyams that I would like to make a film about Clint's production—not something he had previously encouraged. But earlier that summer my wife died suddenly and, although Clint and I have never discussed this matter, I've always believed he approved the idea because he thought I needed a change, a distraction from grief. I've always been silently grateful for that gesture, for working in the deeper reaches of the Canadian West turned out to be a wonderful recuperative experience for me, and my little film turned out all right as well. As, of course, did *Unforgiven*.

Not that anyone saw it coming. Clint played it very low key, though he did cast better-known actors—Gene Hackman, Morgan Freeman, Richard Harris—to costar with him than was his habit. But I remember that in its summer preview piece the *Los Angeles Times* briefly mentioned the picture as a routine western and characterized Clint as Warner's "fading house star." Uh-uh—the wise-guy press authoritatively peddling misinformation.

There's no need to reprise the astonishing critical and popular success of *Unforgiven*, though I think even Clint was surprised when the Oscar buzz started. He had once told Hyams that he didn't think he would ever do well with the Academy. He was, he believed, too much a populist for its more middlebrow tastes. Which, considering that it won Best Picture and Best Director, and considering how often in the years since his films have been in the Academy's eyeline, proves only that Clint is not an entirely infallible prognosticator.

Unforgiven is certainly a study in two definitions of masculinity. Gene Hackman's Sheriff Daggett is a hard-assed lawman running a tight town—all gun control and ill-controlled sadism. I have one or two right-wing friends, who think he's the picture's hero. Clint's William Munny is a sometime gunman ("I've killed everything that's walked or crawled…"), a widower believing his late wife had succeeded in reforming him ("I'm not like that any more"), but desperate to claim the reward offered for killing two cowboys who cut a whore in a cathouse fracas. He needs the money to save his children from destitution. In his past, possibly even now, in his guilt-ridden soul, he's no better than Daggett.

But if that were all *Unforgiven* was it would be no more than an above-average western. What sets it apart is how inexplicable fate moves its characters. The cowboy miscreants turn out not to be evil incarnate; they're just a pair of dumb, liquored-up kids. Munny's best friend, Ned (Morgan Freeman), is unable to kill one of them when the time comes. The self-named "Schofield Kid," all hot blood and braggadocio, and tagging along with them, turns out to be near-sighted and useless in a gunfight. If Daggett had not flogged Ned to death when he was captured, there's some likelihood Munny and Daggett might have been spared their final deadly confrontation. But that act gives Munny deadly motive—this is no longer about the money. And this says nothing of all the enriching subplots and secondary characters—Richard Harris's grandiloquent "English Bob," beaten senseless and ridden out of town, a dime novelist (Saul Rubinek), representing the nascent celebrity culture of the late nineteenth century, who is writing a book (*The Duke of Death*) about Bob's fraudulent exploits. There is a whole frontier world—more richly detailed in "Big Whiskey," the raw frontier town straggling down a hillside, than in any western I know. And it is fate that moves William Munny blindly through it. "That's kind of what I like in stories, in movies and plays, where fate takes you in a way that you're totally unprepared for. That's always the intriguing dramatic element."

Unforgiven was a game-changer for Clint, though I've never heard him speak that way about it. It granted him the right to take himself seriously, to be overtly ambitious in his choice of material.

OPPOSITE The actor as director on the set of *Unforgiven*, 1992.

"You know, it goes back to the old thing we used to talk about all the time in acting classes when I first came to Universal: they'd say, 'What would you rather be, an actor or a movie star?' Everybody used to say they would rather be an actor, of course. But after you start thinking about it, you say: 'Wait a second, who gets all the great roles?' Movie stars. You are a great actor and you are sitting there waiting for the phone to ring and it can be a long time running. So you kind of have to throw all that out and not worry about what being a movie star is, so you can get the roles with more challenge to them."

This not to say that in the years ahead he totally avoided straightforward genre pictures (*Absolute Power, Blood Work*). Nor is it to say that all of his more aspiring films (*Midnight in the Garden of Good and Evil*) were always successful. But for the last seventeen years he's mainly been involved with material that, while still addressing his core concerns, does so in a darker and more sobering way.

In the Line of Fire, which immediately followed *Unforgiven*, was a suspenseful yet delightful and beautifully made popular entertainment. But Clint's Secret Service agent was beginning to puff a bit as he trotted alongside the presidential limo. And he was haunted by the fact that he might have taken the bullet that felled JFK in Dallas, but did not. One of the remarkable things about Clint's later career is that he always played his age and always gave the impression that possibly his knees ached a little when he got up in the morning—just like yours.

He's made more than a dozen movies since, of which I think at least seven are "major motion pictures." In that period, he also endured a very public breakup of his longstanding relationship with Sondra Locke—during which he appeared (for the first and only time) sullen and angry, and suffered a brief falling out with the usually adoring press. But, shortly thereafter, he married pretty, bubbly Dina Ruiz, finding what seemed to me an uncomplicated happiness that he had never fully found in the past.

In the mid-1990s I undertook, with his blessing, a biography of Clint. It was, for me, a very agreeable experience—sitting as the dusk gathered about us, the tape recorder turning, as Clint earnestly attempted to recall his life. Usually there were only one or two lights burning dimly. His films are always quite dark—Clint's eyes do not take kindly to high light levels—and, golf courses aside, he prefers his life to be lit in the same way. But the operative word in my description of these interviews is "earnestly."

If I were asked to provide a one-word characterization of Clint the one I'd choose would be "dutiful." If he commits to something—a film, a public appearance, a dinner at Orso's—he will fulfill that commitment, whatever distractions or inconveniences might arise. He is, as you may have gathered by this time, not a man much given to making excuses.

A good example might be *A Perfect World*, the film that followed *In the Line of Fire*. It turned out to be a disappointment in the US, critically and commercially, yet Clint rightly clings to the belief that it is a very good film. Robert "Butch" Haynes, an escaped convict, very well played by Kevin Costner, takes as a hostage a little boy named Phillip "Buzz" Perry (T.J. Lowther) and, eluding a police chase (led by Clint as a Texas Ranger named Red Garnett), they bond. Haynes is a good-humored man with a dark and violent side, the boy has been deserted by his father and has been denied most of the normal pleasures of boyhood (including Christmas) by his mother who, though loving, is a fundamentalist Christian. Butch loosens the kid up, and the kid, in his sweetness and innocence, makes Butch a somewhat more responsible human being—not that he can evade a tragic fate.

It's not that Robert Kincaid can avoid romantic rue in *The Bridges of Madison County.* People wondered why Clint was bothering with this adaptation of Robert James Waller's critically reviled, insanely popular novel. But Clint saw something more interesting in the brief encounter between his wandering photographer and Meryl Streep's mildly, rather humorously restless woman. "I don't think he's out searching for housewives in middle America," he says of Kincaid. "Fate just kind of drives him that way." Suppose Kincaid had turned left instead of right in his search for the eponymous covered bridges and landed up at another farm. Suppose her husband and children had been home when he approached her porch. Suppose, particularly, that he and Steven Spielberg, who was executive producing, had not ordered a slight shading in the script so that Francesca was more active, more complicit in her own seduction, than she was in the book.

OPPOSITE Clint with his second wife, Dina, on his left, and his children from his first marriage, Kyle and Alison, at the premiere of *Flags of Our Fathers*, 2006.

I visited the *Bridges* location in Winterset, Iowa, and, of the several Eastwood shoots I had observed, this was among the happiest. He and Streep were enjoying a very congenial, mutually respectful relationship. The film was not technically difficult and she liked Clint's quick pace—"I almost always like the first reading better than anything we do subsequently"—so this was "heaven" for her. She had worked with other actor-directors and Clint would later recall her saying that "they never stopped directing even when they were in the scene—a little glint in the eye where they're looking at her differently than the character is looking at her. She thought I made that switch pretty well."

The press didn't see any of that. It focused on the tough guy playing his first flat-out romance. And on the fact that he shed some tears on camera. So un-Clint.

8. Clint seemed briefly to be less than aspiring in his choice of material as the century turned, contenting himself with genre pieces (*Absolute Power, Space Cowboys, Blood Work*). There is, however, one exception, *True Crime* in 1999. It's a genre piece, a newspaper yarn, with Clint appearing as a typically feckless reporter on the Oakland *Tribune.* You know the type—a drinker, a womanizer (among his conquests is the wife of his managing editor), a man in the midst of a messy separation. One day he's assigned to do a little color story on a man about to be executed that night for murder in nearby San Quentin. Something about the situation smells wrong to him. Frank Beechum (Isaiah Washington) is obviously a decent guy, and his wife (Lisa Gay Hamilton) and their child, Gail (Penny Bae Bridges), are in very touchingly rendered anguish as they make their last visit to death row. You could argue that the plot, which involves a mad dash with new exculpatory evidence as the prisoner approaches his final moments, is an antique (it resembles, as much as anything, the "modern" story in D.W. Griffith's *Intolerance* of 1916). But the Beechums are another hard-pressed Eastwoodian family in need of rescue, trying to maintain an air of normalcy in utterly abnormal circumstances. Their little girl has lost the green crayon she needs to complete a picture she's drawing for her dad, and the whole prison staff, portrayed with great humanity, goes on the hunt for it. When, at last, she is led out of her father's prison her wail of despair is heartbreaking in its helplessness (the child actress had bumped her chin during the lunch break, and Clint, seeing that she was upset but not really in pain, took advantage of her condition to record a moment of astonishing intensity).

I don't want to make too much of what remains essentially a genre film. On the other hand, it is like a number of other Eastwood films in that it blends the comedy of the quotidian with an intensely suspenseful story. More important, in the power of its jailhouse sequences, it transcends the norms of genre-movie acting. And, perhaps, portends the run of great pictures that have preoccupied him during the first decade of the twenty-first century. Arguably, it is the greatest series of back-to-back successes in the history of movies, made more impressive—to others, not to Clint—by the fact that their director turned seventy in 2000.

Mystic River, Million Dollar Baby, Letters from Iwo Jima, Gran Torino—these are all very good, possibly great movies (time will, as it always does, make the final judgment), with *Flags of Our Fathers* and *Changeling* quite impressive as well. Almost all of them were financially and critically successful, several of them did very well during Awards season (with *Million Dollar Baby* winning Best Picture and Best Director Academy Awards, as well as Oscars for Hilary Swank as Best Actress and Morgan Freeman as Best Supporting Actor).

We can risk a few generalizations about them. Setting the World War II pictures aside for the moment, the rest of the films all, in one way or another, deal with family issues. *Mystic River* is the most complex of them—and maybe the most psychologically complex of all Clint's films. It begins with three boys playing in the street. One of them is abducted and sexually abused, his life ruined almost before it has begun (he is played as an adult by Tim Robbins, who won an Oscar for Best Supporting Actor for the inarticulate eloquence of his work). The other two boys turn out to be a smalltime crook (Sean Penn, also a richly deserving Oscar winner) trying to go straight, and a cool-seeming but tormented police detective (Kevin Bacon), who takes over the case when the former's daughter is murdered. Penn's raging performance, both towering and subtle, is a great one, justly praised and honored at the time. If Clint is, as we've seen, obsessed with the workings of fate, then this is the most detailed tracing of its mysterious effects—on more people than *Mystic River*'s three protagonists, and over more years than he has ever covered. The picture ends on something less than a triumphant note. It ends, in fact, on a wrongful and unpunished death, with the survivors' lives somehow proceeding along their unknowable paths.

But let's pause for a moment here to note that with one exception—*Flags of Our Fathers* (which has a subtext of quite another kind)—all of these late films end on a note of tragedy—sometimes a resounding one. *Million Dollar Baby* (misunderstood as "a boxing picture" by Warner Bros., which refused, as it had with *Mystic River*, to fully back what Clint correctly saw as "a father-daughter love story") ends with Hilary Swank's female boxer in a vegetative state and Clint as her grieving surrogate dad euthanizing her. *Letters from Iwo Jima* ends with virtually an entire army wiped out. *Changeling* ends with Angelina Jolie's heartbroken mother unable to find her abducted son. *Gran Torino* ends with Clint's Walt Kowalski sacrificing himself for the immigrant neighbors he has reluctantly come to love. I don't think we need to add that all but one of these films also deals with families, or their simulacra, under heartbreaking pressures of one kind or another.

I think we do need to add a few glosses to the foregoing:

ON GENRE: These films can be understood (or misunderstood) as genre exercises. On a certain level, *Mystic River* is—well, sure—a murder mystery. We can perhaps afford to recognize that, in its way, *Million Dollar Baby* is, okay, a "boxing picture," especially in its flavorsome depiction of Frankie Dunn's rundown gym, with its none-too-promising *habitués* and Frankie's tough-guy ways. *Letters* and *Flags* are, of course, "war pictures" while *Changeling* is in the not-unfamiliar "missing child" vein. *Gran Torino*'s Walt Kowalski is a recognizable type—the inappropriate Old Guy, crankily watching the world hustle past his disapproving eyes. But that's not saying much. As we've observed, almost all of Clint's films always had lineaments of genre about them, whatever their real business may sometimes have been. The difference now is that they also bear the weight of his years, his hard-won authority. Who now would dispute his seriousness? Or fail to recognize his right to comment on large topics? Who now could name another American filmmaker with a similarly indisputable record of taking up sober themes in ways that are largely palatable to a mass audience?

ON IDEAS: Let's take up the matter of euthanasia in *Million Dollar Baby*. Clint is a secularist, lifelong I believe, and his pictures have occasionally portrayed clerics in a less than heroic light. But, as he said to me, he had no desire to proselytize in public for the right to die in certain hopeless situations. But honestly I, like a lot of people, did not notice anything like that going on in the film, so tightly, so logically, was the mercy killing woven into its narrative, which was primarily about a man estranged from his daughter, a woman estranged from her awful family, finding a few months of happiness in a marginal world. This was a case of tragic inevitability overwhelming ideology.

ON THE PERSISTENT DIRTY HARRY DREAM: Among Clint's hardcore fans there has long been an almost comical yearning for one last *Dirty Harry* movie. Fans mention it to him. They have even

mentioned it to me. Clint and I have once or twice laughed about that curious desire. We imagined Harry eking out his pension as a part-time security guard. One night some bad guys invade the warehouse. Harry goes for his gun and gives chase. Whereupon, as Clint put it, "SPLAT—there goes Dirty Harry." But there was, even among a few critics, a desire to see Walt Kowalski in *Gran Torino* as a Harry Callahan clone. Clint merely chuckles at the idea: "Dirty Harry would probably have settled that situation much, much sooner. And—well—handled it a little differently." Besides, Clint is increasingly resolute about a couple of matters. One is his increasingly firm desire not to "suit up," as he calls acting under his own direction—it is exhausting work and he came off the *Gran Torino* shoot more tired than he had anticipated (mostly, I surmise, because his cast was almost exclusively amateur, and required more directorial attention than he anticipated). Then there is his resolute desire always to act his age. As he says, there are not many roles for men of his age, however lightly he wears it. I can imagine him doing a cameo in one of his own productions, or perhaps in someone else's. But I do suspect Walt may be his farewell to performance. Remember, this is the guy who never made another western after *Unforgiven*, on the grounds, as he put it, that he didn't have anything more to say in that form.

ON *DUTY*: The most singular film of Clint's most recent decade is, I believe, *Letters from Iwo Jima*, because it is the one that takes up, in a disguised form, the quality that, as I've said, is the one that is central to his nature—his sense of duty. The press and the public's interest in the film was directed to the fact that he made it virtually simultaneously with *Flags of Our Fathers*, even grabbing a few shots for *Letters* while he was making *Flags*, so this theme went largely unnoticed. It is not unprecedented for a director to make two films in this fashion, but it is quite rare. It is unprecedented for an American director to make a battle film that portrays a former enemy in a sympathetic way. He was drawn to the general topic out of curiosity and because a slender volume of letters home from the Japanese soldiers that fought on Iwo Jima piqued his interest. Then, too, the more or less speculative screenplay by Iris Yamashita, who was doing research for Paul Haggis on the *Flags* script, turned out to exceed Clint's expectations.

But I think what most interested Clint was its central character, the Japanese commanding general, Tadamichi Kuribayashi (Ken Watanabe). He was, putting it simply, Clint's kind of guy. There is reason to believe that he was assigned to the hopeless task of defending Iwo Jima as a kind of punishment for his independence by the Japanese Imperial Staff. He was, as well, a man who had spent time in America before the war, admired its spirit, and thought war with the US was a very bad idea. In the film he is always armed with a pearl-handled Colt .45 revolver, presented to him by American officers.

But the main thing about Kuribayashi is that he knows his cause is hopeless; he expects to die on Iwo Jima. But he will die trying, mounting an imaginative defense against the opposition of many of his officers. He will also die as a kind of humanist. In her great book, *The Rape of Nanking*, Iris Chang argued that the enormous cruelties the Japanese army heaped on its enemies and their civilian populations was the direct result of the cruelties practiced on them by their own officers. Kuribayashi will have none of that, either. He is, perhaps, the most tragically fated character in Clint's filmography which, as we have seen, focuses in recent years almost exclusively on such figures. Making the film, Clint (abetted by Watanabe) slightly revised the script; he arranged that the general's suicide, once the battle was lost, would not be accomplished by the ritual sword. Instead—and there is a bitter, but not emphasized, irony here—he uses his American revolver to kill himself.

9. Does Clint believe a sense of duty leads inevitably to dark dismay? I don't think so. His own life belies that notion. But one time we were talking about his frustrating early acting days, when he was "a gangling kid from Oakland wearing my Troy Donahue corrective shoes," and that set me to thinking about the almost infinite distance he has since traveled. It is easy enough to put his early failures down to typical Hollywood blindness, its tendency to believe whatever its going collective wisdom is until it goes—well—SPLAT!

But still, I had to admit that Clint had come from far back in the pack. He had been acting in movies since 1955 without attracting much attention, and though his role on *Rawhide*, for 217 episodes between 1958 and 1965, brought him a measure of security, it was more an agreeable show than a must-see. Indeed, Clint's good-natured presence became the show's chief attraction—particularly to young women, not normally a demographic that TV westerns appealed to. Even so, it was hard to see William Munny or Wes Block or Frankie Dunn in this young man's future. And the Sergio Leone films? Yes, they suggested a darker, more powerful presence. But still, Italian westerns were a place for the slightly shopworn or the somewhat less-than-promising. Clint remains the only major star they ever produced.

So his subsequent career must contain an enormous amount of will—masterfully disguised by his ambling pace, his manifest dislike of tooting his own horn, his refusal to make grandiose predictions of vast success for his next enterprise. He seems to me to have successfully surrendered himself to inscrutable destiny—to, yes, fate.

My biography of Clint was published in 1996, and he agreed to do a little publicity for it with me in New York. Our big appearance was sponsored by the 92nd St. YMHA, and took place in a vast, packed synagogue on the Upper West Side. With the film scholar Jeanine Basinger we did a pleasant Q&A, after which we were scheduled to sign some books. "Nothing elaborate," said my editor, "a little cheese and wine."

Sure. We were escorted through a basement kindergarten to some book-stacked tables behind closed doors. On the other side of which we heard what amounted to a growling mob, uncomfortably lined up on a staircase. There was no security beyond a couple of slightly alarmed publicists. When the doors were thrown open we were confronted by a mob, the mood of which was just this side of confrontational. Most of them were there to buy signed books, but some were armed with posters, 8x10 glossies, special pens that make autographed photographs look more authentic when they're hawked on the Internet. Neither cheese nor wine was in evidence—just a sort of vague hostility. At this level of fandom, which I had never encountered before, anger and adoration are very evenly balanced.

It took a tense hour to satisfy their needs, and as we were being led back through the kindergarten, I said to Clint, "Wow, that was kinda scary."

"Yeah," he said. "You notice that one guy? When he reached in his pocket I didn't know exactly what he was gonna pull out."

I mentioned that though I'd been in his company a few times when we had confronted substantial crowds, I'd never seen anything quite like what we'd just encountered.

"Yeah," he said, striding along. "But when you sign on, you sign on for the whole ride."

His tone was equable. But I had the feeling I had been vouchsafed a life lesson. One that had guided him through a much longer ride than he, or anyone, might have anticipated—and one that is by no means over. We went on to a nice dinner at Elaine's.

From REVENGE OF THE CREATURE to RAWHIDE 1955–59

Discharged from the army, Clint found himself adrift in the early 1950s. This was not a new feeling for him. Before being drafted, he had wandered around the Pacific Northwest, doing hard labor in unrewarding jobs. His military service had been an exercise in boredom—enough of that to last a lifetime. His parents were, by now, living in Seattle and his best thought at that time was to attend a community college somewhere and get his grades up to a level where he could apply to Seattle University, which had a first-class, virtually unique, academic program in jazz.

Instead, however, he drifted down to Los Angeles and enrolled at Los Angeles City College, where he decided to major in business administration, a course, as he says, that attracted lot of guys who had no firm career ideas.

He got a job managing a small apartment building and he was also courting a tall, slender young woman named Maggie Johnson, whom he had met when she was studying at the University of California, Berkeley, and who was now living with her parents in Altadena while she worked for a manufacturer's representative. They married on December 29, 1953.

OPPOSITE The aspiring young actor already with a taste for wheels.
ABOVE The young hopefuls focus on Marlon Brando at Universal's talent school, with Clint back row, center, with the height advantage.

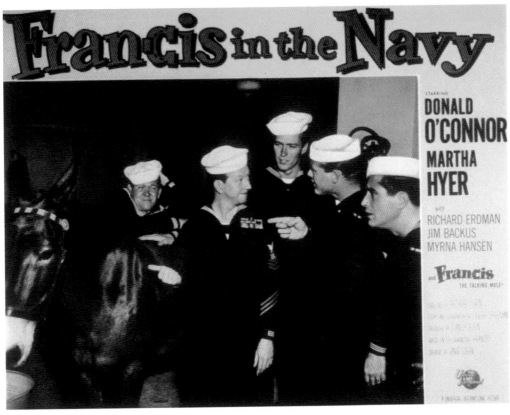

By now, Clint had begun visiting friends who had jobs at Universal Studios, and he found himself intrigued by life on the lot. "Shit, people get paid for doing this," he remembers thinking as he observed the actors strolling the studio's streets. Curious about what their lives might entail, he began observing acting classes around town. This was the great age of Stanislavskian instruction, and Clint had luckily fallen in with good people. He particularly liked the classes taught by George Shdanoff, who in turn was a disciple of Michael Chekhov, an Oscar-winning character actor (Hitchcock's *Spellbound*), the author of a book, *To the Actor* (which Clint recommends to young actors), the nephew of the immortal Russian playwright. He had, as a young actor, worked with Stanislavski at the Moscow Art Theater, so it was with some authority that he advanced a method of playing that was in opposition to The Method as it was then being promulgated by Lee Strasberg. Chekhov was not particularly interested in the actor probing his memories for material to animate his playing. He stressed the ensemble and the interrelations of its members, and he offered a lot of sound, practical advice, particularly about how the actor might achieve rapport with his audience. It must have sounded, to Clint, a lot like the way jazz players worked and, after a time, he ceased observing acting classes and, for some time, he was an active participant in them.

Around this time he and Maggie became friends with a cinematographer named Irving Glassberg, who was working a lot with Arthur Lubin, a long-term contract director at Universal.

Glassberg shot a test of Clint, which was good enough to get him, at $75 a week, into a talent-development program at the studio. He also showed it to Lubin, who took an interest in Clint. The talent program was reasonably well-managed, with courses in acting, of course, as well as dancing, fencing, riding, and so on. The young actors played small parts in the studio's productions, and did other chores around the studio—looping, playing in other people's screen tests, even appearing at premieres. The studio was not looking to the program to swell its ranks of character actors; as one instructor later said, they thought if they could get one or two stars out of it, it would be worth its cost. It sort of worked out for, in addition to Clint, the likes of David Janssen, Gia Scala, John Gavin, and Mamie Van Doren passed through the program on their way to widely varying degrees of fame.

Clint's first movie appearance was in *Revenge of the Creature* (he was a lab assistant who briefly mislays a white rat) and he appeared equally briefly in *Lady Godiva, Tarantula, Never Say Goodbye, Star in the Dust*, and *Away All Boats*—his work as unmemorable as the movies were. His best gig at Universal was for Lubin in *Francis in the Navy*. This was, of course, the series about a cynically talking mule, which the director, who had a little specialty in verbalizing animals (he also created Mr. Ed, the talking horse, for TV), invented. Clint never has more than a couple of lines of connected dialogue, but his part, as an eagerly innocent sailor, runs through most of the picture and he is agreeable enough in it.

OPPOSITE Clint quickly learned how an actor "might achieve rapport with his audience," as such early publicity photos confirm.
ABOVE Lobby card for *Francis in the Navy*, 1955.

But not exactly memorable. It's quite amazing that such a good-looking young man did not attract more attention at the studio, and he thinks he was just not the type it had in mind for stardom. Who knows? What we do know is that shortly thereafter the studio dropped his contract. He got two jobs from Lubin, now working at RKO, in *The First Traveling Saleslady*, a particularly inane comedy in which Ginger Rogers played a woman selling barbed wire in the Old West, with Clint in a decent role as a soldier being lasciviously eyed by Carol Channing. He had another job, this time as a day player, in another Lubin film, *Escapade in Japan*, and he got a little television work in shows like *Highway Patrol*. But mostly the Eastwoods were living on Maggie's salary and what Clint could pick up doing odd jobs, which included digging swimming pools.

His disappointments were mostly small, typical for a young actor struggling to make his mark. He did, however, suffer a larger one. William A. Wellman, one of the best directors of the movies' Golden Age, was making an autobiographical film, *Lafayette Escadrille*, about the World War I flying squadron, composed of American volunteers, in which he served. He responded strongly to Clint's shy presence and vowed to get him the lead in what would turn out to be Wellman's last movie. The studio thought otherwise. Tab Hunter had been flirting with the stardom he never attained for most of the 1950s and was certainly better known than Clint, so naturally he got the job. Wellman gave Clint a consolation-prize supporting role, and he enjoyed working with the decisive Wellman, whose *The Ox-Bow Incident* remains one of Clint's favorite films.

THIS PAGE Clint Eastwood and Carol Channing in *The First Traveling Saleslady*, 1956.
OPPOSITE LEFT The cast of *Rawhide*, which launched in 1959 and was to run for 217 episodes.
OPPOSITE RIGHT Following the success of *Rawhide*, Clint recorded a number of cowboy/country record albums.

Whereupon fate finally took a benign hand in Clint's life. One day he dropped by CBS to visit Sonia Chernus, who was one of the Eastwoods' best friends (she would later work as a story editor for Clint's company). She was working there as a reader and wanted to introduce him to a network executive she thought might be helpful to him. But strolling along a corridor, a man named Robert Sparks popped out of an office, spotted Clint, asked him if he was an actor, and promptly asked him to meet with Charles Marquis Warren, then producing a new western series to be called *Rawhide*. Both thought Clint might be right for the role of Rowdy Yates, second in command of a cattle drive that for seven years and 217 episodes never reached its destination. In a matter of weeks Clint was approved by the network brass and had the part.

Westerns were all the rage on TV at the time and *Rawhide* proved to be a solid performer in the ratings, with Clint's pleasant, incrementally maturing presence offsetting the rather dour, slightly off-putting, work of Eric Fleming as the trail boss. He was low-keyed, ingratiating, and well—yes—sexy, bringing in a demographic not usually drawn to westerns, young women. The show even had a hit theme song. For seven years, it was all Clint did professionally, in the process learning almost everything he needed to pursue his craft while saving his money against the day he would once again be out of work—which, of course, did not happen.

A lead role in a long-running television series is, often—perhaps even usually—the apogee of a career. With few exceptions such work leads on, at best, to leading roles in other series. In any event,

The film failed on every level—with Hunter giving an extraordinarily limp performance—but shortly thereafter Clint got a decent role in a B western, *Ambush at Cimarron Pass*, which he believes—and no one would argue with him—is the worst film he ever made. He was paid $750 for an eight-day shoot in the deeper reaches of the San Fernando Valley for a picture shot in black and white CinemaScope. It's about a mixed group of travelers making their way through Apache territory—mostly on foot since the production could not afford horses for more than half the schedule. Clint plays a Confederate sympathizer who reforms as the film shambles along. The lead was played by Scott Brady, a crude heavy drinker who generally played heavies. He made everyone's life miserable and the picture eventually slipped into release as the second feature on double bills. Clint and Maggie saw it in a neighborhood theater and he left vowing to quit the business, go back to college, and make something of himself in another field.

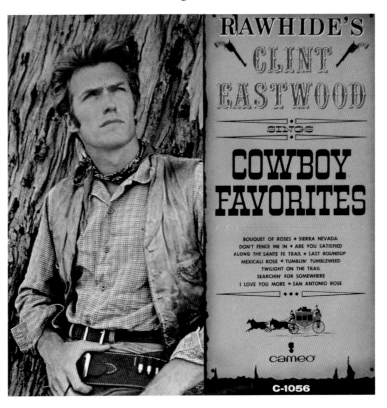

"I remember when I first got in the movie business, when I was first acting and I was doing a lot of bit parts over at Universal, the head of the acting group or the producers would say, 'Well, come on in and play it with balls.' They'd say, 'Play it ballsy.' And I didn't even know what they were talking about. It was hard for me to fathom, 'cause I'd never even heard that expression."

Rawhide did not make him a star, that is to say, it did not insert him prominently in the consciousness (and unconsciousness) of the nation. He was a really cute, very likeable guy, of which there were not a few on TV, and he thought—not without justification—that he was never given the opportunity to explore aspects of Rowdy's character than went much beyond the juvenile. What he lacked at that point was that air of mystery (and occasional menace) that is required of movie stars, and there seemed to be no way of exhibiting those qualities in American film. He was an actor stuck in grade.

But fortune favors the brave. He was at least well enough known so that, as a second or third choice, he could carry a small-scale Italian western. He was also undeterred by the modest salary on offer. He just thought it might be an amusing way to spend his summer vacation from *Rawhide*. Most important, he doubtless saw in the paucity of the script's dialogue, in its relative lack of back story and complex motivation (which he succeeded in cutting further during the shoot), precisely those mysterious and menacing notes he had not previously been able to sound in his work. His was among the more circuitous routes to stardom in modern movie history. But now, in April 1964, when he arrived in Rome to make what was then called *The Magnificent Stranger*, he was, at thirty-four, belatedly about to grasp a destiny that, only in retrospect, seems inevitable.

OPPOSITE Golf was an early passion; here Clint practices his swing on the *Rawhide* set.
ABOVE At home in 1961—could this have been the script that was to change his destiny?

A FISTFUL OF DOLLARS 1964

The script, when it arrived, was a fourth or fifth carbon, typed on onionskin paper. It was more novelistic in form than a traditional screenplay, though Clint immediately recognized it as a knock-off of Akira Kurosawa's *Yojimbo*, a movie he'd always thought could be converted into quite a good western. He was not the first actor the director, Sergio Leone, had thought of to play the part, and the offer to do so was not princely —$15,000. But still, he thought the idea was a pretty good one—even if everyone told him to collect his money in advance, Italian producers being notorious for skipping out on salary payments.

So Clint signed on for *Il Magnifico Stragnero*, as it was originally called, and flew off to Rome carrying his *Rawhide* pistols and gun belt, a flat hat he picked up in a costume shop, some black jeans and several boxes of the nasty little cigars—they made him feel "cantankerous"—that would become his character's trademark. He and Leone spoke only a few words of each other's language, but Clint liked the excitable, rotund, bespectacled director, who had learned his trade as an assistant director on dozens of films, and he liked the idea behind the film, which was to shake up the genre conventions which he thought had brought the western to "a dead space."

He thinks his largest off-camera contribution to the film was paring down its excessive, over-explanatory dialogue. ("Okay, Sergio," he remembers saying, "in a B movie we tell everybody everything. In a real class-A movie we let the audience think." Given fewer words to spout, Clint was able to play "very ironic, dry, and a little bit sardonic."

It's a spare little story they were telling—two gangs of thugs are in contention for control of a miserable little Spanish-American town. It is Clint's task to ride in and restore peace, mainly by killing off both factions. Toshirô Mifune's great portrayal of this character is much more colorful—scratching, shrugging, hyperactive—but Clint's is equally effective, as he takes the classic western hero's taciturnity to new levels of silence. As if to make up for his minimalism,

Leone's style is more maximalist than Kurosawa's. For one thing, his film can be read as a version of Christ's Passion, complete with a resurrection. For another he had a unique style, alternating huge panoramic shots with super-tight close-ups, quite unlike anything John Ford ever imagined. As for the picture's alleged violence, it is very sparse. What made it discomfiting to traditionalists were the lengthy build-ups to the shootouts—protagonist and antagonist stalking, circling one another until the tension between them becomes unbearable and it is released in a burst of gunfire.

Clint left the location late in June, not at all certain of what he had participated in, but with his hopes of learning how people made movies elsewhere more than fulfilled. It was over a year before

OPPOSITE Actor becomes Icon: Clint in the poster art for *A Fistful of Dollars*.
RIGHT The excitable Sergio Leone directs a scene with Clint and Margarita Lozano, 1964.

he began reading in the trades about a surprise Italian hit called *A Fistful of Dollars*. Wait a minute! Could this be? Inquiries were made and there arrived a phonograph record of Ennio Morricone's groundbreaking score, which astonished Clint. Almost simultaneously, there arrived phone calls from the producer, begging for his services in a sequel. Soon a print of the picture arrived and Clint screened it for a group of friends, and even with the dialogue still not dubbed into English, they loved it. It was just so damned … different.

There were legal hurdles still to be cleared—Kurosawa and his people were not entirely amused—but the fact was that this strange little film, released without publicity in a single theater in Florence in order to qualify for Italian government subsidies, was an authentic populist triumph. It ran and ran in Michelangelo's city—as it did

elsewhere in Europe and eventually in the United States. At first critically reviled (except for a few honorable exceptions), it and its sequels eventually did, for a time, revitalize the western, give it a bite, a sexiness, a modern relevance, that had long been absent from the form.

It seems to me Clint has never received quite the credit he deserves for taking this large, instinctive chance on a very risky proposition. He, no less than the genre itself, needed to break out of the genteel box in which not only this form, but his presence, had been encased. He would, of course, go on to make more respectable, more critically revered, films. But I don't think he would ever make a more usefully revolutionary gesture than he did in this and the two Leone films that followed it.

ABOVE AND OPPOSITE Clint played it "very ironic, dry, and a little bit sardonic." The movie reinvented the western, with minimalist performances and stark imagery, filmed on location in the rainless plains of Spain.

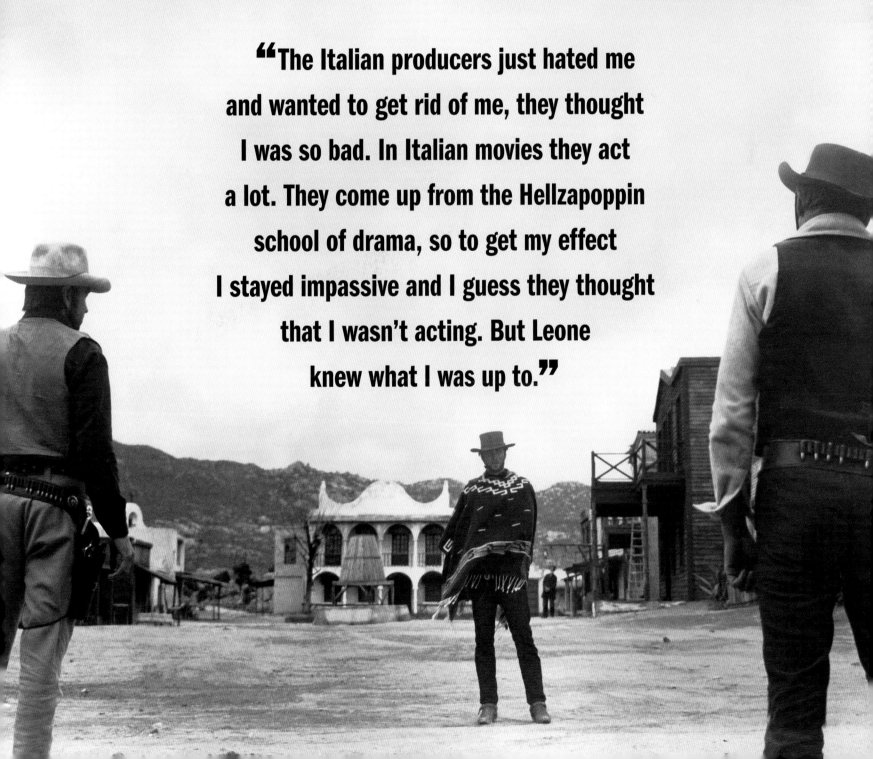

"The Italian producers just hated me
and wanted to get rid of me, they thought
I was so bad. In Italian movies they act
a lot. They come up from the Hellzapoppin
school of drama, so to get my effect
I stayed impassive and I guess they thought
that I wasn't acting. But Leone
knew what I was up to."

FOR A FEW DOLLARS MORE 1965

This is undoubtedly the most balanced of Clint's three films for Sergio Leone. It is not quite as simply structured as its predecessor, but not quite as outrageously epic in ambition and scope as *The Good, the Bad and the Ugly*. Its characters have a little more depth than *Fistful* and, best of all, it has, in Lee Van Cleef, a costar who can gracefully hold the screen opposite Clint. Van Cleef was a sort of second-string heavy in westerns, a slender, saturnine man whose career had been bedeviled by drink and physical ailments. He got this job because Henry Fonda, among others, had turned it down and, as Colonel Mortimer, a former Civil War officer, he revived his career with a coolly impassioned performance.

He and Clint's character meet cute in a gun duel that, had it continued, quite possibly might have ended with both men standing in the street in their skivvies, so adeptly do they shoot off items of each other's clothing. The colonel is a man on a mission, seeking vengeance on El Indio, played by *Fistful*'s leading psycho, Gian Maria Volontè, who, we eventually learn, raped the colonel's sister on her wedding night, causing her to commit suicide. Both the colonel and El Indio carry identical watches; it is the latter's habit to have it play a wistful little Morricone tune which, when it ends, is the signal for everyone to draw their guns and start plugging one another.

Clint's character is more simply motivated. Monco (he was never "the man with no name" in these pictures—that was the belated invention of an American marketing expert) is making an amoral living as a hired gun, with designs on bank robbery. But he is impressed with the colonel's manner and manners, and forms a temporary alliance with him—almost a father-son bond. That turns out to be a good thing for the colonel, with Monco backing him in the film's climactic gun battle—another of Leone's brilliant triangular shoot-out stagings.

Once again, this turned out to be an excellent adventure for Clint. The pay was better, he enjoyed Van Cleef's company, and the picture, if anything, prospered even better than *Fistful* had. This was good for Clint, as his long-running role in *Rawhide* was beginning to draw to an end.

LEFT Clint Eastwood as The Stranger and Lee Van Cleef as Col. Douglas Mortimer with their prize, El Indio, played by Gian Maria Volontè. OPPOSITE No more the newcomer, Clint is now the star in *For a Few Dollars More*.

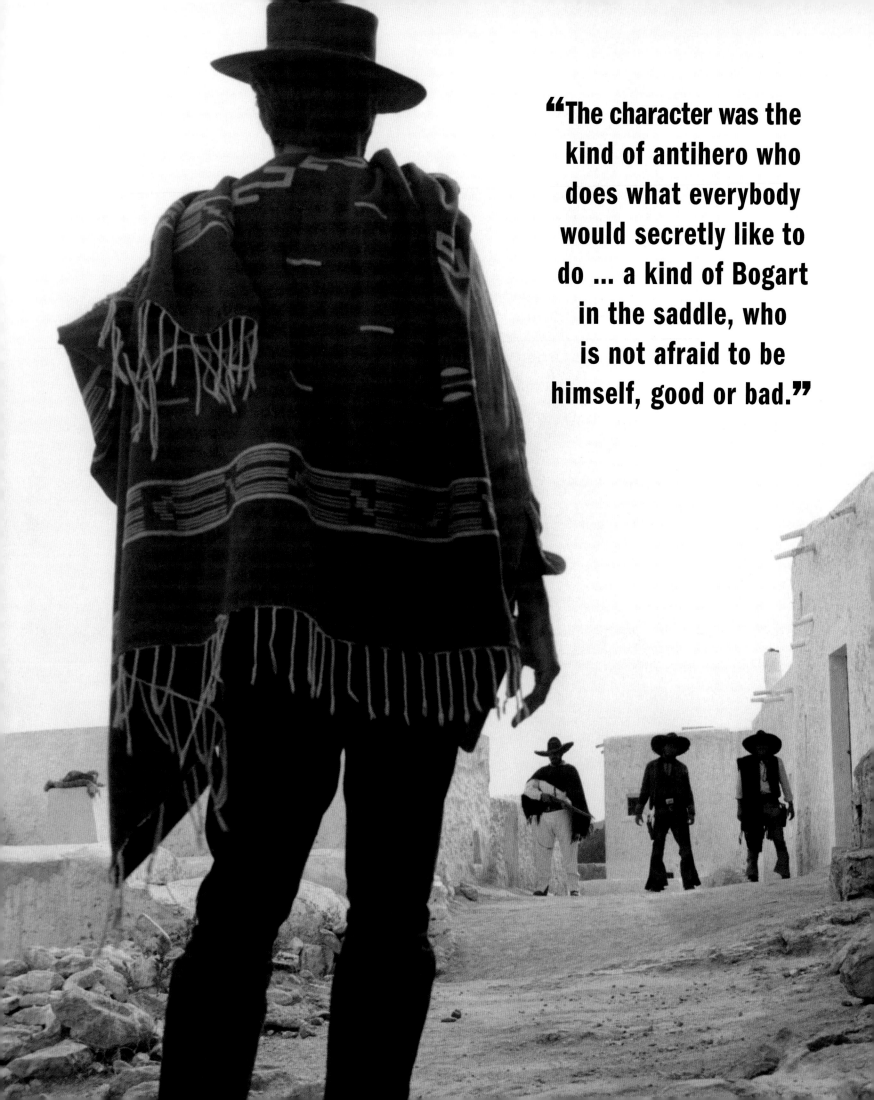

"The character was the kind of antihero who does what everybody would secretly like to do ... a kind of Bogart in the saddle, who is not afraid to be himself, good or bad."

At this point, one would not necessarily have predicted the kind of stardom that would soon be his. But he was beginning to make the kind of transition to feature-film work that television's leading men dream of making but only rarely achieve. And he was doing so on his own unlikely terms. Maybe fate was blindly driving him on. But I think it was more a matter of trusting his instincts, of sensing that there was something right for him in these Italian films, despite their slightly dubious provenances, despite the initial failure (by American critics in particular) to see that Leone's work was more sophisticated than that of his many competitors, that his films would have a near-to-revolutionary impact on the western genre—much more so, I think, than Sam Peckinpah's more blood-drenched work that, at the time, was getting much more critical attention.

OPPOSITE Clint in trademark poncho, "the man with no name" was the belated invention of an American marketing expert.
ABOVE Cool in crisis: Clint, his gun, and his ever-present cigar.

THE WITCHES 1967

The Italian title *Le Streghe*, under which *The Witches* played its few release dates in Europe, was a kind of vanity production. It was mounted by Dino De Laurentiis in an attempt to revive the career of his wife, Silvana Mangano, which had declined since her very sexy and promising work in *Bitter Rice*, and the string of very decent films she had done in the 1950s and 1960s for some of Italy's best directors. This film was to be an anthology piece—five episodes directed by more fine directors (Luchino Visconti, Pier Paolo Pasolini, Franco Rossi among them)—and it would star many of the better-known international stars of the moment.

The idea was that these disparate stories would showcase the range of Mangano's talent. Clint says he had long ago fallen in love with her on-screen image and, better still, his episode was to be directed by no less than Vittorio De Sica, one of Italian Neo-Realism's founders (*Shoeshine, The Bicycle Thief, Umberto D*) and cowritten by his brilliant screenwriter-collaborator, Cesare Zavattini. Clint was offered a choice of payments, a flat $25,000 or $20,000 and a free Ferrari automobile. He naturally chose the latter, on the grounds that he would never be able to afford such a splendid vehicle and that its cost would not be commissionable by his agents.

The story was minor. He plays Mangano's husband, a dull middle-management banker, who is nonetheless rather smugly self-regarding. Mostly he complains about the noise of Roman traffic, which prevents him from getting much sleep. One dull evening at home, Mangano gets to fantasizing about a richer life and finds herself dreaming about a night when she is sexily sashaying down the Via Veneto, with a crowd of eager males trailing her. She leads them to a stadium where Clint, in a black cowboy outfit, shoots them. Later, inside the arena, she does a very genteel striptease, with Clint watching from a light pole, brandishing a gun—with which he eventually shoots himself.

The episode has a somewhat expressionist air, and it is the most developed of the stories offered in *The Witches*, which is not saying much. But Mangano spoke excellent English, had, Clint thought, the most beautifully expressive hands he'd ever seen, and he enjoyed working with her, as he did with De Sica. The Italian didn't give him much direction, which was fine with Clint, though, curiously,

OPPOSITE Directed by Vittorio De Sica, Clint played the husband to Silvana Mangano in this vanity production. RIGHT The poster for the Italian production of *Le Streghe*.

he mimed every move and gesture for Mangano to imitate. More interesting to Clint, De Sica cut the picture in the camera, leaving editors and producers with no choice but to put the picture together the way he envisioned it.

De Sica was a compulsive gambler and generally spent his weekends at Europe's grandest casinos, but on one of these jaunts he stopped off in Paris to introduce Clint at the French premiere of *A Fistful of Dollars*, warmly praising him as a "fine, sensitive" actor, with the possibility of becoming the next Gary Cooper. That—and the experience of being directed by a truly world-class filmmaker—is about all Clint got out of *The Witches*, although we might note that it was his first languidly humorous attempt to subvert his macho image, an activity he would return to, perhaps more consciously, certainly more effectively, in the years ahead.

And then, of course, there was that Ferrari, which was shipped to New York, where his wife met him, the idea being to drive across country in the vehicle. That did not work out too well—they had too much luggage, which they strapped to the sports car as best they could. Clint thought they looked a little like the Joad family as they made their way westward, albeit it in a more stylish auto (which, after being sold on, was auctioned in 2004 for $481,800).

As for the film, it played mainly in Italy and did little for Silvana Mangano's career. It was not released in the US until fourteen years later, and then only in a few film festivals and other special situations. Nonetheless, Clint had no regrets about it—he had enjoyed a pleasant little vacation-cum-learning experience under one of the few world-class directors—setting aside himself, Sergio Leone, and Don Siegel—he ever worked for.

ABOVE Clint said that he had long ago fallen in love with Mangano's on-screen image and that, and the Ferrari (*right*), were good enough reasons for taking the role.

THE GOOD, THE BAD AND THE UGLY 1966

It was long. It was brutal. It was often quite funny. It was expensive, for this time Sergio Leone was backed by a major American company, United Artists. It was also going to be Clint's farewell to the spaghetti western; his costar, Eli Wallach, was convinced of that before a single camera turned on the production. He had, by now, gotten everything he needed out of this quirky little (now not-so-little) genre.

The Good, the Bad and the Ugly is everything-but-the-kitchen-sink filmmaking. It features, among other set pieces, a gigantic Civil War battle for a bridge; a lengthy passage in an Auschwitz-type prison camp, where the band is ordered to play loudly in order to cover the cries of the tortured; a gunfight with one protagonist firing from his bathtub. The "Good" is nominally Clint's Blondie. The "Bad" is Lee Van Cleef as Angel Eyes, a particularly sadistic mercenary. The "Ugly" is Wallach's energetically amoral Tuco, cheerfully stealing the picture under Clint's flintily amused gaze. The picture has a subtext—whatever cruelties men do to one another in pursuit of their petty goals, it is nothing compared to the large-scale viciousness of war—but really its three protagonists are in search of, yes, buried treasure.

But that's no more than a pretext for its far-flung, high-flown, virtually nonstop action, all of which is well staged by Leone, who finally has the wherewithal to indulge his desire for spectacle. The director may sometimes have looked like "Yosemite Sam" to Clint, a chubby little man excitedly miming activities for his actors to imitate, but he was also Clint's kind of guy, a solid, knowledgeable professional, bringing a lifetime's experience to his craft. On the set, Clint continued to have a good time working for

OPPOSITE "The Good" surveys his domain.

56

"The cigars put you in the right mood–cantankerous."

Leone, though he cautioned Wallach to watch his ass—the crew was not always up to Leone's standards and, indeed, one explosion went awry and they were endangered by falling debris. Working on the same sequence, the production was delayed when a bridge was accidentally blown up before the multiple cameras were ready to roll.

Wallach, however, was largely enchanted by the experience. "He allowed me to have my romp with this little guy," he said of Leone. In that comment he illuminates one of Leone's great strengths—which is for getting up close and personal with his character's wonderfully exaggerated obsessions. In a way, what Clint provided Leone in all their films together was bemused rationality; he is most basically the taciturn observer of human folly—and the instrument by which reason is finally restored to a feverish world.

It was a very smart choice on Clint's part. However carried away we are by the lunacy of Leone's world, in the end we look to Clint's character for the restoration of order to it. And, as our surrogate, he never fails us. In the years ahead, Clint would often enough embrace eccentricity and obsession in his own roles—in his mind playing the straight man, the uncomplicated hero, is the surest road to boredom. But, for the moment, he was content not to sue the audience for attention, content to let it drift toward him as relief from Leonian lunacy.

Leone and Clint had a falling out when Clint refused to sign on for the director's next picture—*Once Upon a Time in the West*—and Leone said cruel and stupid things about Clint. The latter, however, put those comments down to frustration—Leone had his troubles getting his increasingly epic visions financed. Not long before the director died, they reunited in Italy and made their peace. Later, Clint dedicated *Unforgiven* to "Don [Siegel] and Sergio," a graceful acknowledgment of his two great directorial mentors.

OPPOSITE Poster art for *The Good, the Bad and the Ugly*: Leone's and Eastwood's energetic, operatic final collaboration.
ABOVE LEFT Clint as the "Good," Blondie, with what will be one of many nooses, ready to hang.
BELOW With the "Bad," Lee Van Cleef as Angel Eyes. ABOVE RIGHT With the "Ugly," Eli Wallach as the amoral Tuco.

HANG 'EM HIGH 1968

Clint returned to American filmmaking—he had not made a feature in his native land for a decade—with this modest, but not entirely uninteresting western, insisting that agreeable Ted Post, who had directed him in twenty-seven *Rawhide* episodes, direct the film. It begins arrestingly, with Clint, looking and playing a young innocent in the Rowdy Yates manner, being strung up—unjustly, of course—for rustling a small herd of cattle. He is dangling from the end of a rope, gasping for air, when Ben Johnson, driving a "tumbleweed" wagon, transporting a group of criminals to the territorial jail, rescues him.

Clint's Jed Cooper is understandably upset by his near-lynching and vows vengeance on its perpetrators. Rather quickly clearing his name, he signs on as a deputy for a hanging judge (Pat Hingle). Their deal is that Jed can pursue his own vengeance if, at the same time, he rounds up miscreants who have escaped the judge's jurisdiction. Clint enjoys a brief romance with Inger Stevens, a woman who has also been ill-used, but his obsessive attention is on the men who wronged him. Eventually he brings most of them to justice, though at the end of the film he still has two of them to round up—not to mention all the other criminals he has not yet met, but whom, it is implied, this once decent young man will devote the rest of a harsh life to running down.

OPPOSITE The prodigal returns to the American western.
ABOVE Clint Eastwood and Inger Stevens take a ride in *Hang 'Em High*.

"It had a certain feeling about capital punishment and injustice... I felt it was time, even though it was a smaller film, to go ahead and challenge myself in that way."

Hang 'Em High has several other points of interest. For one thing, it explores the resurrection theme that was a feature of *A Fistful of Dollars*, as well as several future Eastwood features. For another, it was a gloss on the theme of one of Clint's favorite boyhood films, William A. Wellman's *The Ox-Bow Incident*, in which innocent cowboys, also driving a herd of recently purchased cattle, are lynched. The one thing the film was not was a spaghetti western, though several critics identified it as such when it went into release ("Only because I was in it," Clint later snorted). It is, in manner, a much tidier, less raffish, much more talkative western than the Leone films, and quite conventional stylistically. The critics were still nattering over what they saw as the upsurge in violence in their beloved western form, not seeming to notice that there was not necessarily more violence in the new westerns, but violence of a different sort. In the past, dozens of anonymous cowpokes were shot off the roofs of western streets. Now the conflicts were visibly bloodier and much more regularly staged closer to the camera.

Big deal. Or so it seems to me. If we are to have violence in our movies (from which it has never been absent) then its consequences should, I think, be visible. And painful. To a degree *Hang 'Em High* was also affected by the bloody political events taking place on the national stage during the awful summer of 1968, when it appeared in theaters, with even the President of the United States wondering if those events were inspired by what was appearing on our screens.

This was balderdash, of course. And it had no effect on the film's box-office performance. When its takings were finally toted up, it ranked twentieth on the year's list of top grossers. It was a terrific performance, both for this modestly mounted, tightly budgeted little picture and for a star beginning his transition from faintly exotic realms to the American mainstream.

OPPOSITE Another noose and another set for *Hang 'Em High*, directed by Ted Post. The star begins his transition to the American mainstream.
ABOVE Western domesticity and silver service with Inger Stevens.

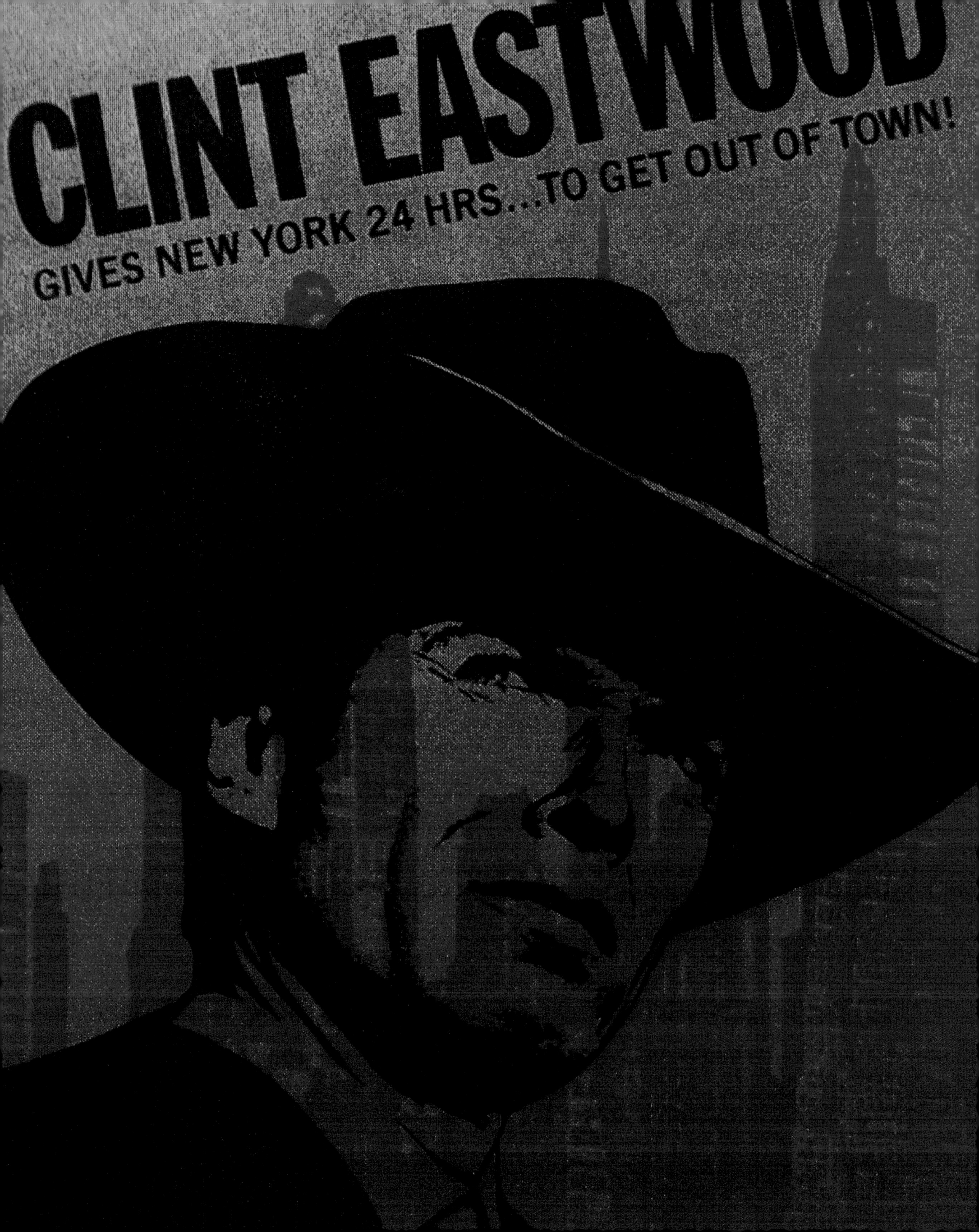
CLINT EASTWOOD
GIVES NEW YORK 24 HRS...TO GET OUT OF TOWN!

COOGAN'S BLUFF 1968

Coogan is a quiet, Gary Cooperish lawman arrived in New York to apprehend, and return to his Arizona jurisdiction, an escaped killer. It was originally intended to be a made-for-TV movie, but Jennings Lang, a powerful executive at Universal, where Clint had just signed a three-picture deal (later extended), thought it might be developed into a big-screen feature for the actor.

The latter saw it as a way of bringing his screen character out of the past and into a big-city environment, possibly broadening his appeal. It was not the most exalted—or original—idea, this country mouse, shrewder than he looks, teaching a thing or two to the city slickers.

And there were other problems to be solved—several draft scripts, none of which was ideal, a looming deadline (Clint was very shortly due in Europe to begin *Where Eagles Dare*), and, above all, the lack of an acceptable director. It was in solving the last problem that *Coogan's Bluff* had its largest significance in Clint's career, in that Don Siegel got the job.

He was a tough, no-nonsense guy, educated in part at Cambridge, but doing his best to hide that credential. He had been around the business since 1934, at first working in the montage department at Warner Bros., later making Academy Award-winning short subjects, before graduating to low-budget features, some of which (*Invasion of the Body Snatchers*, *Riot in Cell Block 11*, *Flaming Star*, the best of Elvis Presley's movies) were highly regarded by cinephiles. But he was stuck in grade; Hollywood continued to regard him as no better than an efficient lowbrow. He desperately needed to hitch his wagon to a star.

Which turned out not to be so easy. He and Clint liked each other at first glance, and set to work (eventually with Dean Riesner's help) cobbling together a shooting script. Some problems and some scratchiness were encountered, but eventually they set off for New York to begin shooting.

The narrative issues posed by *Coogan's Bluff* were never fully resolved. Clint is often charming as the faux innocent. But the movie as a whole has a brutal air, particularly in its treatment of women, who are very casually used and abused. That doesn't entirely square with the essential sweetness of the Walt Coogan character. Or with the developing feminist zeitgeist. It's as if all

concerned thought that perhaps a muscular assertion of traditional maleness might simply quash the female need not to be so harshly objectified. On the credit side, *Coogan's Bluff* contains some well-staged action sequences, in particular a cue-wielding fight in a pool hall, and decently written exchanges between Coogan and Lee J. Cobb, playing a cynical New York detective who cannot abide the interloper's persistent questioning of his and his department's encrusted stupidities.

The picture was mildly successful, but it did not do much to improve Clint's image and it did not do much, immediately, for Siegel's career. That would come a little later, when he became Clint's go-to guy as he more and more forcefully asserted himself as something more than a "component" in the picture-making process.

OPPOSITE Poster art for *Coogan's Bluff*, Clint's first cop movie. RIGHT Clint is measured for position on set at Universal Studios. OVERLEAF The Triumph motorbike was one of many iconic machines owned—and is still owned—by Clint, here with Tisha Sterling on pillion and (*right*) Andy Epper gets snookered.

"Don Siegel always
used to joke …
if the idea works
I'll take credit for it;
if it doesn't work,
it's your idea."

WHERE EAGLES DARE 1968

Quentin Tarantino, one of the movie's few fans, accurately characterized *Where Eagles Dare* as a "bunch-of-guys-on-a mission" movie. In essence it is about a group of spies parachuted behind German lines in World War II, ostensibly charged with recapturing from an Austrian *schloss* a general who is said to know the secrets of the impending allied invasion of Europe, but really (or also) looking for a double agent operating in their midst. As Tarantino also said, it is essentially about incredibly inept German soldiers congregating at places convenient for Clint to mow them down *en masse*.

The attraction for Clint was costarring with Richard Burton, just then beginning his boozy decline from almost movie stardom to almost brain-dead irrelevance. Clint's representatives at that moment had in mind a two-tier career for him: modestly scaled genre pictures for Universal on the one hand, big-budget, star-studded international spectacles on the other. In the event, Clint's major duty was keeping Burton reasonably sober when they were

on the set. He liked Burton, respected him as an actor, and seems to have been bemused by the expansive lifestyle—private jets, huge entourages, much jewelry—that he enjoyed with his wife, Elizabeth Taylor, whose company Clint also liked.

It is possible that the main thing he learned from them was how not to comport himself as a movie star—not that that was much of a temptation for him.

OPPOSITE Clint relaxes between takes. ABOVE A convivial moment in *Where Eagles Dare* with Ingrid Pitt, Mary Ure, and Richard Burton.

That was particularly true as he observed Burton at first hand. With his mellifluous voice and his vast fund of show-biz anecdotes, Burton could be a charming companion, but there was, as well, something impenetrable about him, some disconnect between his good-natured mask and his deeper emotions. He was, I've always thought (I knew him slightly when he was acting in *Camelot* in New York in 1960), a near-tragic example of what can happen to gifted people when they are thrust into celebrity's fast lane.

In the event, Clint did not have much to do in the film. All the other actors in the invading group spoke German, while he did not. This rendered him mute in a number of crucial scenes while he patiently awaited the opportunity to apply, as needed, such muscle as the plot required. A lot of his time was spent placating Burton's woozy demands and pretending to match him drink-for-drink when they were not on set. Toward the end of the shoot, Clint was eager to get finished so he could return home to attend the birth of his long-awaited first child, Kyle—an event he missed by a couple of days.

The movie that was eventually released proved commercially viable and almost totally without resonance. Based on an Alistair MacLean novel, it was just another decently mounted "Boy's Own" adventure, of the kind that dominated the screen in the years before special-effects extravaganzas began to take over a market segment largely composed of teenage boys. It also proved, if any proof was needed, that Clint could effectively carry pictures produced on a somewhat larger scale than his previous efforts had been.

"Richard Burton and I killed so many Nazis in two hours, it made me wonder why the war took so long."

THIS PAGE With Richard Burton on and off set. The older actor proved a charming, if inebriated, companion.

They must do what no army can do...go where no army can go...
penetrate the "Castle of the Eagle", nerve-center of the Gestapo, and blow it up!

Metro-Goldwyn-Mayer presents a Jerry Gershwin · Elliott Kastner picture starring

Richard Burton · Clint Eastwood · Mary Ure

also starring

"WHERE EAGLES DARE"

Patrick Wymark · Michael Hordern · story and screenplay by Alistair MacLean

directed by Brian G. Hutton · produced by Elliott Kastner · Panavision® and Metrocolor

THIS PAGE Eastwood on and off set in *Where Eagles Dare*.
ABOVE The drinks continue off set, this time with
Elizabeth Taylor and Ingrid Pitt joining the men.
LEFT Poster art for *Where Eagles Dare*.

PAINT YOUR WAGON 1969

From Clint's viewpoint, it seemed like a good idea at the time—a musical that could lighten up his image and—probably more important to him—show off his musicality. He had been—skillfully—playing jazz piano since he was a child, was a passionate *aficionado* of modern jazz, and had a pleasing light baritone voice. And, besides, the proffered musical was, in its way, a western—thus an easy and attractive transitional vehicle for him. Why not take a chance on *Paint Your Wagon*?

Actually, there were lots of reasons to have skipped it. For one thing, the source material was perhaps the least of Alan J. Lerner's and Fritz Lowe's Broadway musicals. For another, it was being personally produced by the neurotically nervous Lerner. Besides, it was to be shot on location deep in the Oregon woods, where a whole mining town was built—on rockers, so a concluding earthquake could be persuasively staged. Finally, the director was to be Joshua Logan, an expert Broadway hand, but not a man who would be comfortable picking his way through the mud and mess of this setting in his nice little Italian shoes.

So everything that could go wrong did. To begin with, an over-zealous gate guard refused Clint admission to the Paramount lot when he reported for rehearsals. By which time, the script, which originally had a certain arcane charm about it, had been updated to match an imaginary Sixties sensibility (essentially it was now about a frontier *ménage a trois*), with Lee Marvin as a charmless old goat, Clint as his innocent "Pardner," and Jean Seberg as the object of their affections. Once on location Marvin, who did not tolerate directorial insecurity comfortably, became more or less permanently drunk—if rarely overtly disorderly—and essentially unmanageable by Logan, who soon found himself fighting to retain his job, as Lerner reached out to more take-charge directors, like Richard Brooks, as replacements. As the movie fell more and more behind schedule, Clint undertook a relationship with Seberg, who was not herself a model of stability. They basically absented themselves from the set whenever possible, hopping on Clint's motorcycle to canoodle in the beautiful countryside.

RIGHT Clint with Lee Marvin and Jean Seberg, the object of their affections.
OPPOSITE "I Talk to the Trees" was Clint's memorable song from an unmemorable movie.

Don Siegel dropped by for a visit, agreeing with Clint that they could have made two or three pretty decent westerns on the $30 million budget that was dribbling—no, flooding—through everyone's fingers up here in the wilds. Eventually the picture was finished, with the studio insisting on playing it as a roadshow attraction (two-a-day showings, with tickets sold on a reserved-seat basis), where, of course, it bombed, not only because of the film's stammering pace, but because that method of releasing generally overblown productions had run its course.

In the end *Paint Your Wagon* did Clint no harm—the public tends not to blame performers wounded by exploding bombs. Indeed, Clint took a very useful lesson from the experience. Obviously, in any career, one can get caught up in a mistake. But from here on out, he vowed, all the mistakes would be of his own making. "I came to the conclusion, after the fifth month, that I was going to get really active with Malpaso [as he had named his own production company]. I was going to go back to doing just regular movies." It was, he said later, "a turning point in my career." As, indeed, it would prove to be.

ABOVE Clint and Lee in action. BELOW Clint consults with Alan J. Lerner.
CENTRE Clint and Jean Seberg enjoyed each other's company on and off set.

"It was a disaster, but it didn't have to be such an expensive disaster."

ABOVE Poster art for *Paint Your Wagon*.
BELOW Clint with Lee Marvin on location in the Oregon woods.

TWO MULES FOR SISTER SARA 1970

This is another fine mess—that, in the end, turned out more or less all right. It is the story of a hooker (Shirley MacLaine), disguised as a nun, who is seeking funds for the Juaristas rebelling against the Emperor Maximilian in Mexico in the 1860s. She is saved from rape by Clint's Hogan, an American mercenary, also serving the Juarista cause as a dynamite expert, assigned to blow up a government fortress.

The first script was the work of Budd Boetticher, widely and correctly admired for a series of austere little westerns he directed for Randolph Scott. One imagines that this film might have been in that vein, but he unwisely sold his screenplay to the loathsome producer, Martin Rackin, who promptly signed Albert Maltz for a rewrite. He was one of the Hollywood Ten, whose first credited work after a long period on the blacklist this would be. It was not work that was particularly congenial to him and Clint judged his script neither better nor worse than Boetticher's, that it was perhaps a bit more—er, well—colorful. Originally, Elizabeth Taylor was set to costar with Clint, but, with her career now somewhat in disarray—she endured a string of pretentious flops at this time—she disappeared, to be replaced by MacLaine. More surprising, considering that the movie was directed by Siegel, Clint appears looking very much like one of his Leone protagonists—unshaven, taciturn, very rough hewn—as MacLaine's rescuer from the fate worse than death. They then join forces, a fighting love story ensues, and eventually they destroy Maximilian's fort and ride off into the sunset together. Ennio Morricone's score reinforces the notion that this is a Leone knock-off, though that's not really the case.

The film is entertaining in its little way but it is an odd product for Siegel, who did not typically do comedy-romances, and it's an odd one for Clint as well, who at the time was eager to shake even a superficial identification with his spaghetti western past. Indeed, around this time he rejected Leone's attempt to cast him in *Once Upon a Time in the West* (his role was eventually played by Charles Bronson), which is the probable cause of the Italian's subsequent estrangement. One gets the impression that Clint was unsure about

how long his newfound success might last—"It takes a long time for an actor to get over the thought that whatever he's doing at the moment may be his last job," he said to me many years later. His ceaseless work in this period was, I suspect, motivated by that idea. It is possible, too, that he was building up his savings account, so that he could sustain himself more comfortably when he ceased being an actor for hire and embarked on a new, more risky career as an independent filmmaker.

In any event, no harm done. *Two Mules* was a success. And it gathered a few admiring reviews. A new breed of less tradition-bound reviewers was beginning to emerge and one of them, Roger Greenspan, in *The New York Times*, called it "a movie-lover's dream," adding that, "it stays in the mind the way only movies of exceptional narrative intelligence do."

Well, not really. But Clint was just one picture away from beginning to establish his exceptionalism.

RIGHT *Two Mules for Sister Sara*, Clint leading the mules with Shirley MacLaine, who played the hooker disguised as a nun. OPPOSITE MacLaine, Eastwood, and Siegel consult in the heat of the Mexican landscape.

"It's really a two-character story and the woman has the best part

THIS PAGE *Two Mules for Sister Sara* was a pleasant, picaresque western with strong echoes of Clint's work in Italy for Sergio Leone. Shirley MacLaine made an unlikely but intriguing costar, and the score by Ennio Morricone contributed to the film's success.

—something I'm quite sure that Shirley noticed.
It's kind of *African Queen* gone west."

KELLY'S HEROES 1970

It was supposed to be a blend of two genres—a straight adventure story in which a group of military misfits go on an unauthorized mission behind enemy lines to steal $16 million in gold bullion from the Nazis for their own profit, and a *M*A*S*H* style satire on soldierly ineptitude. Shot in Yugoslavia with a group of actors including Don Rickles and Donald Sutherland, whose company Clint enjoyed, it turned out not to work very well on either level, especially the satirical one.

Directed by Brian Hutton, in the same (literally) explosive manner he had brought to *Where Eagles Dare*, it is, as we look back on it today, less focused than the previous film. *Eagles* may not have been a model of originality, but this one is like several dozen similar big battle films. This was a particular disappointment to Clint. The boredom of his own military duty (mostly as a swimming instructor at Fort Ord, Ca.) and the stumbling incompetence of the army's bureaucracy had always rankled him. Moreover he deplored the miscalculated adventure of America in Vietnam. He thought *Kelly's Heroes* might at least inferentially criticize military mindlessness.

OPPOSITE Clint astride his Norton Commando 750S while on location for *Kelly's Heroes*.
ABOVE With a bunch of agreeable actors that included Donald Sutherland and Don Rickles. Clint thought this "could have been one of the best war movies ever."

The shoot went well enough, and Clint moved on, almost without a break, to his next picture, *Two Mules for Sister Sara* (which was released ahead of *Kelly's Heroes*). But the producing studio (MGM) was under new management, led by James Aubrey (a.k.a. "The Smiling Cobra"), and he decreed that the film should be severely re-edited so that its satirical elements were largely excised. Hutton fought the good fight for his cut of the film and Clint, with increasing anger, joined in this struggle—to no avail. He was on a remote Mexican location by this time and unable to bring his angry physical presence to the executive suites in Culver City. His mood was not greatly improved when he learned that the studio planned to open *Heroes* at virtually the same time that *Two Mules* would be going into theaters. "How much can they tolerate of the same actor?" he asked, not unreasonably.

More, apparently, than he imagined. He was still, relatively speaking, a fresh and attractive face, and both pictures did all right at the box office, although *Kelly's Heroes*, much the more expensive of the two, grossed only about $600,000 more than its more modestly priced competitor. As for Clint himself, he was trying hard to measure up to the demands of the press for interviews, an effort that had, for the moment, mixed results. He is, inherently, a shy man and far from glib. One gets the impression, perusing the clippings that recount these encounters, that he was trying as hard as he could—perhaps too hard—but that it really wasn't working for him. He's not sullen or hostile; he's just rather puzzled and somewhat inarticulate.

It was something he would have to work on—which through the years he did. It's part of his dutifulness. Nowadays, especially when he's talking to people who ask him serious questions about his work, he's good-humored and able unpretentiously to articulate his intentions, especially as a director. Back then, though, he was still a stranger in the strange land of movie stardom.

"The film could have been one of the best war movies ever. And it should have been; it had the best script, a good cast, a subtle anti-war message. But somehow everything got lost. The picture got bogged down shooting in Yugoslavia and it just ended up as the story of a bunch of American screw-offs in World War II."

OPPOSITE Clint with Rickles and Sutherland.
THIS PAGE Adrift amongst "a bunch of screw-offs," including, additionally, Telly Savalas (*top right*), his view that the film was a missed opportunity was echoed by the critics.
LEFT CENTER With the director, Brian G. Hutton.

THE BEGUILED 1971

Clint speaking, some years later, about *The Beguiled*, said, "I wasn't sure an audience was ready for that, or wanted that, but I knew I wanted it." It remains the darkest, oddest, and, to my taste, one of his most interesting films. It is Southern Gothic, based on a novel by Thomas Cullinan, which came to his attention by means no one can quite remember anymore. Clint interested Don Siegel in the book and, such was his power at the time, it got an unlikely green light from stodgy Universal.

It is the tale of a feckless Union soldier, found wounded behind enemy lines in the Civil War by a student at an isolated and rundown female seminary. Taken to the school and nursed back to health by its headmistress (an unimprovable Geraldine Page) and her charges, he is soon having his way with her and some of her students. He is a cocksure and careless man—Clint's first attempt to play the ambiguous side of masculinity. When his unfaithfulness to Page's Martha Farnsworth is discovered, she claims that his leg wound has become gangrenous and, while he is knocked out by a fall, she amputates it.

But wait! There's worse to come. Eventually she arranges, with the complicity of her students, his death (poisoned mushrooms). Occasionally *The Beguiled* totters on the brink of black comedy, but the intensity of the playing in the claustrophobic space of the school does not permit that. It retains its tension. And its charged sexuality.

Not that its tonality was easily achieved. There were many drafts of the script, with Albert Maltz again taking a hand and arguing for a happy ending. He just couldn't bear to think of those sweet young things harboring such darkness. Eventually, a script that was faithful to the novel was cobbled together by the film's associate producer, Claude Traverse, who—how typical of Hollywood—received no credit for his efforts except in the grateful memories of Eastwood and Siegel.

It was a happy production. Clint and Page enjoyed working together, as he had previously enjoyed working with another major Broadway star, Lee J. Cobb. Like him, he found Page "ready to go, ready to roll, no BS … they just step right up to bat." We might pause here to note that Clint was never just the lucky, handsome hunk the press in those days took him to be. I recall that in his younger days he had been an earnest student of method acting, studying with serious Stanislavskians. In general, it can be said of him that if he perceives a weakness in himself, he will bend every effort to address it. You can see it in his attempts to manage his encounters with the press more successfully. You can see it in the way he addressed his fear of flying, rooted in a near-death experience in a plane crash during his army days. Eventually, he became the owner and pilot of a helicopter, which, to this day, he flies himself on his far-flung errands around the West Coast.

OPPOSITE At the gates of the seminary, Clint, as antihero John McBurney, unaware of his fate. ABOVE The Union soldier before the fall.

85

The movie, however, was an unambiguous flop. In those days, people would accept the possibility that Clint might endure some setbacks on his heroic path. But they expected that eventually he would explode in righteous rage and set things violently to rights in the final reel. They could not endure him subsiding more or less quietly into death—particularly at the hands of a bunch of schoolchildren. And that says nothing about the film's bleak view of carelessly questing masculinity and of murderous femininity. There is probably no hope of rescuing *The Beguiled*'s reputation at this late date. But it is a haunting film. And it is of major importance as an assertion of Clint Eastwood's determination to define his stardom on his own terms.

"You know, he is totally justifiable. What guy wouldn't try to save his life in a situation like that? With seven girls hauling you around on a stretcher say, 'Hey, well, I will grab a little nookie while I'm here, and who cares?'"

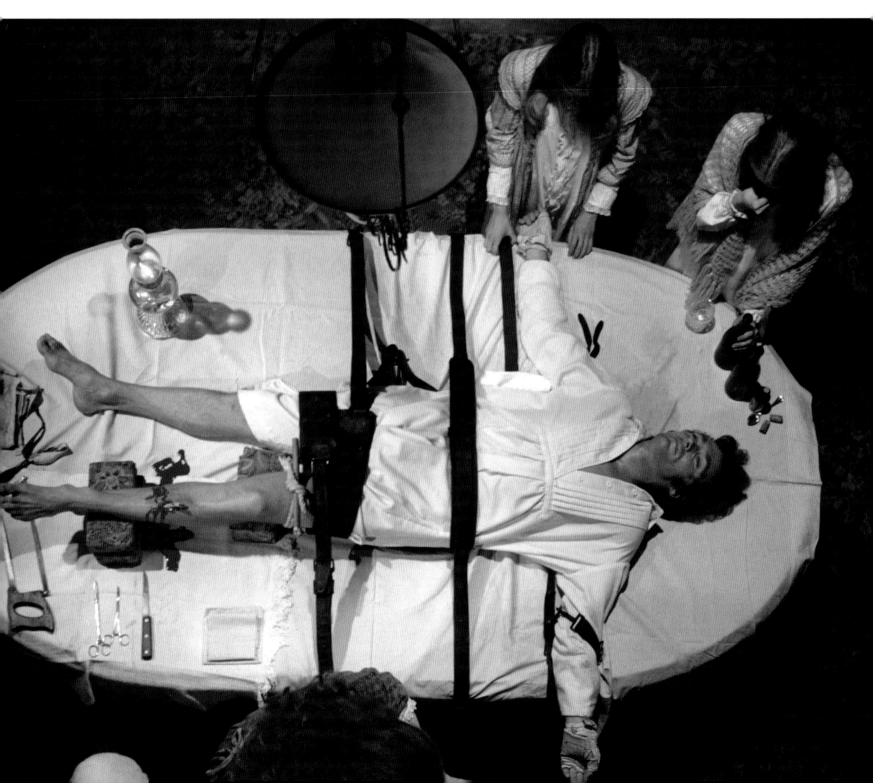

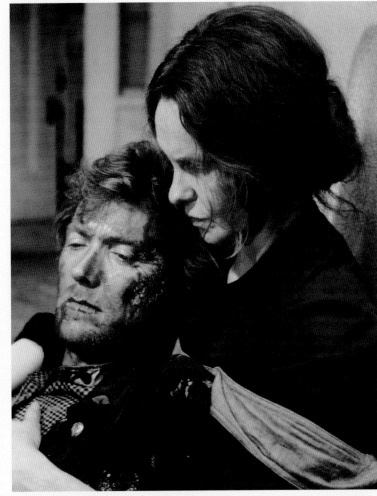

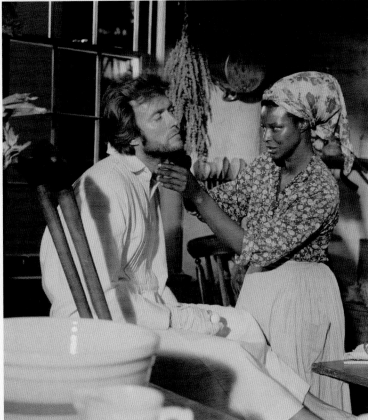

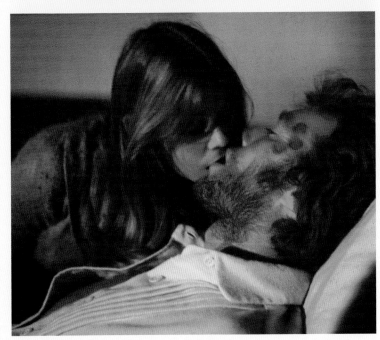

OPPOSITE AND THIS PAGE Scenes from this Southern Gothic tale, which occasionally totters on the brink of black comedy but retains its tension. ABOVE RIGHT With Geraldine Page. BOTTOM LEFT With Mae Mercer. ABOVE With Jo Ann Harris.

PLAY MISTY FOR ME 1971

It was time for Clint to realize his long-held dream of directing. It had taken root during his *Rawhide* years, when he thought, for a moment, that his request to direct an episode would be granted. Then the producers demurred, citing previous bad experiences with actor-directors. The incident puzzled and angered Clint. Over the program's many episodes he had studied the largely veteran directors who had jobbed on and off the show on a weekly basis, learning what to do from the good ones, what not to do from the bad ones. He had done the same thing during his feature career. As an observer of the production process, he was already a canny veteran.

And now he had what he correctly thought was a perfect script for a beginner. *Play Misty for Me* was written in treatment form by Jo Heims, a sometime legal secretary who was an old friend. Clint had once held an option on the property, which had subsequently passed to Universal, where he proposed making it. The studio was dubious, but with Clint working for Screen Actors and Directors Guild minimums, it could be made for less than a million, which triggered minimum payments to craft workers, too. Clint knew what the studio bosses thought—let him get this out of his system and then he'll do a couple of westerns for us, which is, indeed, what happened.

But Heims had a nifty idea: a smooth-talking, small-city disc jockey, cool and solipsistic, meets an attractive woman (Jessica Walter), has a casual sexual encounter with her—not the sort of thing that was unknown to him—which she regards as anything but casual. Indeed, she turns out to be a psychopath and when he rejects her she begins stalking him and his girlfriend (Donna Mills) with almost fatal results for them. "Why would you want to play in a picture where the woman has the best role?" the studio brass wondered. "I don't know," came what was about to become his typical reply. "Why does anyone want to see anything? But it's a good suspense piece."

It also had a small, thus easily manageable cast, it could be made on the Monterey Peninsula, which he had fallen in love with while soldiering at Fort Ord, and where he and his family now mostly lived. He was even able to do a sequence at the Monterey Jazz Festival, which, given his musical passions, was a big plus.

But just as he was about to start shooting, his beloved father died suddenly of a heart attack and that loss hit him hard. It might be argued that working on his film was an anodyne for his grief. It might also be argued that his emphasis on fitness, a healthy diet, and the other good habits took an upsurge after this first close brush with mortality. I'm not so certain of that. As I've said, he's a dutiful man and he seems to have always known that an actor's first duty is to his own appearance. His great trick is not to expend any visible sweat on that activity.

ABOVE Clint the small-city disc jockey.
OPPOSITE With Jessica Walter in *Play Misty for Me*.

"I just thought I could do it. I picked a small show, a small—not a big—cast, not a tremendous production problem. And *Play Misty for Me* was written by a friend of mine. It was a success because it cost us seventy-two or seventy-three thousand dollars. I can't quite remember exactly. But it was very inexpensive and the studio didn't really jump on it because they thought, 'If this guy does a couple more westerns and a few detective dramas, what the heck? So we'll just let this one sort of sneak out.' But it hung out out there and it gathered an audience and it gathered a following."

90

The day before he made his first shot was devoted to careful preparation, and he hit the sack convinced that he was completely ready—until he sat bolt upright in bed, realizing that the one thing he'd neglected was studying his own lines. But he burned a little midnight oil and was reassured as well because he'd talked Don Siegel into taking a small, almost talismanic role as a bartender. The director did a couple days of work, opined that Clint had things nicely under control, and departed.

It was a trim, suspenseful, scary little picture. Jessica Walter was terrific as the mad woman and Clint captured the sleepy egotism of the DJ perfectly. He obviously knew what it was to be handsome and much hit-upon, and how to play up those qualities—in a fiction, though not in real life—as an entitlement. Given that the film followed so closely on *The Beguiled*, one has to believe that Clint's thoughts, as his star ascended, were suddenly focused on the darker aspects of the privileged male's existence.

The picture was not particularly well handled by Universal; it should have been more profitable than it was—as witnessed by the lingering fondness in which his audience holds it. People somehow keep rediscovering it—not least when it was widely noticed that the much more successful *Fatal Attraction* of 1987 basically ripped off *Misty*'s crucial plot device more sensationally, but not necessarily more effectively.

OPPOSITE The calm before the storm in *Play Misty for Me*, and the poster art.
ABOVE Clint Eastwood the director at work on his debut, ushering in a whole new phase of his career.

DIRTY HARRY 1971

It is rare to be able to identify the precise moment when a star becomes a super-star. But in the case of Clint Eastwood that moment is self-evident. It occurs early in *Dirty Harry*, when, eating a hot dog in a greasy spoon, alarm bells in the bank across the street go off. "Aw, shit," says Harry Callahan, as he rises from his stool and, still chewing on his food, strolls over to foil the robbery. In short order, he comes upon a wounded criminal, itching to go for his gun, which is just inches from his fingers.

Whereupon Harry launches into his now immortal soliloquy. "I know what you're thinkin'. Did he fire six shots or only five..." Clint looks almost boyish as he delivers his lines, an ironic smile playing about his lips. If you want to get fancy about it, he is acknowledging the Dostoyevskian bond between the criminal and the cop pursuing him. But let's not go there. It has become a standard trope in both popular and high-toned fiction, no less effective for its familiarity.

The point is that Clint, in his presence and in his playing, makes his character irresistible. I believe that, from that moment on, he was ours. Or we were his. Or some combination thereof—always excepting the sourpusses among us, who for a long time persisted in the belief that Clint and all his works posed clear and present dangers to the republic. And that *Dirty Harry*, in particular, had, as Pauline Kael put it, the "fairy-tale appeal" of "fascist medievalism."

That's a pretty weird description of a movie so grittily realistic in manner. If it were true, then Harry would be firmly aligned with the police and municipal bureaucracy who, in fact, do everything in their power to thwart his monomaniacal pursuit of the psychopathic killer who is stalking the streets of San Francisco. Admittedly, his tactics are not subtle or pretty, and they do, rather obviously, shade the letter of the law—in particular the Escobar and Miranda

OPPOSITE Harry Callahan makes his presence known.
OVERLEAF A traffic-stopping moment from *Dirty Harry*.

93

"I tried being reasonable, I didn't like it."

Harry Callahan

decisions of the Supreme Court, which slightly tipped the legal balance away from the victims and toward the criminal. Clint himself shared that view of their effect. But that didn't make him a wing nut. A lot of Americans, of many political persuasions, felt the same way. Some years later, David Thomson, the movie encyclopedist, quite sensibly wrote: "Those saved by the social revolutions of the 1960s were only ever a few. Eastwood guessed, or knew in his bones, that Harry's 'dirtiness' was a refreshing reclaiming of common sense and direct action as far as middle America was concerned."

Another way of saying that is that Clint would not have pursued this script over the years and through several incarnations merely because it made an ideological point. As an actor, he liked the bleakness of Harry's character and his situation as a widower who is oriented exclusively toward his job, because there is nothing else that claims his attention—no woman, no fine dining, no sailboating on the bay, not even a movie. What fun he has is confined to insubordinate wisecracking to his superiors, not excluding the mayor. It is the movie that sealed his bond with ordinary Joes.

And under Don Siegel's hard-driving direction (which yet takes time for comic and suspenseful diversions that have the effect of humanizing Harry) it is a very well-made movie—even Kael had to admit that. It was one of the factors that made it seem so dangerous to her. She, like a number of other critics, liked to strike an anti-intellectual pose, pretending that popular success was often a better measure of a movie's merits than the praise of the Mandarins. On the other hand, she understood that the unguided masses were volatile and easily misled—particularly when "corrupt" Hollywood, in this case led by those roughnecks Eastwood and Siegel, was having its way with them.

The result, in this instance, was an utterly false argument. If you go back to *Dirty Harry* today you will still find in it what it always was, an extraordinarily effective and artful popular entertainment, about which no apologies need be made. In fact, the only thing that seems wrong with it now is its relatively modest gestures toward the ideological arguments of its moment. Conversely, what shines more brightly now is the complex character of its protagonist—sad, lonely, angry, funny, driven, and quixotic. It is a remarkable portrait of a certain American type, fuming, puzzled, close to the end of decency's rope, yet clinging desperately to it as modernity, in all its ambiguities, keeps fraying it.

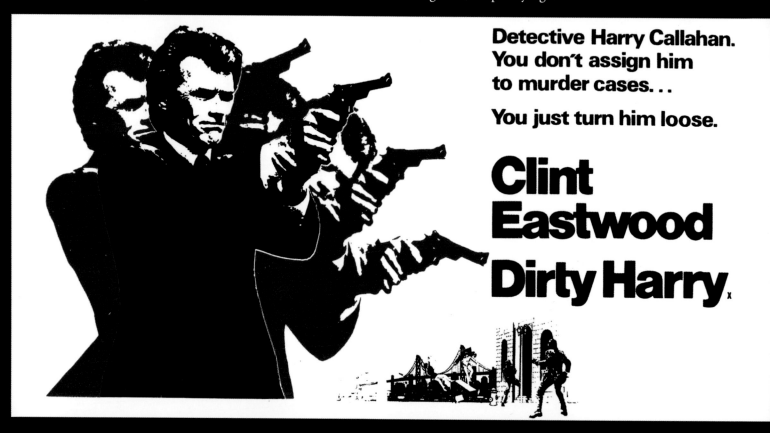

ABOVE Legendary poster art for *Dirty Harry*.
OPPOSITE Clint on and off the set of *Dirty Harry*, the dazzling urban thriller that gave him his second iconic characterization.
TOP LEFT On location, son Kyle learns some stunts from his father.

lint Eastwood in
resence and in
aying makes his
cter irresistible.
Harry in pursuit
e hijacked school
n the final
es. Clint said
the stunts,
e you're in
cter you can

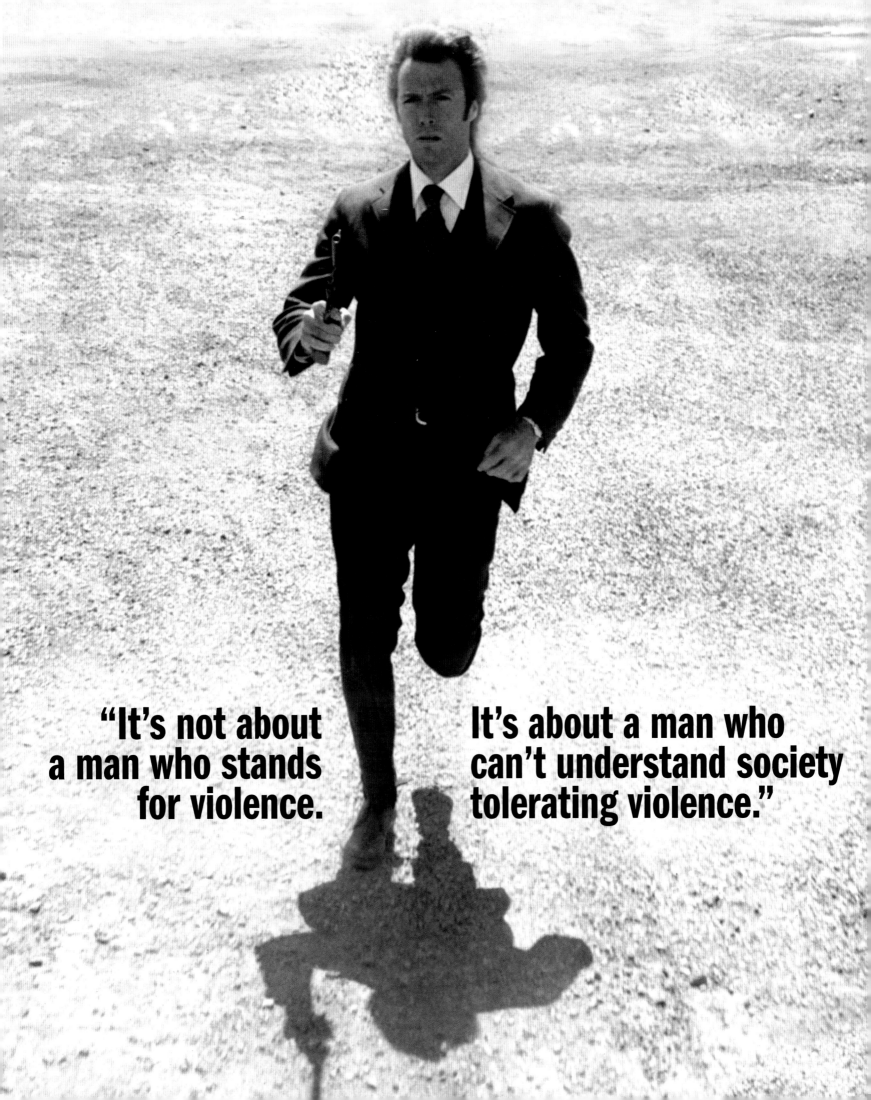

"It's not about a man who stands for violence. It's about a man who can't understand society tolerating violence."

JOE KIDD 1972

Time, now, to discharge the obligations Clint owed Universal as a result of the *Misty* deal. Sure enough, they turned out to be, as he had predicted, a pair of westerns. The first of them, *Joe Kidd*, involved quite decent talent. The screenplay was by Elmore Leonard, not yet the beloved master of witty popular fiction he would soon become, but a competent craftsman; the director was John Sturges, whose credits included *Bad Day at Black Rock*, *The Magnificent Seven*, and *The Great Escape*, as well as a number of much more routine movies.

In support was Robert Duvall, giving a rambunctious performance as a cattle baron engineering a land grab at the expense of Hispanic ranch owners. Clint appears first in Duvall's employ, then switches sides to support the downtrodden.

Leonard's script kept being rewritten by the producer and, worryingly, the production began without a firm ending. But Clint liked Sturges, a director who, like Siegel, kept barreling along toward some sort of logical—or in this case illogical—conclusion. There was a narrow-gauge railroad that ran down the street of the western town that was the film's chief location, and the director kept eyeing it. He had always wanted to stage a train wreck and he wondered if, with Clint at the throttle, the engine could jump the tracks that ran close to a saloon and massively intrude on its barroom, where a number of subsidiary heavies were gathered. Clint thought: sure, anything to bring the picture to some kind of conclusion. (His second child, Alison, was due and he was eager to be on hand for her birth as he had not been for Kyle's.) So it was done.

Joe Kidd eventually went forth to decent business and weak reviews. Clint was now regularly listed on the annual list of top box-office attractions, and one critic made an interesting point when he observed that Clint brought an "authoritative normalcy" to his playing in this film. It was, I think, his default setting in those days. If nothing else, he could be counted on to bring solid professionalism to his work in the kind of genre movies that seemed to be all that the studios—especially Universal—could imagine him doing. But he was growing restive in this situation, and he had already noticed that his friends at Warner Bros. had been much more forthcoming than Universal ever had when it came to

discussing the advertising and promotion for *Dirty Harry*, seeking his opinions, drawing him into their process. His old friend and attorney, Frank Wells, now running business affairs at Warner Bros., was already urging him to jump ship. But Clint still owed Universal some pictures, and for the next three years he made them while also undertaking roles at other studios. It's always better to be busy than to be idly awaiting someone else's big idea.

ABOVE Clint on location for *Joe Kidd* with director John Sturges.
OPPOSITE A more traditional cowboy in a more traditional western.
OVERLEAF Riding the trail with Robert Duvall in *Joe Kidd*.

"I liked John Sturges and they made a good pitch."

"I'd never done this
before, start a picture
and not have an ending."

HIGH PLAINS DRIFTER 1973

He rides out of a shimmering heat haze, a stranger in a flat hat and a frock coat—this time, for the first and last time, literally a "man with no name," identified in the credits only as "The Stranger." His destination is Lago, a raw little town, all of its buildings unpainted, on the edge of Mono Lake, which is, in reality, almost a dead sea, its water drained off to feed Los Angeles' insatiable need for fluid assets.

As imagined by screenwriter Ernest Tidyman, who usually specialized in urban settings (i.e. *The French Connection*), Lago is a cesspool of corruption, its previous sheriff beaten to death because he threatened to expose the fact that the mine on which it depends for its livelihood is located on government land, which means that it is not entitled to the proceeds of its operation. His killers were an outlaw band, hired by the town to enforce its secrets. In turn they were betrayed by the townsfolk and now, freed from jail, they are heading toward Lago with vengeance on their minds. The oncoming Stranger may possibly be the slain lawman's brother, though it is also possible he is his ghost or possibly even a freelance apparition. Clint has never said who he is, only admitting that he played him more as the vengeful brother than as anything else. He thought audience speculation about his identity was good word-of-mouth advertising for *High Plains Drifter*.

In any event, the town hires The Stranger as their designated gunslinger, and he organizes a defense force, orders that the town be painted bright red and renamed "Hell," and allows its citizenry to be largely wiped out by the marauders before he finally kills them all.

It is a one weird little western, its spirit closer to the Leone films than any of Clint's other American movies. Full of brutal action and rough sexuality and, under Clint's direction, with a huge assist from Bruce Surtees' cinematography, it is probably the bleakest of his movies—an exercise in virtually unrelieved, sun-baked nihilism.

I like it a lot, precisely because of its essential amorality. Certainly I liked it more than John Wayne did. A little later, Clint had a film he thought might be right for Wayne, who in the course of rejecting the offer made some affronted comments about *High Plains Drifter*, largely because it was so anti-John Ford in its outlook.

Putting it mildly, it was a rejection of the basic Ford trope about decent people taming the wilderness, building a civilization where none had previously existed.

Well, sure. Duke Wayne got that right, but he was now becoming a beloved back number. Anarchy was the ruling passion in the modern western, no matter how much the traditionalists mourned that fact, which was reflected in the reviews of this film. They were, on the whole, blandly acceptant of its transgressive spirit, which even Clint later admitted might have been a bit much. He would never again make a film that took so dismayed a view of human nature, or one in which, at its end, the restoration of moral order seemed so much a matter of chance.

OPPOSITE Poster art for *High Plains Drifter*. RIGHT Eastwood lines up a shot on his first western as director, here with cinematographer Bruce Surtees.

" John Wayne didn't like *High Plains Drifter* and let me know it. He wrote me a letter putting it down, saying it was not the West. I was trying to get away from what he and Gary Cooper and others had done.**"**

OPPOSITE *High Plains Drifter* rides forth; audience speculation about his identity was good word-of-mouth advertising.
RIGHT The ambiguities of *High Plains Drifter* extend even to the exact nature of Eastwood's enigmatic central character in this semi-supernatural western.
ABOVE With Mariana Hill.

"I like to direct the same way that I like to be directed."

BREEZY 1973

This is the slightest film Clint ever made, a sweet, somewhat improbable romance between Frank Harmon (William Holden), a jaded real-estate salesman in his fifties, and a seventeen-year-old hippie (Kay Lenz), whom he finds at the bottom of his driveway, sobbing over a dog wounded by a passing car. They bundle the animal off to a vet—he's repaired, of course—and the almost annoyingly cheerful girl enters Frank's life, restoring an anxious cheer to it. He's embarrassed to be seen with her when they encounter his friends but, in the end, they decide to stay together. Probably won't last a year, he grumbles. To which she replies, "Just think, a whole year."

The script was once again by Jo Heims and Clint and his producer, Robert Daley, figured the film wouldn't make a dime, which was all right, since it wouldn't cost more than a nickel. They liked the innocence of the story. And Clint liked the idea of working with Holden. He had been a sort of Wasp *beau ideal* in the 1950s, offering an intriguing mixture of cynicism and idealism in a devastatingly handsome package. A heavy binge-drinker and a man never entirely certain that acting was suitable work for a gentleman, he had nevertheless been, for roughly a decade, Hollywood's leading star. Now his career—despite his great, wintry command of *The Wild Bunch* in 1969—was in decline. But he was very much Clint's kind of guy—reserved, untemperamental, and completely professional on the set, very courtly with Lenz, with whom he shared some potentially discomfiting love scenes.

This was, once again, a chance for Clint to practice his directorial skills in a low-pressure situation, and he did quite well with material that needed more dramatic tension. There should have been more visible emotions at stake in a relationship where the age difference between the principals is a daunting four decades. In the end, the film is a sort of fairy tale told in a rather realistic manner. It does, however, make the point that happiness is not easily found and that people are right to grab for it, however unpromising their circumstances.

From the studio's point of view, this was probably an inexpensive indulgence for a star whom they surely saw growing increasingly restive with the material they were offering him and with the cluelessness of their promotional efforts, well exemplified by the way *Breezy* came and went virtually without notice.

OPPOSITE Clint Eastwood and William Holden on location for *Breezy*.
RIGHT Time out during production.

THIS PAGE A gentle, romantic picture, *Breezy* confounded expectations and alienated many of Eastwood's fans. This was his first non-starring film as director.
ABOVE AND OPPOSITE William Holden and Kay Lenz, a four decades' age difference between them.

MAGNUM FORCE 1973

It was John Milius's idea. The screenwriter is an avid gun collector, often identified as a rare neo-conservative in an endemically liberal Hollywood—he's really more of a libertarian-anarchist with a taste for grandiose heroics and sometimes antic, sometimes flaccid, action sequences.

In the early 1970s, he became fascinated by news stories out of Brazil about their "Death Squads"—police officers who took to murdering figures they regarded as menaces to the body politic. At first, it was said, they were moved by idealism, but they were soon corrupted, and became killers for hire. What if, Milius wondered, such a unit infected the San Francisco police department? He approached Clint with his idea and he responded enthusiastically.

He has always said that he thought of it as nothing more than a good idea for a *Dirty Harry* sequel, but it is hard to escape the notion that it would also give him the opportunity to answer the liberal charge that Harry Callahan was some sort of fascist troglodyte. By the end of *Magnum Force*, the cop is defending liberal democratic ideals against the assaults of the secret police, whose leader is a smooth-talking Hal Holbrook.

It's a serviceable conceit for a well-made police drama, which was not easily realized. For one thing, Milius was offered the chance to direct *Dillinger*, another script he had written, so Clint was obliged to press into service Michael Cimino, who was then polishing up Clint's next film, *Thunderbolt and Lightfoot*. Clint hired his old friend, Ted Post, to direct, but that, according to Post, turned into rather an unhappy experience. According to him, Clint, now of course a director himself, intruded on Post's prerogatives as he had not on *Hang 'Em High*, leading first to wrangles, then to a sort of passive resistance on Post's part. Asked about this situation years later, Clint professed puzzlement. He retained a large affection for Post and remembered the shoot as a pleasant one.

Post thought Clint's performance "draggy." So too did the implacable Pauline Kael, who thought his "inexpressiveness" was the key to his mass audience appeal. "Educated people," she opined, expected something more, well, you know, "expressive." Hal Holbrook, a thoughtful observer of his own profession, correctly thought the opposite: "That silent containment of his is his most powerful instrument," he later said. Whatever the particulars of the matter, this much can be said with certainty: ideology makes no difference to the action-movie audience. They really don't care whether the film's moral tow is liberal or conservative. They're just present for the kicks, and *Magnum Force* provided them in generous measure. The dialogue may not be quite as sharp as it was in the first *Dirty Harry* film, but he is still a rebel against authority, this time with better reason; these guys are actively malevolent instead of being merely routine incompetents. And the picture's success at the box office assured the *Dirty Harry* series status as a franchise, which Clint would come to regard ambivalently. Over the next decade and a half Harry Callahan would not entirely lose his edge. He would always retain his ability to snap-shoot one liners amidst hails of bullets. But there were obvious limits to this character and, despite the fact that he became a less obstreperous figure as the years wore on, Clint eventually came to feel that he probably extended the series one or two more films than he ideally should have done.

LEFT The second *Dirty Harry* directed by Ted Post, here on set with Clint.
OPPOSITE The poster art.

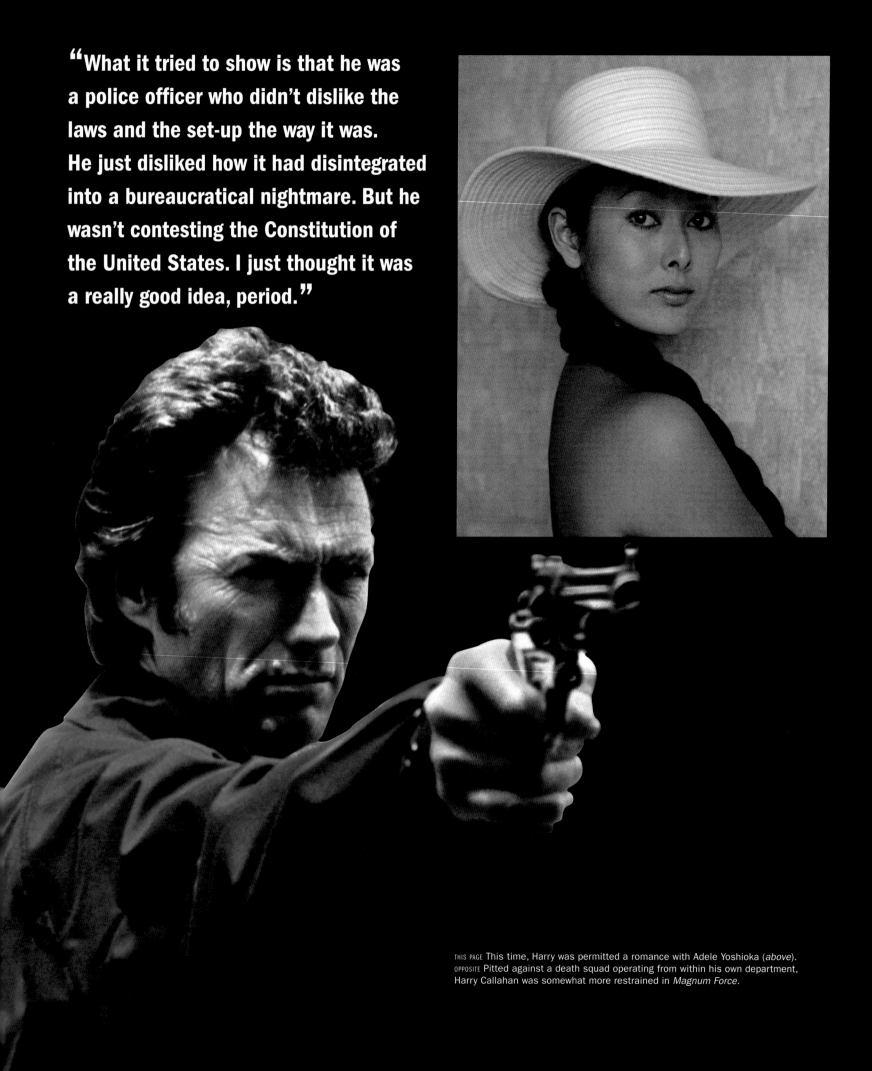

"What it tried to show is that he was a police officer who didn't dislike the laws and the set-up the way it was. He just disliked how it had disintegrated into a bureaucratical nightmare. But he wasn't contesting the Constitution of the United States. I just thought it was a really good idea, period."

THIS PAGE This time, Harry was permitted a romance with Adele Yoshioka (*above*).
OPPOSITE Pitted against a death squad operating from within his own department, Harry Callahan was somewhat more restrained in *Magnum Force*.

THUNDERBOLT AND LIGHTFOOT 1974

This is possibly the most forgotten of Clint's better movies—not even available at the moment on DVD in the United States. Yet, as written and directed by Michael Cimino, just before his great success, *The Deer Hunter*, and his even greater failure, *Heaven's Gate*, *Thunderbolt and Lightfoot* is a loose, wry, genre blend—a road movie, a buddy film, and a caper comedy that ultimately touches on the tragic. Possibly it was too much of a good thing for the mass audience, but for Clint, playing the straight man in a nest of nut jobs, it represents his first experiment with the sort of mixed-intention movies (*Every Which Way But Loose*, *Bronco Billy*) that would intermittently attract him in years to come.

Clint is an eerily composed bank robber, in search of some loot that has gone missing from a previous job; Jeff Bridges is a sort of semi-hippie, drifting around the West, getting into minor scrapes. The developing fondness between the cool older man and the less-than-thoughtful younger man suggests the possibilities of intergenerational bonding. But there are problems, centered around a pair of Thunderbolt's former confederates (a sadistic George Kennedy and a feckless Geoffrey Lewis), which are enlivened by the gang's chance encounters with all sorts of American weirdos—a wacko driving around with a trunkful of white rabbits, a filling-

ABOVE Clint Eastwood and Jeff Bridges up against a sadistic George Kennedy.
OPPOSITE *Thunderbolt and Lightfoot*, the first of the mixed-intention movies that would appeal to Clint.

station attendant with strange theories of American capitalism, an encounter with a kid who objects to the way Lewis is running an ice-cream truck (don't ask). What's best about the movie is the unblinking way Clint and Bridges accept the insanities and inanities that dot their path. Hey, this is working-class America, generally driven crazy by the hopelessness of its lives and its dreams.

Eventually the fractious gang decides to replicate a previous heist, which improbably involves blowing a hole in a bank depository with a military cannon—not to mention Bridges getting himself up, rather fetchingly, in drag. They pull off the job, fall out in its aftermath, with Lightfoot grievously wounded by Kennedy's character—who gets his comeuppance in an encounter with a murderous guard dog. Clint and Bridges eventually recover the proceeds of the previous robbery (it was hidden behind the blackboard of a one-room school that has been repurposed as a roadside attraction), though, as a result of his beating by Kennedy, the latter does not live to enjoy the loot.

The movie runs at a nice, unforced pace, and its appeal now is almost that of a period piece. Thirty-five years later, America is a much more homogenized place than it recently was; we work out our craziness—somewhat more dangerously, I think—on the Internet rather than in person on our roadsides, our convenience stores, our motels. You can't make movies about people typing out their goofiness at their computers, in their basements, while the respectable world gets its shuteye. Our loss, I think. I like them out there—the way they are in *Thunderbolt and Lightfoot*—giving us the wild eye in person.

ABOVE More used to being the sole focus of attraction, Clint fitted easily into this costarring buddy movie, allowing Jeff Bridges equal chance to shine.
OPPOSITE Thunderbolt hits the road.

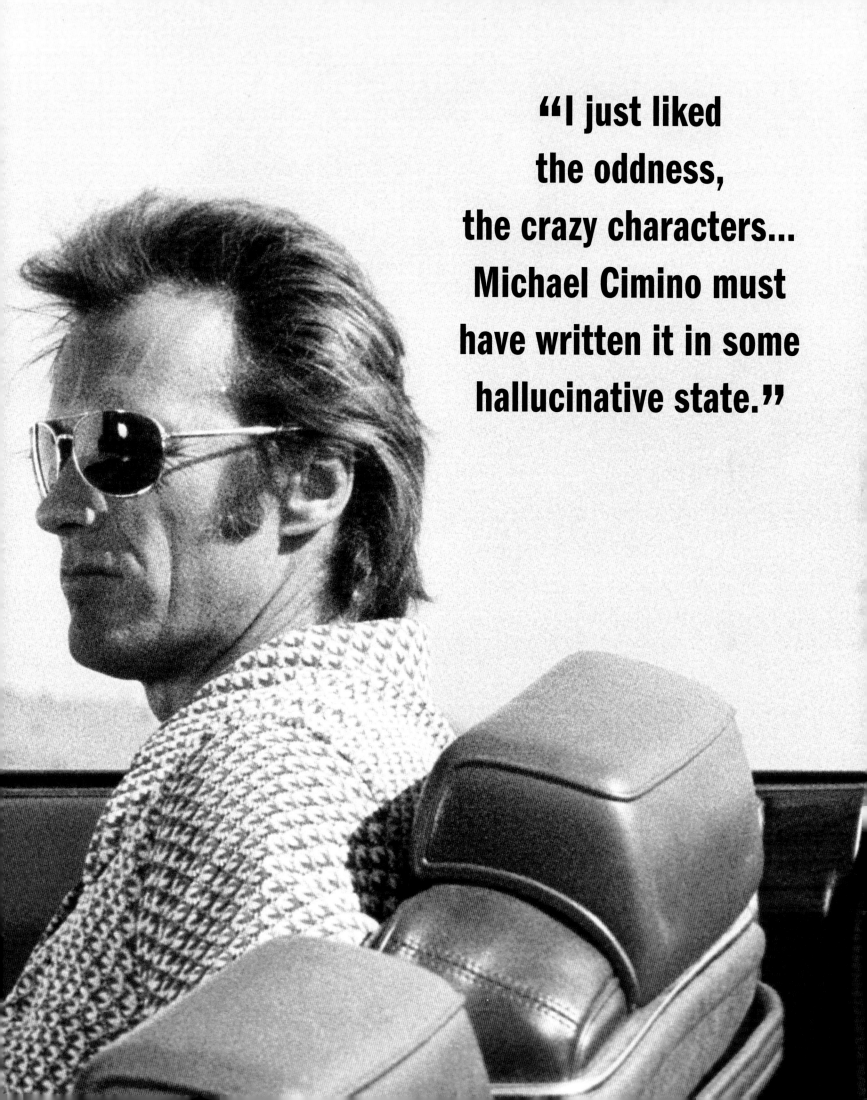

"I just liked
the oddness,
the crazy characters...
Michael Cimino must
have written it in some
hallucinative state."

THE EIGER SANCTION 1975

The novel, a bestseller, was the creation of a man named Rodney Whitaker, a writer of several pseudonyms, the most famous of which, "Trevanian," he employed here. His protagonist was called Jonathan Hemlock, an art historian by day, a hit man for the CIA by night. His assassinations were codenamed "sanctions," hence the title, and the Hemlock books, he always claimed, were intended as satires on the James Bond series, though that motif is not particularly clear either in the novel or in Clint's picture.

His filmography is not notable for an interest in espionage, but the movie rights were controlled by Richard Zanuck, with whom he was friendly, and David Brown, and they were then working at Universal, to which Clint still owed a picture. He also thought the property offered a good opportunity to test a theory of production which he has pretty much held to ever since: take a relatively small cast and crew to an isolated location and make a movie, taking advantage of the efficiencies of small scale, and largely free of interference from the studio suits.

So off they went to Switzerland, where the object was largely to record a thrilling mountain-climbing sequence strung along a plotline that is blessedly lost to memory. The production, however, was bedeviled by tragedy. One of the several highly skilled mountaineers employed in it was killed in a rockslide. It was no one's fault, but Clint considered shutting down the production. The climber's colleagues, however, argued that the man knew the risks of their profession and that if the production was canceled then his death would be robbed of whatever—admittedly minor—meaning it might have.

They decided to clamber on—often in very scary circumstances. At one point Clint found himself dangling from an overhang by what seemed to him a very slender rope. He could hear the cowbells jangling in a valley thousands of feet below, he could see the hotel where the production was comfortably housed. He could not, for the moment, imagine what he was doing here. The action required of him was to cut his lifeline and ostensibly tumble several thousand feet down the mountain. The rope, of course, was a fake—he would only fall a few feet to a ledge outside the camera's range. But still … or as one of the climbers said to him later—it goes against every mountaineer's instinct to cut a lifeline, even a fake one.

Of course, he gulped and did it—no harm done. Clint later allowed that *The Eiger Sanction* "probably wasn't the best film I ever made," but he did take justifiable pride in the authenticity of its climbing sequences. But, again, the studio's marketing efforts were clueless in his opinion. He was willing to do whatever was required of him promotionally, but he was largely ignored. "What can we do about it?" Bob Daley, his line producer finally inquired. "Well, what we do is we don't release any films here for a while." Which is precisely what happened. Clint was moving on.

ABOVE Clint and George Kennedy hear the cowbells ringing. OPPOSITE Filmed in Switzerland, there were many dynamic mountain-climbing sequences in *The Eiger Sanction*.

"I could see this pasture
way down below, and I
could hear the cowbells
ringing, and I thought,
why am I not sitting
out there with those
cows sunbathing?"

THIS PAGE Although he thought *The Eiger Sanction* "probably wasn't the best film I ever made," Clint took justifiable pride in the authenticity of its climbing sequences. Though received coolly by critics, the film is notable for some breathtaking and hazardous stunt sequences, many of which Eastwood performed himself.
OPPOSITE Eastwood as CIA hit man Jonathan Hemlock undertaking *The Eiger Sanction*.

THE OUTLAW JOSEY WALES 1976

Clint's line producer, Robert Daley, grabbed the scrawny, badly printed book off the office slush pile—something to read over dinner that night. Whereupon he found he could not stop reading what was then called *The Rebel Outlaw Josey Wales*. He finished the book in one sitting, excitedly called Clint in Carmel, and they agreed that Daley would ship it to him by airplane the next day.

Soon thereafter they optioned the book—and embarked on one of the weirder adventures of Clint's career. The book's utterly unknown author was one Forrest Carter, who turned out to be a bundle of nasty contradictions. To begin with, the creator of one of Clint's best characters—a loner, a hard case, yet a man capable of gathering hugely sympathetic feelings to him—turned up in Los Angeles roaring drunk, having missed his flight because he had been jailed in Dallas for drunkenness. He proved to be incoherent in his meetings with Daley, and that evening he pulled a knife on a woman who was his dinner companion, threatening to kill her if she didn't marry him. He was quickly shipped home—to be heard from subsequently only when he demanded more money for his book.

What no one then knew was that Carter, previously know as Asa Carter, was—or had been—a rabid racist, author of many a scurrilous pamphlet, and a sometime speechwriter for the virulently segregationist Georgia governor, George Wallace. This information did not become public knowledge until a second book, *The Education of Little Tree*, began attracting attention in the literary and film communities (Clint was briefly interested in it as well). That book, purporting to be a memoir of Carter's childhood, in which he claimed to have been raised by Native American grandparents, was, incidentally revealed to be largely fictional.

OPPOSITE The outlaw and the tools of his trade.

In the meantime, having completed his obligations to Universal, Clint made his move to Warner Bros., with him mentioning to his new studio that he had this little western he was interested in. By now, Sonia Chernus, Clint's story editor, was writing the first draft of the *Josey Wales* screenplay, which was then turned over to Philip Kaufman, who provided a spare, elegant shooting script, which he was signed to direct, an arrangement that did not last long. There are conflicting views of what happened on location, but Clint has said that he found Kaufman to be indecisive and in danger of losing control of the production. He has also said that firing Kaufman was the hardest thing he has ever done in his career, raising his recollections of the hard circumstances he had endured as a struggling actor.

Thereafter, *The Outlaw Josey Wales* proceeded in an orderly fashion, with Clint and Sondra Locke forging the long-term relationship that was among the things that brought his first marriage to an end. The picture had a spacious air—Clint had learned his lessons in panorama from Sergio Leone very well—and despite its many action sequences, it had an easy, unforced pace. But it is typical of Clint's directorial work at this time in that its cast is relatively small, composed of characters that are all loners and ostensible losers, looking rather hopelessly to find new, peaceful, and more promising lives on the frontier. He does not at first completely share these goals, for he is lost in bitterness because his farm has

ABOVE Sondra Locke as Laura Lee. BELOW Chief Dan George played Lone Watie, another key member of the surrogate family. OPPOSITE *The Outlaw Josey Wales*, now considered one of Eastwood's most important pictures, and another milestone in his career as director.

been destroyed and his family killed by Civil War border raiders. What he can supply the waifs and strays that accrete around him is the ability to employ his killing skills in their defense. It is only later, and then by inferential means, that he forges them into a surrogate family, with himself as their reluctant *pater familias*.

As he rescues them from disorder, he rescues himself from bitterness. In the end he staves off an attack by hostile Indians, with a moving "live and let live" speech, and he also gains satisfying vengeance on the man who destroyed his first family. He was conscious, of course, that the movie could be read as a metaphorical statement about America's war in Vietnam, and that pacifistic message was fine with him. But he was more interested in the "saga" he was telling and in the development of his character—"this hard put upon and desperate man"—into a man capable of a kind of ironic and wintry affection for ordinary humankind, whatever its foibles. I don't think he consciously saw the film as his

first exploration of his preoccupation with families—or in this case a surrogate family—needing succor in a harsh and violent world.

No one else perceived that subtext, either. And, in fact, the film's reviews were generally bad. One critic, Richard Eder, a particularly pompous and impenetrable book reviewer briefly slumming as a *New York Times* movie critic, said Clint's character, "seems to be thinking and feeling nothing, and is therefore almost invisible to the camera." Another reviewer thought *Josey* inferior to the long-gone B westerns starring Chester Morris and Richard Dix. Clint obviously and correctly thought otherwise. As he continues to do. In his mind the film is every bit as good as *Unforgiven*. It is just that it appeared at the wrong time in his career, when the critics were still convinced that he was just another dumb and violent hunk, incapable of nuance or—dare one say it?—soulfulness. Even when those qualities were manifest, in plain sight, in this handsome, thoughtful, and authoritative movie.

"I do all the stuff Wayne would never do. I play bigger-than-life characters, but I'll shoot a guy in the back. I go by the expediency of the moment."

"At the time I felt that it was a statement that mankind has to find a better solution than just battling themselves into the ground."

ABOVE AND BELOW The director at work on one of his most important films, and a personal favourite. OPPOSITE Relaxing on location, Sondra Locke and Clint at the commencement of their relationship.

THE ENFORCER 1976

Dirty Harry Callahan never took kindly to new partners; left to his own devices he always preferred to work alone. But this—this is too much. He's assigned a woman. She's named Kate Moore and when he meets her for the first time, it is a disaster. She's earnest, she's over-eager, she has it in her to be a real pest. About the only thing to be said for her is that she is not a glamour puss.

Tyne Daly is not entirely unattractive—there is a sort of nicely scrubbed luminosity to her countenance. But let's face it, her figure is less than grand—kind of chunky if the truth be told.

But she seemed to Clint just the sort of woman Harry would go for; he never saw him falling for a model or a TV anchorwoman. He would want a Plain Jane—and, of course, someone who would plausibly prove herself, competent, hardworking, and brave, which Daley's Kate surely is. Gradually, Harry learns not to patronize her, and she learns that he may be something more interesting than a hotheaded gunslinger. They never consummate their relationship but they do become flirtatious, and the two actors even improvised a scene in a bar that makes us certain that, if they ever get a moment, they will embrace some more extensive dalliance.

The idea for the film came to Clint in an odd way; a couple of young would-be screenwriters from San Francisco left a treatment with the head waiter at The Hog's Breath, a pleasantly low-key Carmel restaurant of which he was the principal owner. He thought their effort better than some other ideas for another *Dirty Harry* sequel he had seen. So he optioned the treatment, and turned it over to the more seasoned writing professionals, Stirling Silliphant and Dean Riesner, for fuller development.

The plot is nothing much: Harry and Kate are pursuing a group of local terrorists—they resemble the Symbionese Liberation Army, at the time newsworthy for their kidnapping of Patty Hearst—but Harry is a little different than he was. His fuming impatience with bureaucratic bungling has now passed over the line into self-parody, which enlists a sort of affectionate regard from the audience. He's like a splenetic, slightly eccentric cousin or uncle we can't help kind of liking however outrageous his opinions may be. Indeed, he suggests to a minister who works with the poor, who asks him why he is so devoted to his work, that he is a kind of people's tribune,

defending the defenseless against the criminals who victimize them more than any other class. What's next, one wonders—Dirty Harry casting a ballot for Jimmy Carter in the 1976 election?

But the thing that makes *The Enforcer* memorable is its ending. Pursuing the murderous radicals, who are making a final stand at the now-deserted Alcatraz prison, Kate is shot. And killed. And the anguish on Harry's face is terrible to behold. Her last words to him are "Get 'em," which of course he does. It's a genuinely surprising but entirely plausible conclusion, and one that adds a certain weight and memorability to the movie.

The critics, naturally, were uninterested in Harry's developing humanity and probably the audience wasn't either. But it must be said that, under James Fargo's direction (he had been a longtime assistant director on Malpaso films), this remains the best of the *Dirty Harry* sequels, a movie which grants its hero something of an inner life and something of an outer life that contains a certain warmth and, yes, even a certain vulnerability.

OPPOSITE Poster art. *Dirty Harry* is back—this time with a female partner.
RIGHT The new partner, Tyne Daly as Kate Moore.

"I asked a police captain, who was a very experienced homicide captain, 'What's it like with women officers?' And he says, 'Awful'. And he went into this thing about why this wouldn't work and this wouldn't work, and he had a very prejudicial response. And I said, 'Yeah, but just think about it now. Think about women doing a job that a man could not do, you know, undercover stuff, different kinds of things.

Has any woman officer you know ever done something that's really interesting?' And he started thinking. And the more he thought about it, he'd come up with these great anecdotes about female police officers and how they'd done something interesting, especially undercover work… And he came up with some tremendous ideas after, once he'd got past the misogynistic kind of response of, 'Oh, no, no way.'"

"The girl's part is a terrific role, not just token window dressing like in so many action pictures. Her part is equal to the male part, if not more so."

THE GAUNTLET 1977

Ben Shockley, the detective Clint plays in *The Gauntlet*, is the anti-Dirty Harry, an alcoholic cop just barely able to carry out routine duties—like escorting a Las Vegas hooker to Phoenix, Arizona, where she's supposed to testify in a gangland investigation. The prostitute may be a college graduate, but she's also a shrill, profanity-spouting, and hostile feminist, who so hotly resists removal from jail that Shockley orders her bound, gagged, and strapped to a gurney for the first leg of their journey. Clint thought it a good thing to cast Sondra Locke, who usually played "waify" types, as he put it, and she delivered a terrific performance—high-energy and darkly comedic.

It soon becomes apparent that her Gus Mally is a person of more than routine "interest" to a party or parties unknown. Powerful people want her dead, and if Ben gets caught in the crossfire, so what? Early in the picture, they take refuge in her shotgun bungalow in Vegas. It has been staked out by the local cops and there ensues a truly remarkable sequence—they pump something like 250,000 rounds into the house (it was, of course, wired with squibs) and after they have all exploded, the house groans, creaks, and collapses in on its foundation. It is one of the great, strangely comic excesses in action-movie history, suggested, Clint said, by some news footage he had seen of an assault on—here they are again—a Symbionese Liberation army hideout.

The picture quickly becomes, and stays, an exercise in nonstop violence, blended, curiously enough, with a foulmouthed version of a romantic comedy along the lines of *It Happened One Night*. On their wayward way, Shockley and Mally naturally discover true love—and the man behind the attempt to murder them, Shockley's boss, the Phoenix police commissioner (the smooth and elegant William Prince), who has also forced Mally into a perverse sexual encounter with him.

Shockley hopes that if he delivers his prisoner in a spectacular and public way, he can expose the criminal conspiracy. To that end he armors a bus with heavy sheet metal and drives it down a main Phoenix drag, where, like the bungalow at the movie's beginning,

OPPOSITE Clint as Ben Shockley, the anti-Dirty Harry, in *The Gauntlet*.
ABOVE Scenes of the broad, almost comic, mayhem that distinguished this movie from Eastwood's other cop thrillers.

135

it takes an equal number of bullets. Improbably, the ploy works—eventually the impressed cops refuse to fire on their colleague (whatever else has happened, they are awed by the sheer nerve of the man).

From first to last *The Gauntlet* is a wildly improbable film. But if you can set aside the customary hopes audiences carry for at least an air of realism in their movies, if you can bear its hail of bad language, almost as thick as those opening and closing hails of bullets, it is a lot of lowbrow fun. It is also the first movie in which Clint experimented with a notion that would appeal to him several times in the future—playing a guy who is not entirely bright. There is some part of him that likes to subvert his heroic image, to undercut the boredom that their all-knowing perfection, their always smart ideas, their perfectly honed instincts, can engender—especially if you are ever-restless Clint Eastwood. He cheerfully let Locke have all the snappiest lines and confined himself pretty much to supplying guns, muscle, and the wide variety of vehicles they required to keep moving through a desert landscape.

A lot of Clint's colleagues—including Don Siegel—thought the movie simply silly. Sure, all action films set tasks for their protagonists that lie beyond the realm of plausible execution. But this—this was too much for them and Clint was a little miffed by their attitudes, especially since this was his riskiest venture to date. Despite the fact that Clint was acting and directing for scale, and the rest of the above-the-line talent were not highly paid, *The Gauntlet* was, at around $5 million, the most expensive picture Malpaso had yet made. But it proved profitable and one lonely critic, writing in the *Village Voice*, noted the emergence, "slow and crude," of something new in Clint's character, "a vulnerable male who needs a woman to lean on." I would date that emergence to its somewhat shyer statement in *The Enforcer*, but I do agree, as Clint surely did, that this was "a much more audacious concept than the preening [wait a minute, "preening"?] invincibility of Harry Callahan."

BELOW Clint and Sondra Locke take to the road in their second collaboration, and one in which she delivered a high-energy and darkly comedic performance.
OPPOSITE Poster art, by fantasy artist Frank Frazetta, as over the top as the film itself.

"Every advisor I had said, 'Don't do the orangutan movie. Don't do *Every Which Way but Loose*. You can't do this. This is not you.' I said, 'Nothing's me. I'm just plain.'"

EVERY WHICH WAY BUT LOOSE 1978

There comes a moment in every male star's career when, if he's wise, he will openly send up his image. If he doesn't, people will start getting the idea he's uppity. That moment arrived when Clint read the script for *Every Which Way But Loose*.

The husband of one of his secretaries hoped to produce the film and also hoped Clint might give it a read and pass it on to his friend, Burt Reynolds, who had a much more lowbrow persona, and had recently had a huge hit with *Smokey and the Bandit*. Instead, of course, Clint nabbed the property for himself.

Everyone he worked with hated the idea, except Sondra Locke, who thought there was "something hip about it in a strange sort of way." Which, of course, was true. Clint plays Philo Beddoe, a trucker and bare-knuckled boxer, living in a tumbledown house with his dimwitted manager (Geoffrey Lewis), his hilariously cranky mother (a wonderfully snarling and perpetually impatient Ruth Gordon), and, yes, his pet orangutan, named Clyde who, despite Locke's presence as a rather mysterious country and western singer, provides the star with the love interest that really counts in the picture.

Clint has a profound affection for animals. He doesn't hunt and has never, as far as one can tell, spoken an angry word to or about animals. It's not "a religious thing," he says; rather he thinks they have a right to peaceful coexistence with mankind. There are multiple reports of him intervening on his sets to spare the lives of creatures as lowly as the cockroach. I've seen him in a swell seaside dining room in Cannes patiently attempting to lure a pigeon into his hands with crumbs of bread. So, of course, he quickly bonded with Manus, the immature orang who played Clyde (grown-up orangs can be dangerous). His feelings were reciprocated and the ape was cuddlesome with him to the point that his owner-trainer became mildly jealous of Clint. In the course of the film, the creature joined Philo for beers, gave the finger to a comically harassing motorcycle gang, and so on. In its best moment, after Clyde has stolen some Oreo cookies from Ruth Gordon's character, Clint points a finger at Clyde, who throws up his arms. "Bang," says Clint, and Clyde flops down, pretending to be mortally wounded.

But Clint tends to his every need—even sneaking him into a zoo, so Clyde can get laid by its resident oran. There are women all over the world who are less attentively attended than Clyde. Which

may be one of the inferential points the movie wanted to make. Another of them may come at its end, when Philo throws a big fight that he's in the process of winning; a victory would make him a marked man, the target of every boxer seeking to make a rep. Maybe he's smarter than he looks—or anyway smarter than Clint plays him. And maybe Clint was saying something about his own needs, exemplified by his low-key management of his stardom.

Certainly the movie played better than anyone other than Clint thought it might. It became his biggest hit to date, despite the studio's dubiety, despite its awful reviews. Partly that's because of its release patterns. It opened in the small towns day and date with its big-city releases. "That's where it played, out in mid-America. People would go back. And it would play for weeks and weeks and weeks and weeks." Clint sometimes says of ventures about which others are dubious, "It's the kind of thing I'd like to see, even if I weren't in it." I'm sure that's what he was thinking about this movie when he took it on.

"The orang is an introvert, and the chimp is an extrovert. Chimps love to perform, roll their lips back and do all that kind of stuff. But orangs are kind of cool. They love to study things, and they are kinda shy. You have to coax them into it. I didn't get overly friendly. I would always pretend I didn't notice him, then he would start studying me, because I wasn't looking at him and staring him down. I'd feel him start picking at my ear and looking in my ear, you know doing little things like they do to you. And always grabbing my Adam's apple. Eventually, he got to really like me."

ESCAPE FROM ALCATRAZ 1979

The movie is as straightforward as its title; it recounts, in painstaking detail, the true story of the only attempt to escape from what may be the most notorious prison in history (Devil's Island would be the only other serious contender for the title), on which the books have never been closed. The script—his first—was the work of Richard Tuggle who, when laid off from a magazine job in San Francisco became intrigued by J. Campbell Bruce's book on the subject, optioned it, and eventually started shopping his screenplay around Hollywood, where it eventually caught Don Siegel's attention.

He tentatively set the production up at Paramount, with everyone thinking of Clint to play Frank Morris, the hard-case armed robber who conceived and led the escape plot. Clint, however, was briefly on the outs with Siegel, and Siegel, in turn, was on the outs with Warner Bros., where Clint would have preferred to make the film. These difficulties were fairly quickly ironed out—Clint signed on and Paramount remained the producer—and a very tough location shoot (Alcatraz in the late fall is not the most comfortable place to make a movie) was soon underway. But that chill somehow seeped into the movie, much to its advantage. Siegel later said he had shot as if it were a black and white movie that just happened to have color film in the cameras. It is all spare, muted dialogue,

OPPOSITE A detail of the film's effective poster art.
ABOVE Clint, as Frank Morris, contributed a performance of brooding intensity.

and it concentrates minutely on the details of how the escape was planned and executed, mainly by making improvised tools out of the most primitive objects. It is also sympathetic to prisoners who are maltreated by the elegantly sadistic warden (Patrick McGoohan), which has the effect of enlisting the audience's sympathy in all the cons. This obviates the necessity of inventing hard-luck back stories for them, which some studio executives urged. What the picture offers in that line is one word: a prisoner asks Frank Morris what his childhood was like. His answer is, "Short."

There's no question that Morris and three confederates managed to escape *The Rock*. There is, however, no evidence to suggest they made it to dry land; most people who know anything about the case think they perished in the icy waters of San Francisco Bay. On the other hand, there is also nothing to suggest that their escape failed, either. It is just the kind of open ending that Clint likes; let the audience imagine what they want about what happens to the movie's characters after the picture ends. He rather thought that the escapees died trying to finish the job. But that seemed a little grim, so Siegel shot a little scene where the warden and guards, searching for traces of the prisoners on nearby Angel Island, come upon a carefully placed chrysanthemum (earlier established as a symbol of resistance to authority), which hints that the prisoners are long gone, melted into the American vastness.

But no matter. The film remains one of the best in the Eastwood canon—tough, spare, no words wasted—and it is, to my taste, the best prison-escape movie ever made, not excluding Robert Bresson's *A Man Escaped*, which shares this film's austerity but has a spiritual dimension that, though admired by many, eludes me. But then, like Eastwood and Siegel, I'm a contented secularist, impervious even to implied religiosity.

 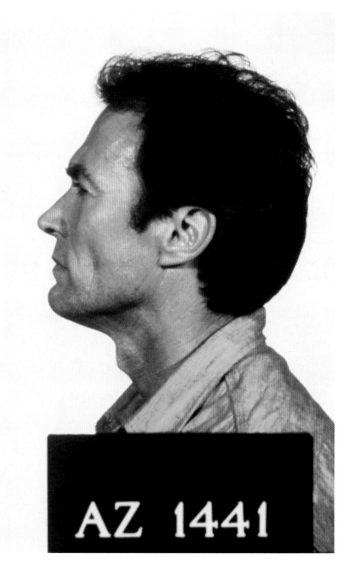

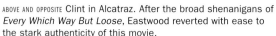

ABOVE AND OPPOSITE Clint in Alcatraz. After the broad shenanigans of *Every Which Way But Loose*, Eastwood reverted with ease to the stark authenticity of this movie.

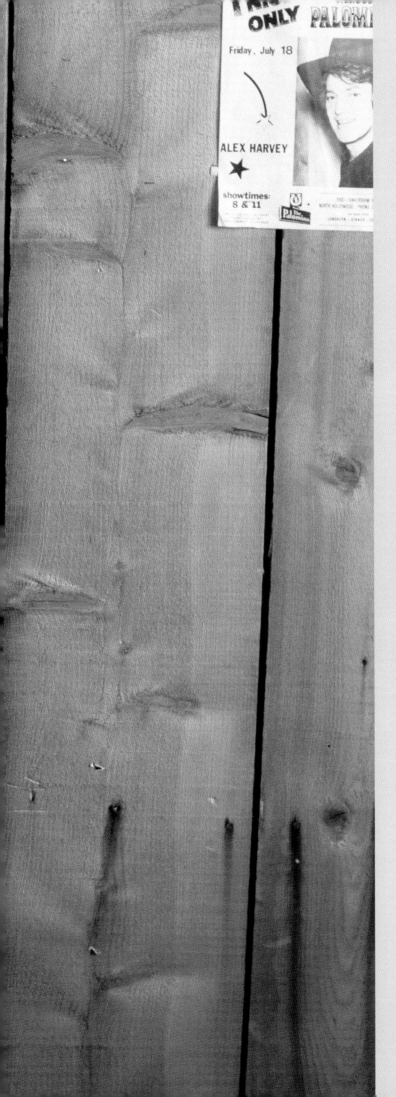

BRONCO BILLY 1980

He acquired the screenplay in a typically casual way: Clint was having dinner with a friend when a young woman approached their table, asking if she could send a script to his office. The next day it arrived and he spotted it on an assistant's desk. Standing there, he began reading, thinking to give it five pages or so, but found himself reading the entire manuscript in that one session. And deciding to make *Bronco Billy* that afternoon. He has often said that he thought of it as his Capra film. That is to say that it was the kind of movie he thought Capra might have been drawn to were he still active as a director.

Once again, Clint is a father figure to a surrogate family, the star and proprietor of a not very prosperous Wild West show, playing small towns in the modern West (the picture was shot around Boise, Idaho). Among its denizens are a Lasso Leonard (Sam Bottoms), who does rope tricks and is a Vietnam draft dodger, a one-armed trick-shot artist, a snake handler who refuses to use nonvenomous creatures in his act and is constantly being bitten ("He's a proud Indian," Bronco Billy equably observes), his pregnant wife, whose condition interferes with her "authentic" tribal dances, and, supplying something like the reality principle, Scatman Crothers as the show's ringmaster. Sondra Locke adds a little romantic *frisson* as a runway heiress.

But it is Bronco Billy McCoy who commands the most interest. Clint does some adept riding and shooting in the arena, but his character is, *in extremis*, a self-made American male, a one-time shoe salesman from New Jersey who is also a jailbird; he's done time for shooting his former wife, whom he caught in bed with his best friend.

OPPOSITE The hero as loser: Clint as *Bronco Billy*.

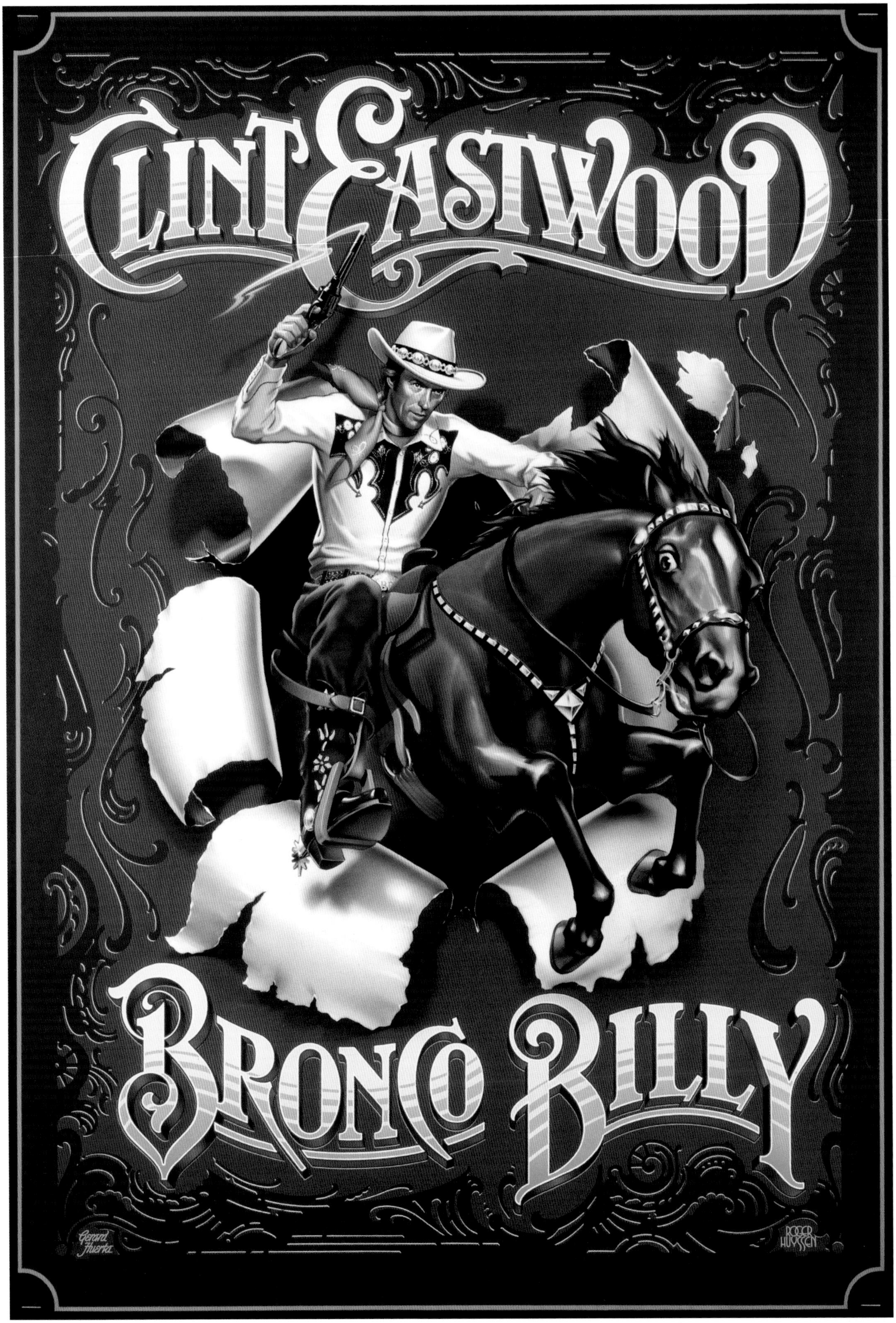
CLINT EASTWOOD
BRONCO BILLY
Gerard Huerta
ROGER HUYSSEN

As he suggests, wives come and go, but good buddies are forever. Billy lives by a simple creed: he loves children and wants to set a good example for them, he is fanatically loyal to his troupe, and he loves the United States of America because of the re-inventive opportunities it has given him. Amazingly, this philosophy sees him and his little show through many misadventures.

Bronco Billy is not quite as simple-minded as Philo Beddoe; he is, in fact, more like Clint himself at this time, devoting himself to small-scale movie enterprises, using casts and crews that were reliable and familiar to him, and depending on his own star power to produce somewhat more solid box-office results than Bronco Billy did. He spoke of himself, in those days, as a singles and doubles hitter who was not aiming for the fences.

"There was something so beautifully naïve about it all: a guy who's a shoe salesman in New Jersey goes out and has this dream of becoming a modern-day Tom Mix or something like that... He had great virtues—though obviously his brain had snapped, and he had gone into another era."

For reasons that remain unclear, *Bronco Billy*, for all its wayward charms, did not do particularly well commercially; neither did a number of other pictures starring the likes of Robert Redford, Burt Reynolds, and John Travolta, all of whom were buried by the summer's continuation of the *Star Wars* phenomenon, *The Empire Strikes Back*. The George Lucas films were game-changers, revising the way movies were imagined, marketed, and released. Yes, they were far riskier than something like *Bronco Billy*, but their potential for reward was far higher, as well. Which is not to say that Clint's film was an abject failure. It cost only $5 million to make and, worldwide, grossed in the neighborhood of $30 million. More to the point, perhaps, it remains, for Clint, a favorite among his films. It is one of mine, too, a sweet, goofy tribute to the naivety of American Dreaming, and to the movies' longstanding affection for the good, simple, dwindling number of people who cling to that dream, without resorting to the now almost endemic lunacy of America's have-nots.

OPPOSITE The appropriately nostalgic poster design for *Bronco Billy*.
THIS PAGE Audiences were not ready for *Bronco Billy*, but it is a film that remains one of Clint's favorites among his work—a sweet, goofy tribute to the naivety of American Dreaming.

149

ANY WHICH WAY YOU CAN 1980

Any movie that grosses over $100 million, as *Every Which Way But Loose* did, is almost inevitably going to demand a sequel, so this movie, which the critics correctly saw as a little more narratively coherent, was made. The cast was pretty much the same, though there was a new orangutan, and a new director, Buddy Van Horn, who had literally been born into the movies—his father had been the chief veterinarian at Universal—going on to become a rider and stunt coordinator, eventually hooking up with Clint very early in his star career. Soft-spoken, weathered, and preternaturally calm, he was Clint's kind of guy. "We kind of grunted at each other," is how Van Horn describes their on-set relationship.

The picture finds Clint once again eager to give up his bare-knuckle boxing career, on the interesting grounds that he was finding himself beginning to like the pain of those encounters. That line is pretty much thrown away, but Clyde's adventures are well-managed and funny. He's once again the picture's always-unmediated id, the creature whose response to all difficulties is completely natural, forthright, and casually funny. Such plot as the film has revolves around a projected bout between Philo and an East Coast champion named Jack Wilson, which Philo keeps evading—until the mobsters kidnap his haughty girlfriend (Sondra Locke, playing the same role as in the previous Clyde movie), telling him he will never see her again if he refuses to fight.

So he does, in a grand-scale battle that endlessly winds its way down the main street of Jackson Hole, Wyoming, with a boisterous crowd following along. It's a well-staged and inventive action sequence in an agreeable movie. Its salient defect, naturally, is that it is predictable. When we first met Philo, Clyde, and their lowbrow pals, they were a complete surprise. Now we know where they're coming from and can predict where they're going—not that this much diminished the movie's fun. Or its profitability.

RIGHT Director Buddy Van Horn oversees the action in this follow-up to one of Clint's biggest successes, again with Sondra Locke (*above*).
OPPOSITE A marriage made in box-office heaven.

THIS PAGE AND OPPOSITE Clyde, this time a new orangutan, nonetheless steals the show. The critics balked at the raucousness of the film, but it immediately followed its predecessor to the top of the box-office lists—and stayed there.

FIREFOX 1982

Loaded with special effects, *Firefox* was the most expensive film Malpaso had ever undertaken, and it remains—to my taste anyway—the least resonant of Clint's purely genre films. When we meet hot pilot Mitchell Gant, he is living alone in the wilderness, trying to recover from the damage done him by his service in Vietnam—in his dreams he keeps reliving the civilian casualties he observed and his own prison-camp experiences. But he is fluent in Russian and his skills as a pilot are undiminished—which means he is the perfect man to sneak into the USSR and steal the eponymous fighter (the most advanced in the world) so the United States can figure out how to counter its power. This he does—abetted by the members of a Jewish underground, some of whom are working on the airplane.

It's hard to say what attracted Clint to Craig Thomas's novel, except for the opportunity to work with special effects, which he had not done before and which were now all the rage. There's nothing wrong with the effects sequences, though they do not really soar in the Lucas-Spielberg manner. There's nothing wrong with Clint's work in the film—he's playing a damaged man in a visibly damaged way—but there's nothing anarchical or eccentric in his playing. He's back to the taciturn manner of his earlier films, but without the sense of fun—or at least irony—with which he sometimes invested those figures. Reviewing *Firefox*, Andrew Sarris rather acutely observed that Clint was not "the establishment figure his East Coast detractors imagine him to be, but rather a mysterious loner with few ties to civilization," who "has always looked ill at ease in uniforms and organizations."

In some ways the timing of this very standard-issue movie was not great. Because, of all things, Clint was finally beginning to be taken seriously in intellectual circles; in this period there were two receptions for him at New York's Museum of Modern Art, and Clint was openly thrilled by this acknowledgment of his films by a high-toned center of serious film study and celebration. Around this time, *The New York Review of Books* ran a not-unsympathetic analysis of him by Robert Mazzoco, somewhat dubiously, but not entirely wrongly, tying him to the new spirit of Ronald Reagan's America in that he combined "the irreverence of the free spirit, and

the ruthlessness of the rugged individualist." He also observed, quite correctly, Clint's resistance to being "absorbed" in genre convention, though in *Firefox* he was not just absorbed by these conventions, he was nearly buried by them.

But no one seemed to notice. Despite its cost, the picture was mildly successful commercially, and his new fans among the more literate filmgoers mostly ignored it. Indeed, it seems to me they were in a sort of transitional stage: not much interested in genre films, except as guilty pleasures, they were more attracted to Clint as a sort of topic for further sociological studies than they were to the idea that they might possibly be witnessing the rise of a potential film artist. It would take them another decade to fully embrace that idea.

OPPOSITE **Ready for blast-off, Clint as hot pilot Mitchell Gant.**
RIGHT **Clint at work on *Firefox* with cinematographer Bruce Surtees.**

OPPOSITE Clint oversees the demanding shoot and most expensive film Malpaso had undertaken. THIS PAGE *Firefox* was an ambitious production, making extensive and—for Clint—unprecedented use of special effects.

HONKYTONK MAN 1982

By 1982, when Clint released *Honkytonk Man*, new management had arrived at Warner Bros. Robert Daly had moved over from CBS television and Terry Semel had risen from the distribution ranks within the studio. They functioned as co-equal leaders and claimed never to have exchanged an unkind word. Eventually they would usher in an era in which the studio placed large—and largely successful—bets on expensive spectacles like the *Superman* and *Batman* franchises. That, however, did not affect Clint's status at the studio; they liked and trusted him, a feeling that was reciprocated.

As witness *Honkytonk Man*, which may be the smallest scaled and least expensive movie he ever made at Warner Bros. and perhaps something of a minor indulgence on management's part. It tells a very simple story: Clint's Red Stovall is a man singing his life away in low dives along America's back roads. He's a feckless, careless, hard-drinking man of modest talents, who suddenly has an invitation to audition for the Grand Old Opry in Nashville, nirvana for country and western singers. He decides to sing his way there, riding in an ancient Cadillac, driven by his nephew, Whit (well played by Clint's son, Kyle), who's as sensible as Red is erratic. For a time they are accompanied by the lad's grandpa, impersonated by that grand old character actor, John McIntire. They have many perilous, yet comic, adventures on the road, where it becomes clear that Red is suffering from tuberculosis, probably fatally. Eventually they attain Nashville, where Red's audition goes well—until he is overcome with a coughing fit. He will soon die, but not before he manages to cut a record of his best songs, on which, we are led to believe, his tenuous claim to immortality will rest.

I think it is a lovely and soulful little movie, reflecting Clint's puzzled affection for, and impatience with, people who sacrifice their talents to self-destruction. They are, if you wish, the world's anti-Clints, and he's said that he'd like to shake some sense into them, though he's never had that opportunity. I am virtually alone in my regard for *Honkytonk Man*, which received almost no good reviews, with a lot of critics making lame jokes about Red's resemblance to Camille. And, curiously, criticizing Clint's

RIGHT Clint directs *Honkytonk Man*, one of his most personal projects, with his son Kyle (*above*), and cinematographer Jack Green. OPPOSITE Poster art for this smaller scale, and least expensive, movie Clint made at Warner Bros.

"Red Stovall's a collage. A mixture of Hank Williams, Red Foley, Bob Wills, all those country singers who drank their whiskey neat, burned up their life on the road and ended up by self-destructing."

strangulated singing. That, of course, was acting—an attempt to suggest the effect of his illness on his voice. There is plenty of evidence, on screen and off, that his natural singing voice is a light, clear, baritone, marked by excellent musicianship.

The picture did enjoy some success abroad, and no less than Norman Mailer wrote that, "It was one of the saddest movies seen in a long time, yet, on reflection, terrific. One felt a tenderness for America while looking at it." But that was too little, too late, and better reviews would not have affected the fate of *Honkytonk Man*. The truth is, especially in those days, the audience did not like seeing Clint as a victim. His character might have his problems, but he was supposed to somehow triumph in the end. You can see this prejudice in the box-office performances of films as diverse as *The Beguiled* and, later, *White Hunter Black Heart*.

This does not mean, however, that Warner Bros. actively discouraged him from making them. Daly once said that you needed "the intelligence and the financing and the guts to stay at the table and play," and, in a way, that's what he and Semel did with Clint. They would stay at the table with him, despite whatever temporary setbacks he endured. They knew—as surely as Clint did—that eventually their patience would be rewarded, that over the long haul he would deliver huge profits. In that context, failures like *Honkytonk Man* were of no consequence.

Clint Eastwood and Kyle Eastwood
Honkytonk Man

OPPOSITE, FAR LEFT Poster art, capturing the film's melancholy atmosphere.
THIS PAGE With scenes set in Nashville at the Grand Ole Opry, the movie
recalled Eastwood's own Depression boyhood, and played tribute to
the music he grew up loving.

SUDDEN IMPACT 1983

Clint reflected as he set forth to make his fourth *Dirty Harry* movie that, "It was a time in my life when I'd try other things and the public didn't flock to them." He is a practical man, and though he scoffed at a studio marketing survey that revealed a large public longing for a return as his signature character, a script by Joseph C. Stinson had about it a certain originality.

Yes, it would contain his most famous line—"Go ahead, make my day"—uttered in the course of a lunchroom robbery, as Harry prepares to mow down the final miscreant. But more interesting to him was the film's central plot point. Men are being killed, apparently randomly, with bullets aimed at their private parts. Fairly quickly, Harry identifies the killer as a painter of strangely haunting pictures named Jennifer Spencer. We soon learn that, with her sister, she was gang raped, that the sister has been institutionalized as a result, and Jennifer (Sondra Locke) is obviously not completely stable herself. But Harry falls in love with her, so the dilemma of the picture revolves around whether or not he should arrest her for her crimes.

It's a solid crime picture, and it turned out to be extremely profitable. But its deeper interest lies in the critical response it engendered. The previous *Dirty Harry* pictures were, as we know, either hysterically castigated or, more generally, routinely dismissed. This one, however, read to many critics as a feminist parable, even though the occasional jocularities of the dialogue mixed rather uneasily with its considerations of the morality of extra-legal revenge. There was, to be sure, a sense in some quarters that the possibilities for a rather serious film were betrayed by the need to oblige genre conventions, but there was also a feeling that *Sudden Impact* was at least trying to go beyond its genre limits. Reviewing it in tandem with another film, *Uncommon Valor*, about an attempt to rescue an MIA soldier held captive in Vietnam, David Denby observed that "They make contact with a stratum of pessimism that runs very deep in this country—a sort of lumpen despair that goes beyond, or beneath, politics. In these movies America is a failure, a disgrace, a country run on the basis of expediency and profit, a country that has betrayed its ideals."

I think that reading may be a trifle overheated, but not entirely inaccurate, either. There is a darkness to the film—as there is to all the *Dirty Harry* films, which to one degree or another always deal with the irrationalities of American life—that is palpable. And surely under Clint's direction it is visually the blackest movie in the series. In the end I think it is best understood as an example of Clint's instinctive determination to add value to a genre film, to suggest, as the cliché holds, that action is character and, more important, that characters like the one Locke portrays here can be more deeply and interestingly drawn than they usually are—more twisted by the cruelty of circumstance than they—or we—might imagine as we set forth on what we blithely imagine to be our routine and unthreatening daily rounds. Bad things do happen to good people, with results of the kind this film portrays quite grippingly.

OPPOSITE The dramatic poster image of one of Clint's most successful pictures.
RIGHT *Sudden Impact* was the fourth *Dirty Harry* movie and the first to be directed by Eastwood.

"Go ahead— make my day!"

Harry Callahan

TIGHTROPE 1984

This may be the most perfect Clint Eastwood genre movie to date (it was released in 1984). It's a good, tense story in which he plays Wes Block, a New Orleans detective pursuing a sado-masochistic serial killer, preying on prostitutes. The film takes full advantage of the city's many colorful locations, and it presents Wes as a troubled family man whose wife has left him and who is doing his best to be both father and mother to two girls, one of whom was played by Clint's own daughter, Alison. It is his first film revolving around a troubled family in which he is not a stranger, an outsider, intervening in their lives; Wes is very much a part of this picture's major problem.

Perhaps more important, there is a significant—indeed, unique—genre twist to *Tightrope*; the detective finds himself drawn to the same sexual dark side as the killer; he too, does not mind putting women under restraint before having sex with them. There have, of course, been many movies in which we suspect the cop of sharing the criminal's perversities, but none which so openly, if discreetly, show them in play. He does have an unspoken motive—that runaway wife whom he might have "tied" more closely to home. And he is fairly easily cured by Geneviève Bujold's rape counselor, who snaps a handcuff to her wrist, then holds out her arms, inviting Wes to lock the other cuff to her free wrist. It is enough to jerk him out of his obsession and lead the film on to a satisfying conclusion.

Tightrope is very nicely pitched; there is an easy naturalism about it that is neither too breathless nor too brooding—paying full heed

OPPOSITE A very different kind of dirty cop in *Tightrope*.

166

to the pursuit of the murderer, it still has room for comedy, for tentative romance, even for a little sightseeing. Much of this balance can be attributed to Richard Tuggle's very well-written script, which is mature in the best sense of the word. It cannot, alas, be attributed to his direction, even though he is the film's credited director. Like a lot of writers, he saw too many possibilities in every set-up, and dithered over his choices while the production pace dragged. Clint has never spoken publicly on this matter, though members of his crew have; unquestionably Clint quietly replaced Tuggle after a few days' work, but kept him at his side until the end of the shoot. He even, later, recommended him as the director for another film. It is an inexplicable curiosity that this good writer (he had, of course, previously written *Escape from Alcatraz*) has contributed so few scripts in the years since.

The picture was very successful at the box office, less so with the critics, who seemed reluctant to abandon their anti-genre prejudices, though this is, I think, a better film than *Sudden Impact*, which caused so much sober thumb-sucking on their part. There was, however, for the first time, intense praise for Clint's performance in some of the best critical circles: "One of the most masterful under-actors in American movies," said one writer. Another spoke of his "forlorn lust," while a third spoke of him as "a very troubled movie icon … he gives a genuinely spooked performance." A grateful studio mounted a "for your consideration" campaign for that year's Academy Award season.

THIS PAGE *Tightrope* cast Eastwood bravely against type as a detective with a disturbing affinity with the killer he is pursuing.
OPPOSITE Eastwood cast his own daughter Alison as his daughter in the movie.

> My appeal is the characters I play. A superhuman character who has all the answers is double cool, exists on his own, without society or the help of society's police forces... But it would never happen that way. Man is always dreaming of being an individual, but man is really a flock animal.

CLINT EASTWOOD · BURT REYNOLDS

CITY HEAT 1984

On paper it looked like a heaven-sent opportunity for fun and profit—two of the moment's leading studs, Clint Eastwood and Burt Reynolds, costarring in a comedy-crime drama, written and directed by Blake Edwards, then at the top of his witty game. What could possibly go wrong? Plenty, as it turned out.

To begin with, Edwards required expensive perquisites (for example, a car and driver to transport him from his Santa Monica home to the studio) to which the ever-frugal Eastwood objected. Then, in his judgment, and perhaps that of others, a rewrite was required, which Edwards did not feel like doing. Soon he was gone, his script revised by someone else and his directorial reins picked up by Richard Benjamin, an actor-turned-director, who had done well with a couple of nostalgically themed movies (*My Favorite Year* was one of them). This seemed to bode well for *City Heat*, which was set in 1930s Kansas City.

The story was pretty routine: taciturn Lieutenant Speer (Clint) and his wisecracking former partner, Mike Murphy (Reynolds), now a private eye, once loved, now loathe one another. Yet they make common, bickering cause against mobsters who rubbed out Murphy's new associate and have in their possession papers that would implicate city officials in a ring of corruption. There's nothing wrong with that tale, though there was nothing particularly stirring in it either. All would depend on what sass and energy the leading men could bring to its telling, which is where the real troubles began.

Reynolds was injured early in the shoot, which sapped him of energy. And made him temporarily addicted to the painkiller Percodan. Clint judged that his old pal was very close to losing it as the shoot—shot in chronological order—moved along to its high-energy action sequences. He was finally telling Benjamin to abandon his well-laid plans for the big shootout. Just get its basic geography laid out, fire off a lot of guns, and hope that they could do more detailed work later, with Clint's character. In this context, the movie lost much of its fizz—what there was of it was supplied

by Madeline Kahn and Jane Alexander, doing excellent character work. What was meant to be a Christmas blockbuster turned into a "disappointment," as a studio spokesman put it. Mostly the audiences were over at Eddie Murphy's *Beverly Hills Cop* that December.

The fault was not entirely Reynolds'. He more or less got by in the film—though it was certainly part of the long, slow, sad decline in his career. Nor was it Clint's or Benjamin's either. Mostly the fault lay with a script that was too complicated for the lightsome spirit everyone was striving for. It's possible that the period setting was distancing to audiences. Who knows? There are as many reasons for failures as there are for successes, and Hollywood has never been confident about avoiding the lessons of the former, embracing those of the latter. What Clint took from *City Heat* was a lesson he already knew: that commercial calculation, the notion that the right stars in the right vehicle was inevitably bound to create a surefire hit, was often very far from the case. Better simply to trust one's instincts and not be misled by big names and big promises, to return to business as he more usually practiced it.

OPPOSITE Poster art for *City Heat*, in which Clint and Burt Reynolds teamed for the first—and only—time. RIGHT Richard Benjamin directs Clint and Jane Alexander.

BACKGROUND Action scenes from *City Heat*, which should have been a box-office powder keg, but the results of this troubled production failed to ignite. It was a learning curve for Clint to know, simply, to trust one's instincts and to return to business as he more usually practiced it.

PALE RIDER 1985

Clint had a point when he once said, "The western is a myth, so you might as well go myth all the way," which he proved with *Pale Rider*. Clint's mysterious rider appears in a muddy little western town, beats the crap out of a bunch of bullies who are menacing Hull Barret (Michael Moriarty), a mild-mannered miner, then rides back with him to his camp, where he and some other settlers are panning for gold. There he reveals himself to be a "Preacher" (well, he does wear a turned-around collar), though he has a taste for whiskey and, eventually for a widow (Carrie Snodgress). More important, he is a magical figure, rallying the "tin pans" in their fight against Coy LaHood (Richard Dysart), who is running an industrial-strength—and obviously ecologically unsound—mining operation, and who, for no reason beyond the fact that he's the head villain, covets their claims.

Clint's character, known only as "Preacher," is a magical figure. Whenever his surrogate family is in trouble he has a way of turning up to defend them. But he's more than that. Fairly early on he takes off his shirt and we see that he is scarred by bullet holes—enough of them for us to assume that he was killed and that what we are contemplating here is a ghost. Why he has chosen to adopt these downtrodden miners as another of his surrogate families is never explained—except by the fact that he is Clint Eastwood, again exercising a longstanding movie habit of befriending and defending the luckless and the helpless. At the end of the film LaHood brings in a corrupt

marshal and his deputies to wipe out the Preacher, at which point we learn that they are the ones who murdered him. This time, of course, he gains his revenge and brings peace to the miners.

To some degree this is *Shane* with a supernatural twist, except that the Preacher is an even more magical figure—perhaps even a Christ-like one, enjoying a resurrection. Another major variant on *Shane* is that the adolescent figure admiring him is a young woman instead of a young lad. But the main thing about it is that it offers further proof of Clint's love of playing characters who have the ability to mysteriously turn up, unannounced, at the moment when they are most needed by people whose options are severely limited. Since Clint is most basically a realist, these characters of his are a way of stretching reality's limits, perhaps even of suggesting that all of us—himself included—require, in certain circumstances, a touch of mystic good fortune if we are going to attain our happy endings. Or maybe it's just a forthright acknowledgment that improbably dauntless movie heroism is never more than a narrative convention, that, in truth, most movie heroes would end up dead, with their causes hopelessly lost, if they didn't have some magic on their side.

Not that the movie—which is rich in dry, amusing ironies—insists on this point. It leaves open the possibility that, like Joe in *A Fistful of Dollars*, the grievously wounded Preacher crawled into some hidden lair, nursed himself back to health, and returned to the world without actually leaving it. But that's an explanation for the dour and the doubting. In this instance, I prefer the more mystic explanation of his immanence, as Clint obviously does as well. It's so much more fun.

ABOVE The bunch of bullies. PREVIOUS PAGES Back in the saddle again: Clint reacquainted himself with the western in *Pale Ride*. To some degree this is *Shane* with a supernatural twist. OPPOSITE Clint as the mysterious "Preacher," with Sydney Penny as Megan Wheeler.

"Well, there was a different kind of a spiritual feeling than there was with *Unforgiven*. In *Unforgiven*, it's about wrestling with the soul and your past. And in this one, you don't know whether he's a man of the cloth or whether he's some sort of apparition or something, but he's definitely an odd character in the spectrum of things. And he preaches a lot of American ethics, in a way that can be violent and that can also be very gentle."

HEARTBREAK RIDGE 1986

Clint once said, *"Heartbreak Ridge* is my ultimate statement about macho. He's supermacho and he's just full of shit—just completely ignorant." He is Gunnery Sergeant Tom Highway, Medal of Honor winner, Marine Corps lifer, yet inherently as much a rebel against institutional authority as Harry Callahan—particularly as it's exemplified by what he sees as the softer, gentler side of the corps *circa* 1986.

He has returned to Camp Pendleton in California, charged with whipping into shape a doofus reconnaissance platoon. He also has a personal mission—reconciliation with his estranged wife, saltily played by a divine Marsha Mason.

Neither task goes particularly well at first. The corpsmen under his command at first remain reluctant warriors—despite the hilariously obscene tirades he directs at them (these sequences compare quite favorably to similar sequences in Stanley Kubrick's *Full Metal Jacket*, which was released a year later). Worse, his wife Aggie, though she remains drawn to him despite her better judgment, is skeptical about his reformation. This includes earnest consultations with women's magazines, urging new male attitudes on men still clinging to their antediluvian attitudes.

Slowly, comically, people begin to respond to his virtues. His platoon begins to shape up and, better still, to forge a sense of identity as a fighting unit. And Aggie begins to soften slightly. Early in the film an officer tells Highway that he ought to be kept in a glass case, labeled "Break Open in Case of War." In other words, much as we'd prefer it to be otherwise, we still have not yet—and doubtless never will—set aside the military necessity, the military virtues, of the likes of Tom Highway.

All of which are needed by the tin-pot invasion of Grenada. It was, as Clint admits, a pretty poor little war, but it was, at the time, the only one on offer, and Highway and his platoon serve heroically and—in my judgment—a little too lengthily in it. They return home to a flag-waving welcome, with Aggie among those greeting them. For the moment at least she and Highway are reconciled.

I don't suppose *Heartbreak Ridge* is among Clint's best films, but yet there's something about it—the parodistic poses of masculinity he strikes, the curious sweetness of his attempts to fit into the strange new world of post-60s America, above all Clint's willingness to play yet another of his Great American knuckleheads. There are,

in this essentially comic portrait, some occasionally acute social observations, and here and there Clint's performance was correctly praised. Certainly it was the most farcical he had yet offered. Maybe, as we have noted, Clint is not entirely comfortable in uniform, but here he has some nice ambiguities to play—his love-hate relationship with the Marine Corps, his love-dismay relationship with the opposite sex. These matters are not forced upon our attention, and they represent the added value Clint imposes on what would otherwise be just another routine—and antiquated—genre exercise, a military comedy.

ABOVE The muscle-bound Marine Corps in *Heartbreak Ridge.*
OPPOSITE "Break Open in Case of War," Clint again cast himself against type as knuckleheaded Gunnery Sergeant Thomas Highway.

"He desperately wants to correct his life, but by the same token, he's the certain type of guy who just can't do it in any conventional way. He's not in the pussy generation, so to speak."

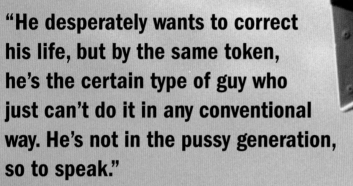

ABOVE The reluctant warriors fall in line. RIGHT Clint, with cinematographer Jack Green, directs his ultimate statement about "macho."

BIRD 1988

Joel Oliansky's script had been floating around for a while, and Clint at one point confessed a certain frustration when it looked as though someone else would make a film about the man who had been his musical hero since he was an adolescent. But when it was controlled by Ray Stark, the producer conceived a fondness for a script Warner Bros. controlled and a straight-up swap of the two properties was arranged.

After that, Clint had to wait a couple of years to put his film into production—he was busy being mayor of Carmel for one thing, and for another, since he was determined to use Charlie Parker's original recordings on his soundtrack, a great deal of highly technical work, supervised by Lennie Niehaus (whom Clint had first met when they were in the army), had to be accomplished. Something over a year and a half's time went into bringing that material up to modern standards. Then, too, Clint did not move the production along at his usual quick pace. This was, in his mind, the most serious film he had ever undertaken and he was not going to make haste with it.

It is probably his darkest film, technically speaking, and perhaps emotionally as well—as befits a short life (Parker died when he was only thirty-four years old) that was spent largely in smoke-filled, ill-lit jazz joints, and one that was passed largely while Parker was gripped by the drug habit that eventually killed him. Clint did not want to romanticize anything about Parker. He did not want to show him as a man surrendering everything to his art or as a man overindulged as a child (which was one theory about the roots of his feckless behavior). It was enough for Clint simply to show a gifted man-boy with no sense of discipline—except when he launched into one of his genius-struck saxophone solos.

THIS PAGE Forest Whitaker as Charlie Parker in *Bird*, sweet as a rose.
OVERLEAF Clint and cast on the set of his second film as director only, and one of his most personal projects.

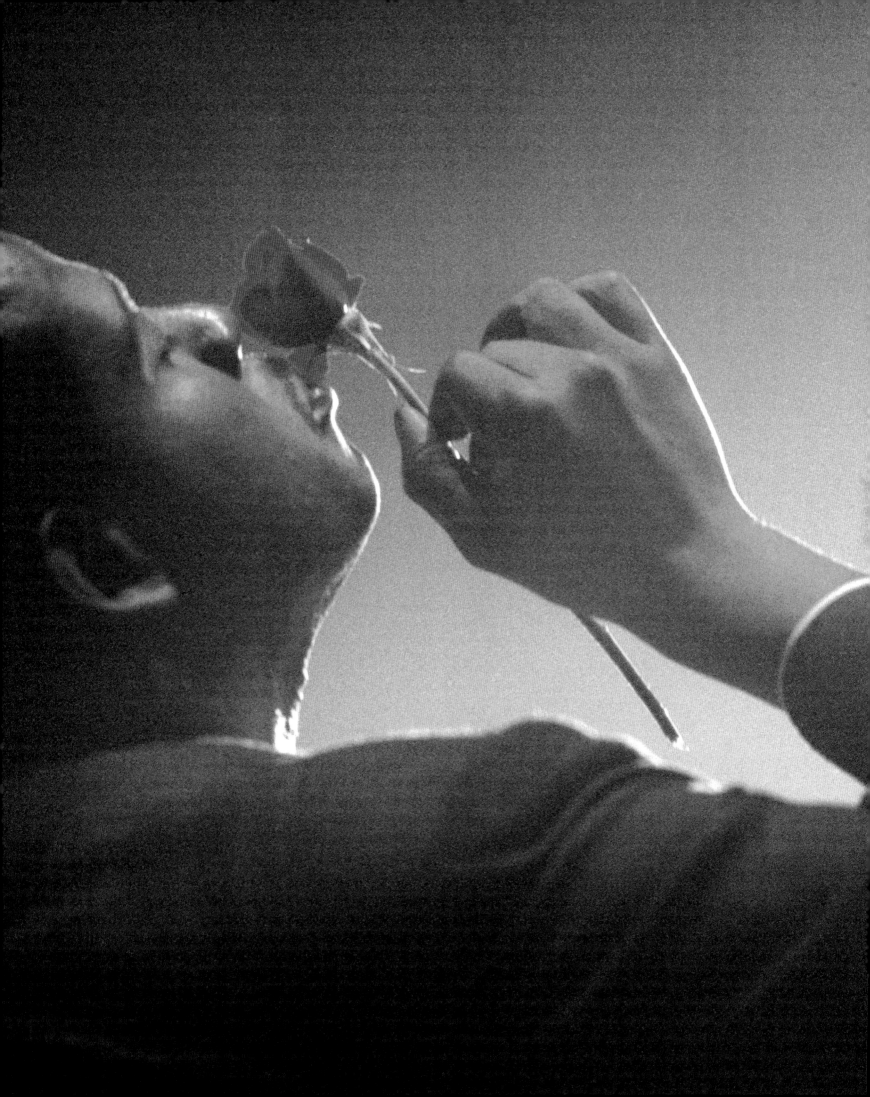

Bird is in many ways an atypical Eastwood movie, especially in its lack of a clean-cut narrative line—it is told as a series of disorderly flashbacks—and its lack of anything like heroic behavior. It displays only a very limited compassion for its well-played (by Forest Whitaker) protagonist. As Clint has repeatedly said, he cannot really understand self-destructive behavior. The best he can do is show it, which he does here without any overt show of compassion. If the movie has a moral, it is spoken by Samuel E. Wright's Dizzy Gillespie, who is Clint's surrogate in the movie— the cool professional artist who understands that, particularly for a black man, it is necessary to maintain your sharpness and your stamina to be, if you can, "a leader of men."

I think the coolness, the objectivity, of the film is its greatest strength. It never disdains Charlie Parker, but it never weeps for him either, as movies about blighted geniuses so often do. It acknowledges the paradox that Clint had observed when he listened to Parker in clubs, that he was "the single most confident individual I've ever seen in my life when he was playing the saxophone," but then just "faded into the woodwork." Clint said a couple of other interesting things around the time of the movie's release. One was that it was the first movie about a jazzman that was created by "someone who really liked jazz." The other was that when he was a young man he often thought of himself as "really a black guy in a white guy's body." I don't doubt that idea for a minute. He had been poor.

And he had been directionless. It was finding a talent and nurturing it that had saved him, as it had for many a black man of his and previous generations.

But *Bird* proved to be a tough sell. Jazz was, to begin with, a minority taste, of small interest to the popular audience, and though many mainstream critics recognized that this was a movie of serious aspirations, they also professed "confusion" over the film's structure, which was nonsensical—it is no more temporally fractured than many another movie that was praised for that very quality. Moreover, there were a number of intellectuals who were invested in various alternative readings of Parker's life and career, and they wrote learnedly about the film's failure to follow their lines. When Clint took the film to Cannes, it was dimly received, with only Whitaker winning a prize for its acting. Later the studio mounted Oscar campaigns for the film for Clint's direction, for Whitaker's playing as well as that of Diane Venora, who was excellent as his wife, but to no avail.

Clint has never fared well at Cannes, and his friend, Pierre Rissient who has long served him as a consultant in his ventures into foreign fields, recalled a jury chairman assuring him, on one occasion, that no prize would ever be awarded to "that Yankee cowboy," which has remained the case. Yes, he had made enormous progress from those kinds of dismissals. But, no, he was still, as of 1988, a Yankee cowboy in the eyes of many people.

A FILM BY CLINT EASTWOOD

BIRD

A FILM BY CLINT EASTWOOD

"We just didn't seem to have enough people in America who wanted to see the story of a black man that in the end betrays his genius. And we didn't get the support through black audiences that I had hoped for. They really aren't into jazz now, you know. It is all this rap stuff. There aren't enough whites who are, either."

OPPOSITE The elegant poster art for *Bird*. THIS PAGE Here with Michael Zelniker (*left*), who plays Red Rodney, and Forest Whitaker (*center*), Clint's work on *Bird* earned respectful reviews, though box-office response was predictably cool.

THE DEAD POOL 1988

There's not much to be said for *The Dead Pool*. It is the fifth, last, and least of the *Dirty Harry* series. The story concerns—well, yes—a dead pool in which participants make lists of people they think likely to die within a year. The winner, of course, is the one who correctly predicts the largest number of people passing on.

Such suspense as the film generates derives from the fact that a number of logical candidates are being murdered well in advance of their natural times.

The film employs some good actors—Patricia Clarkson, Liam Neeson, and Jim Carrey in his first noticeable role; it has a couple of inventive sequences, a car chase between toy vehicles loaded with explosives and the death by harpoon gun of a villain; it takes some satirical thrusts at celebrity culture, in particular at the avidity with which it pursues criminal cases, posing the none-too-pressing question of whether this coverage encourages crime. It makes fun of auteurist pretensions among movie directors, and it even sees to it that an annoying female movie critic—take that Pauline Kael—comes to an unfortunate end.

Under Buddy Van Horn's relaxed direction, *The Dead Pool* is, at best, a routine entertainment, possibly intended to be the most lighthearted of Harry Callahan's adventures, though it does not achieve what anyone would call a frolicsome air. Some critics thought Clint was showing his age in the picture—he was fifty-eight the year it was released—but it seems to me that what he projected was an air of distraction. He had, after all, said before he started shooting the film that Harry had "become pretty much a closed chapter in my mind." Now *Bird*, which he had finished previously, was in post-production and heading for its premiere at the Cannes Film Festival, so Clint essentially left *The Dead Pool* for others to finish. I've never asked Clint the question, but I've always suspected that the movie, the smallest-grossing production in the *Dirty Harry* franchise, was a way of paying back the studio for indulging him in that labor of love.

In any event, no harm done—either to Clint's reputation or to Warner Bros.' coffers. John Ford always called himself "a career man," meaning he understood that, over the years, he had made his share of failures, but that they were outweighed in his mind by his larger number of successes. I've never heard Clint apply that term to himself, but I'm convinced that's the way he looks at his very long life on the screen.

> **"There's only so much you can do with a character, and Dirty Harry was pretty much at the end of his rope."**

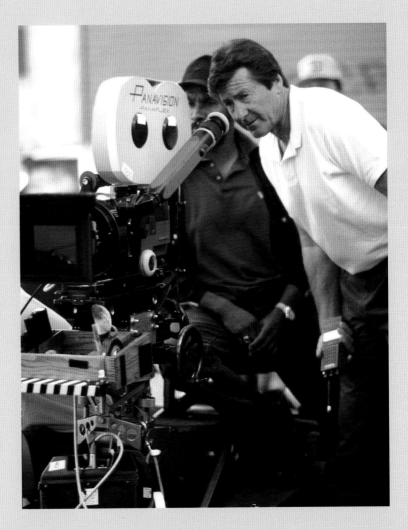

OPPOSITE AND OVERLEAF The last outing for Harry Callahan in *The Dead Pool*.
RIGHT Director Buddy Van Horn supervises the action.

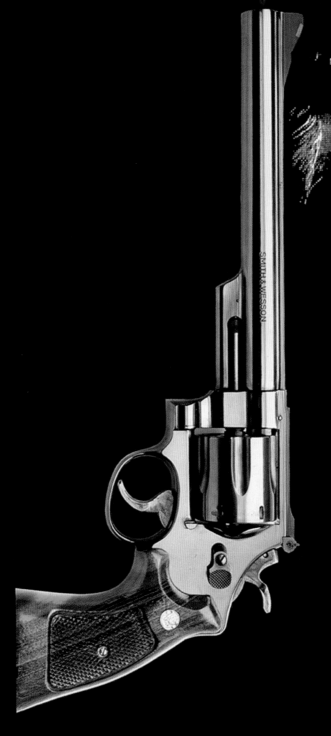

CLINT EASTWOOD

DIRTY
HARRY
IN THE
DEAD
POOL

PINK CADILLAC 1989

In the late 1980s and early 1990s, Clint entered upon the one lengthy downturn in his career—a run of four pictures that were greeted with more than the usual critical dubiety and failed, as well, at the box office. Part of that failure can be traced to his reliance on the open market for his scripts; for some reason there just weren't that many promising screenplays available to him at that time, he would later say. But there were other reasons for this as well. For one thing, his longstanding relationship with Sondra Locke was beginning to deteriorate, and their growing acrimony would prove to be an unadmitted distraction for him. Finally, he would turn sixty in 1989 and there was a feeling that, as an incipient senior citizen, he needed to make perhaps more dignified choices of projects. Certainly, it was generally felt that he shouldn't be fooling around with items like *Pink Cadillac*.

The studio had pushed the project on him, thinking it had some of the knockabout qualities of the orangutan movies (though it was rather obviously missing their salient selling point, the adorable Clyde). Instead, it followed the misadventures of one Tommy Nowack, a skip tracer, a man devoted to pursuing and returning to the law's clutches people who jump their bail bonds and attempt to disappear into the fastness of the American West. In particular, Tommy is pursuing Lou Ann McGuinn, played by Bernadette Peters. She had become a Broadway star—deservedly so—with her kewpie-doll cuteness and her ability to blend innocence and shrewdness. They, of course, fall into a bickering love affair and they have some pretty funny passages in the movie. And some with decent action in them, too. But under Buddy Van Horn's direction the thing doesn't quite come together. It's too casual, too loose. And Peters, adorable as she may be, is not really an accomplished movie actress.

If Pink Cadillac has any minor interest, it is in Clint's determination to play a master of disguise, appearing from time to time as a cowbell-wielding radio personality, a casino sharpster wearing a gold lamé jacket and a pencil moustache, even as a rodeo

RIGHT An uncharacteristic Clint in one of his most uncharacteristic films.
OPPOSITE The dynamic poster art for *Pink Cadillac*, featuring the incipient senior citizen and the vintage automobile.

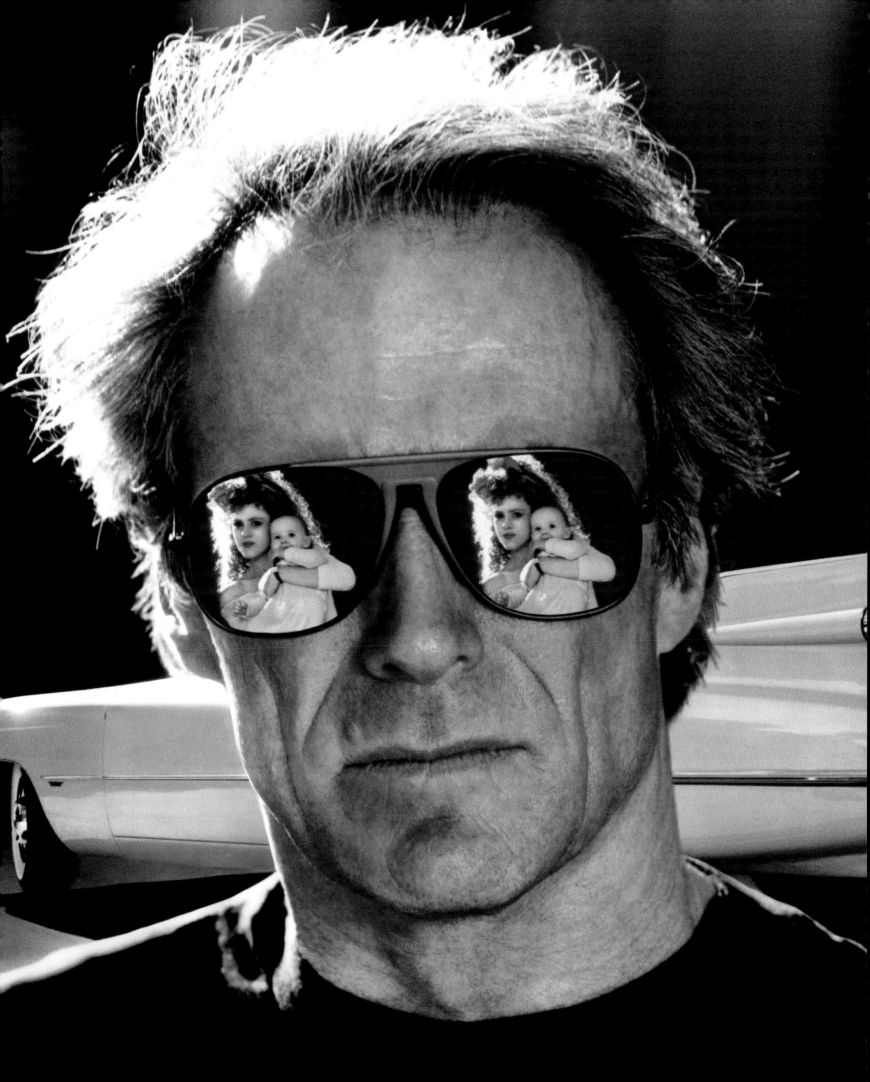

clown. We have had reason to observe that Clint likes to play magical figures, appearing out of nowhere, at just the right moment to turn a plotline or just to astonish the other characters in the movie. You can sense his own enjoyment as he plays these tricks, but they are not enough to carry this limp little movie.

To make matters worse, the studio decided to open it on Memorial Day weekend, which was becoming the traditional launching point of the summer season of blockbusters. The competition that year was *Indiana Jones and the Last Crusade*, Steven Spielberg's bold, bustling, expert assault on what was left of the old mass audience, adolescent males. Indy buried Tommy—taking in $37.7 million compared to the latter's $4.4 million. Not only was it no contest, it was a contest that should never have been run. *Pink Cadillac* never recovered from the blow, and the show-biz press made much of its failure. Clint later waxed philosophical about it: "People wanted me to go another step," he reflected, "and that was all right. At least," he thought, "they wanted me to go somewhere—not just to the door marked 'Exit.'"

OPPOSITE Another magical figure, this time as a rodeo clown.
THIS PAGE Clint with Bernadette Peters, as Lou Ann McGuinn, and the pink Cadillac.

WHITE HUNTER BLACK HEART 1990

This is something of a lost film in the Eastwood canon. It is based on the novel by Peter Viertel, which was, in turn, based on his experiences working with John Huston, polishing the final draft of *The African Queen* on location in the Congo in 1951.

The book was a bestseller and Viertel sold it to Columbia, wrote a screenplay, and then entered upon what may be the longest development period in screen history. Other writers (James Bridges and Burt Kennedy) did drafts, and something like four decades passed before Clint decided to do the film.

Partly that was because he had long admired Huston as a director, partly it was because in his grandiosity of manner he was a sort of anti-Clint, therefore something of an enigma and a challenge to him. Very simply put, the story has the Huston figure (called John Wilson) distracting himself on location with an obsessive desire to shoot an elephant, while, basically, his company sits around waiting for him to abandon his half-mad quest. Jeff Fahey, playing Peter Viertel, calls the idea of killing one of nature's noblest beasts a crime, an idea with which Wilson disagrees. It is worse than that, it's a sin, but one of the few that you can get a license to perpetrate. In the event, he confronts an elephant but funks his shot. The creature charges and succeeds in killing Wilson's native guide, a man greatly admired by the director as a natural man, untouched by civilization's ambiguous values. Wilson returns to the set a visibly broken man. Slumped in his chair he can barely mumble the word "action" to begin his production's first scene.

There is considerable fiction in this story. Huston never actually attempted to shoot an elephant, and there is considerable ambiguity in his confrontation with the beast. Was it simply cowardice that caused him not to shoot? Or was he, finally, just overcome by the magnitude of the crime he came within seconds of committing? Clint has never said. As ever, he wanted the audience to make up its own mind on that point.

OPPOSITE In portraying John Wilson—based on director John Huston— Clint gave a credible impersonation of Huston.

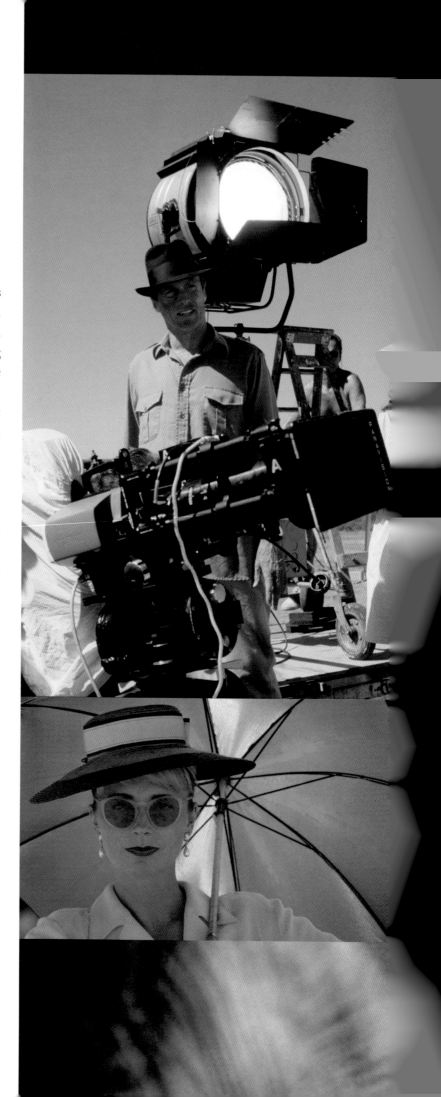

"I constantly quote John Wilson, my character in *White Hunter Black Heart*, who says, 'You can't let eight million popcorn eaters pull you this way or that.'"

Whatever the case, Clint's take on the film stresses other aspects of the Huston character. For one thing, Clint deplores hunting. Beyond that, he had the feeling that Huston needed distraction from the pressure of accomplishing the main task at hand, making his film. "Oh, I've got people that are depending on me. This way he never had to think of that. He was always, 'OK, I'll make the film, but in the meantime, what's going on at Santa Anita?' Or, 'I've got this great-looking chick who lives on the other side of town and I've got to meet her for dinner'—always something that's taking him away from the central thing he's doing."

When the film went into release, the critics found a distraction from the movie's central purpose—the questioning of standard macho posturing. Instead, they questioned Clint's choice of using the Huston accent in the role. I thought he did a credible, creditable impersonation of him. But this toff, swanning about with his bespoke shotgun and swell clothes, spouting grandiose moral sentiments and, worst of all, ending up in a defeated posture, was not Clint as either the reviewers or the audience best liked him. Then, too, the distance of the film's setting, both in time and in geography, was off-putting. The studio gave *White Hunter Black Heart* what can only be described as a reluctant release—an initial run in twenty-five theaters, an art-house sort of exposure, from which it did not expand. Like *Bird*, it returned only about one fifth of its negative cost, without achieving the directorial respect that the earlier film had gained for Clint.

But, that said, I think this is a very good film, a further, somewhat more intellectually serious, exploration of the question that has bedeviled Clint's mind and career all along: what does it mean to be a man, especially when you are an actor who virtually defines the masculine condition for the world at a particular moment in time? It takes some courage to portray such a figure airily, carelessly, antiheroically as he does here.

ABOVE Directing on location in Zimbabwe.
BELOW Charlotte Cornwell coolly played the role of Miss Wilding, John Wilson's assistant.
OPPOSITE In action, Clint's character had an obsessive desire to shoot an elephant.

198

THE ROOKIE 1990

It was another of those scripts that Warner Bros. had lying about and pressed upon Clint, who at that moment had nothing better to do. It represents, I think, a fundamental misunderstanding—or maybe it was just a form of wistfulness—of what Clint was, and what he should be doing, at this stage of his life. Management had enjoyed great success with Clint in action movies and in comedies, and despite its indulgence of his more serious aspirations, they wanted him to go on making more or less youthful entertainments of that sort—even if he was by now sixty years old (even if he didn't look it) and entitled to somewhat weightier enterprises.

The film tries to set up a bantering relationship between Clint's older detective, Pulovski, and his cheeky young partner, Ackerman, played by Charlie Sheen, a rich kid who needs to understand that police work is, actually, serious work. Their exchanges fall flat—not at all in the wise-guy mode of the *Lethal Weapon* or *Die Hard* pictures that were all the rage at the time—and some of the incidents in the story— particularly a sequence in which a villainous Sonia Braga gets Clint tied to a chair and forces him to have sex with her at knifepoint— are downright distasteful.

The picture has a couple of good action sequences—Clint and Sheen hurtling out of a fifth-storey window in a car just ahead of a fireball, and a high-speed chase in which Clint pursues an auto-transporter, which keeps shedding its cargo along the way. Buddy Van Horn, coordinating the stunt, thought it was the most complicated "gag" he had ever attempted.

But no matter. The studio threw the picture into the crowded Christmas release season and it pretty much sank without a trace. "Sometimes these things work; sometimes they don't," Clint later mused. "It's just hard to come up with good material all the time." Yet the truth was he was at a low point in his career—four commercial flops in a row, with the press beginning to speculate that he was in danger of being pushed to the fringes, as other action heroes like Burt Reynolds and Charles Bronson were at the time. It was time, at last, to reach into his pocket and pull out the project that had been resting there for a decade, awaiting its moment.

> "The main thing the director has to do is to know it when he sees it... If you do thirty takes, the big question usually is, 'Was thirty any better than one?'"

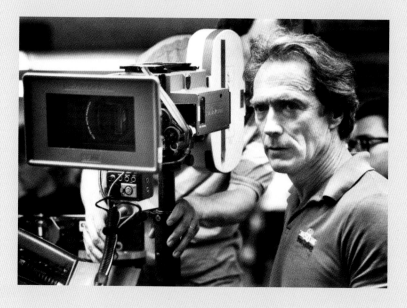

RIGHT The stress on the director shows in making *The Rookie*.
OPPOSITE Eastwood with Charlie Sheen, a teaming that did not pay off.

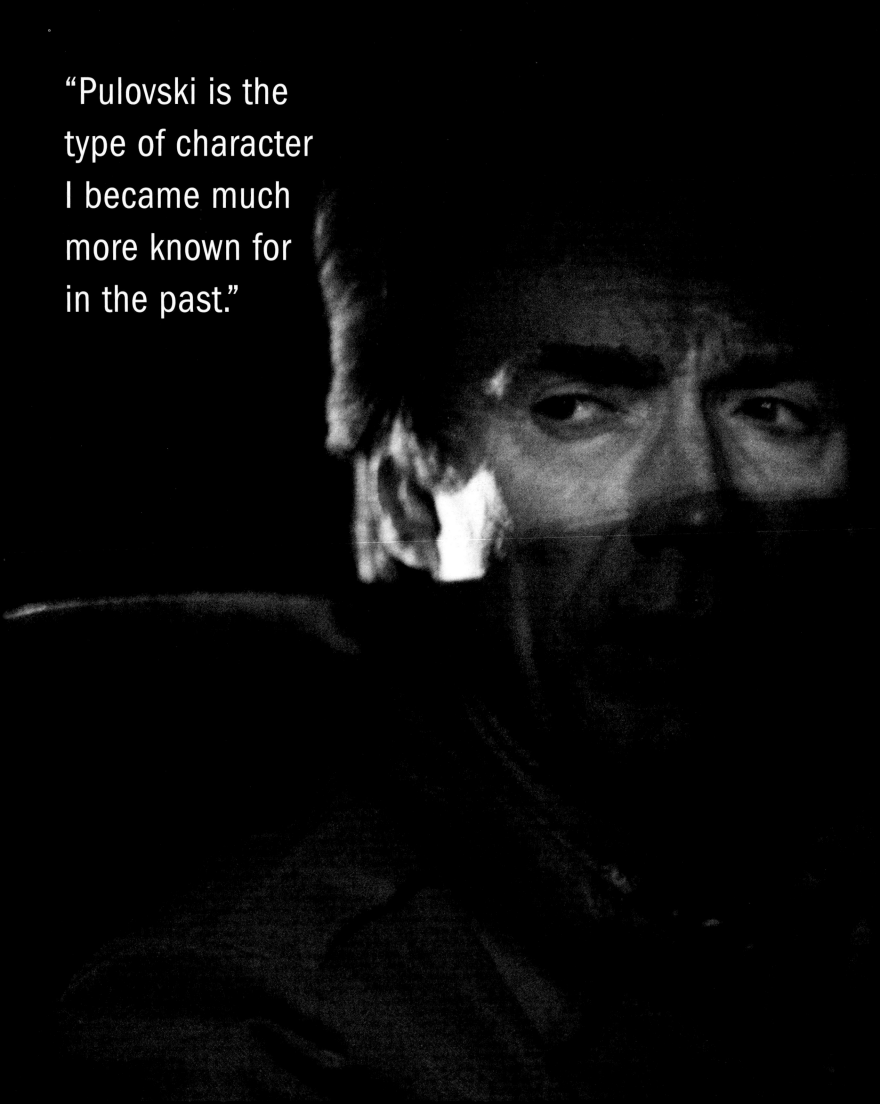

"Pulovski is the
type of character
I became much
more known for
in the past."

OPPOSITE A transitory moment of calm amid many moments of mayhem (*above*).

UNFORGIVEN 1992

A cathouse whore is cruelly disfigured by a drunken, knife-wielding cowboy. He and his partner are, in the judgment of the other prostitutes, insufficiently punished for the crime and they offer a reward for his murder and that of his pal. Word of this opportunity reaches Clint's William Munny, a notorious outlaw who has been reformed (or so he earnestly believes) by the love of a good woman, now deceased.

He can no longer support his children with the proceeds of his forlorn pig farm, so enlisting the help of his former outlaw colleague, Ned Logan (Morgan Freeman), he decides to kill the cowboys and claim the reward. He reckons without the sadistic psychopathy of "Little Bill" Daggett (Gene Hackman), sheriff of Big Whiskey, where the crime was committed. He is, *in extremis*, a law-and-order guy, and he's not going to tolerate disruption in his town. And he is soon proving it, beating William senseless and flogging Ned to death in an effort to make him tell which trail Munny has taken to escape his deputies. At the end of the film Munny and Daggett confront each other, with predictable results.

When the picture was released, many critics identified it as a "revisionist" western, which it is only with an asterisk. The foregoing plot summary shows that it contains many classic genre elements. The revisionist spins in David Webb Peoples' script are largely in its details, in the formality of some of its language, and in the contrasting authenticity of some of its slang, in the centrality of a sex crime instead of, say, cattle rustling, in its plot, in the introduction of contemporary concerns in the plot—the law-and-order theme, for example, and also a primitive celebrity theme, with a dime novelist hanging about, trying to turn sordid frontier criminals into mythic figures for his distant readers. It also turns out that the criminals who cut the whore are not deeply evil—they're actually kind of nice kids operating out of a post-adolescent lack of judgment. "I guess they had it coming," says

OPPOSITE A somber moment at the beginning of *Unforgiven*, on location in Alberta, Canada. Out on location Clint observed, "For a brief moment, whatever the schedule is, you are in another era, another time."

the Schofield Kid, a half-blind would-be gunslinger. "We've all got it coming," Munny sadly observes in response.

Even art director Henry Bumstead's design of Big Whiskey brings a change on our expectations—it straggles down a hill and its main street, far from being dry and dusty, is a sea of mud—as does cinematographer Jack Green's lighting, which is the darkest I've ever seen in a western. Putting this in the simplest possible terms, Clint and his team responded to Peoples' work with an intensity and sense of detail that was unprecedented in the body of Clint's work.

We have previously noted that Clint's best work as a director has occurred when he is encouraged to explore the outer reaches of genre convention, and that is what he does with an unprecedented vitality and commitment in *Unforgiven*. I was frequently on location with the movie in Saskatchewan, Canada, making a documentary film about it and, as always on his sets, Clint was good-natured, self-deprecating, a perfect host to a cast and crew working in rugged conditions. If he felt any pressure to come up with a winner after his string of recent failures, he was not showing it. He was, if anything, even more serene than usual.

When the film went into release almost a year later, critical recognition of his achievement was unhesitating; it was almost as if no one—Pauline Kael and her acolytes excepted—remembered all the dubiety they had previously accorded his films. It was almost as if that "revisionist" tag they hung on the film was their way of saying that Clint was obviously a new man, some sort of born-again filmmaker. "I'm not like that no more," Clint says to Morgan Freeman when they are discussing Bill Munny's bloody past. Something like that was implicit in the film's critical reception—with everyone except his small band of critical supporters—forgetting that Clint had been working his way toward this apotheosis almost since the beginning of his career, when he worked in the more obviously "revisionist" Leone films.

In due course, the Oscar buzz for *Unforgiven* started up, and I think that spooked Clint a little. Only two westerns had previously

CLINT EASTWOOD

GENE HACKMAN

MORGAN FREEMAN

RICHARD HARRIS

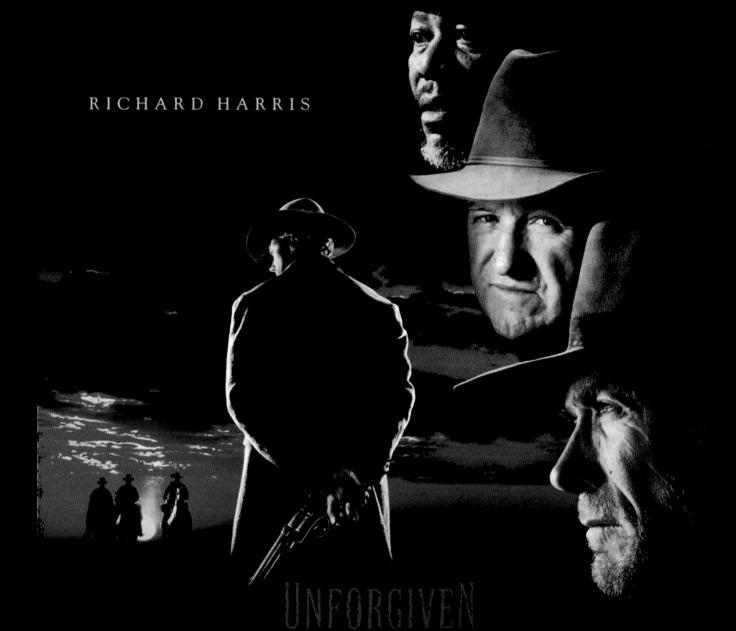

UNFORGIVEN

"I like it that the good guys aren't all good and the bad guys aren't all bad. Everyone has their flaws and everyone has their rationale and a justification for what they do."

ABOVE Bill Munny, closing in on his nemesis. OPPOSITE "I thought it was very important to do a film where violence not only can be painful, but has consequences for the perpetrators as well as the victims."

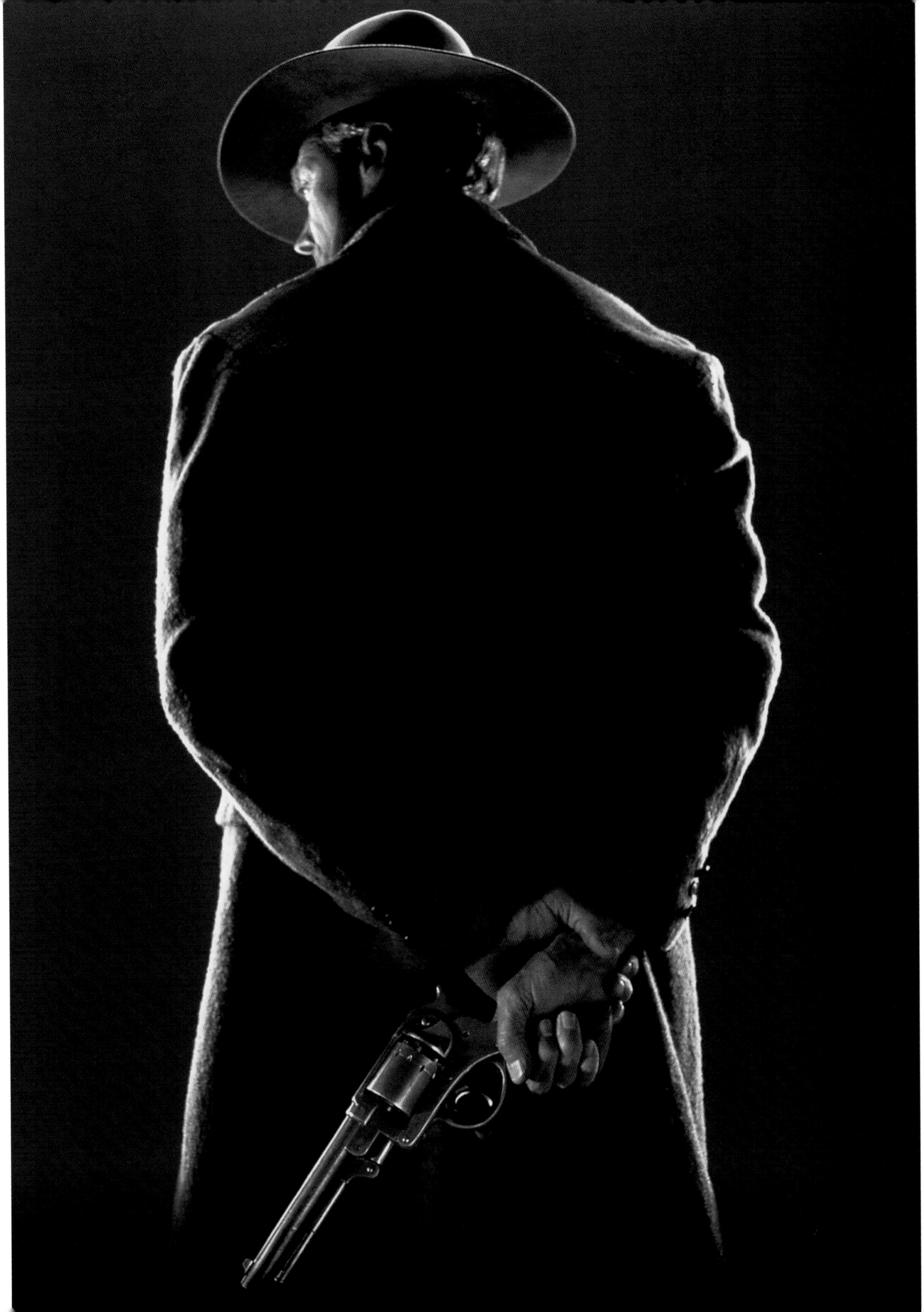

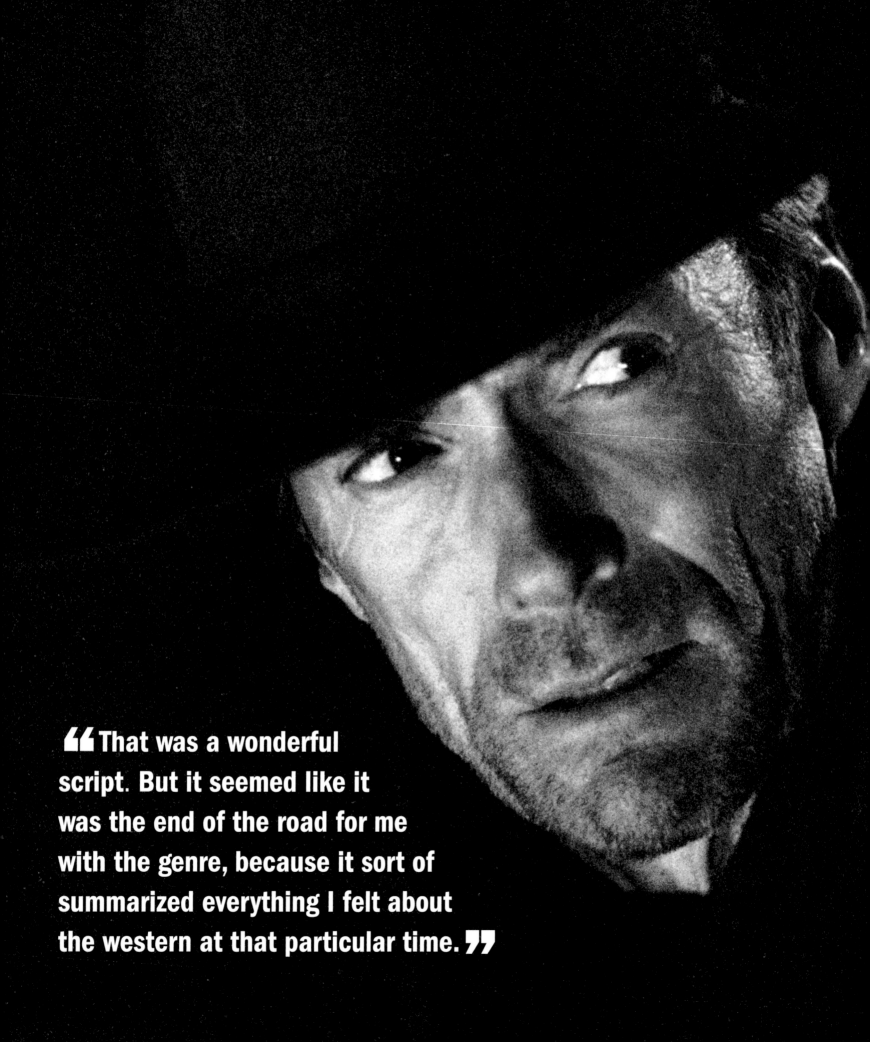

"That was a wonderful script. But it seemed like it was the end of the road for me with the genre, because it sort of summarized everything I felt about the western at that particular time. "

won Academy Awards and he was not at all certain the Academy membership was completely ready to forgive his humble movie beginnings and his devotion to genre filmmaking. That, of course, proved not to be the case, though I felt that David Peoples deserved the screenplay prize and that Clint himself was a far more plausible choice for Best Actor than Al Pacino.

But no matter, really. There is often a good deal of buyer regret after the Oscar season passes into history. But that has not been the case with *Unforgiven*. It is generally accepted as a great film—perfect evidence that a film deeply rooted in genre can be an austere and serious statement about large themes. I generally avoid superlatives, but I remain convinced that *Unforgiven* is the greatest western ever made, so much richer thematically and even visually than all the *High Noons* and *Shanes*, all the handsome, somewhat empty John Ford movies that people continue to treasure—if only because it is not so much a revisionist work but a modernist one.

You are, naturally, free to disagree with this evaluation. But one thing you cannot disagree with: *Unforgiven* granted Clint Eastwood his freedom. He would continue to cling largely to genre conventions, of course, but henceforth he would also be given leave—not least in his own mind—to follow his own aspirations wherever they led him.

OPPOSITE Possibly Clint's farewell to the western. ABOVE On location with Morgan Freeman: "That is part of the appeal of a western. You get out on location, the air is fabulous, and if you didn't go back into town in the evenings, you'd eventually think, yeah this is the world for me."

IN THE LINE OF FIRE 1993

Frank Horrigan describes himself in the film as a "white, piano-playing, heterosexual male over the age of fifty," which is, not incidentally, an excellent description of Clint Eastwood at this stage of his life. The difference between them is that Horrigan is a haunted man—the Secret Service agent who holds himself responsible for John F. Kennedy's assassination in Dallas. This may not be entirely true, but that's what Frank thinks, and that's all that counts.

In the Line of Fire, which is a near-to-perfect entertainment, recounts the duel between Horrigan and John Malkovich's Mitch Leary, a disaffected (not to say psychotic) former CIA agent, who is determined to murder the current president as a way of working out his grievances against the government. Malkovich gives a wonderfully creepy, darkly humorous performance as the nut job, and Clint, who upon first reading the script commented that it was "almost as if it were written for me," is a wry and cagey adversary. He also finds himself drawn to a much younger colleague, Rene Russo's Lilly Raines, with whom he is soon engaged in a bantering, sexy affair—a tone that he had not struck in any of his previous roles, where his comparatively rare romantic encounters were edgier.

Clint had been mired in his bad patch when Jeff Maguire's script was making the rounds, and at that point *Unforgiven* looked to be just another western, which was, in any case, a down-and-out genre. Hollywood was looking for a younger stud to play Horrigan, forgetting that that would obviate Frank's whole JFK back story. When, at last, Clint became aware of this smart script, something more than a good story replete with suspense and romance began driving him. He saw Frank as a sort of anti-Dirty Harry.

The former is a man committed to self-sacrifice, the latter to self-assertion. His first duty is take a bullet for the president (or whatever VIP he is protecting), not to fire one on his behalf. This intrigued Clint: "If anybody told me I had to jump in front of somebody and be shot instead, I'd say, 'You've got me confused with somebody else.' That mentality, that you take the bullet for somebody you might not even respect, is very hard to understand, but at the same time admirable."

OPPOSITE Clint as the Secret Service agent, Frank Horrigan.
RIGHT With Rene Russo's Lilly Raines—Clint observed, "it's always appealing to play a character who has to overcome himself as well as an obstacle."

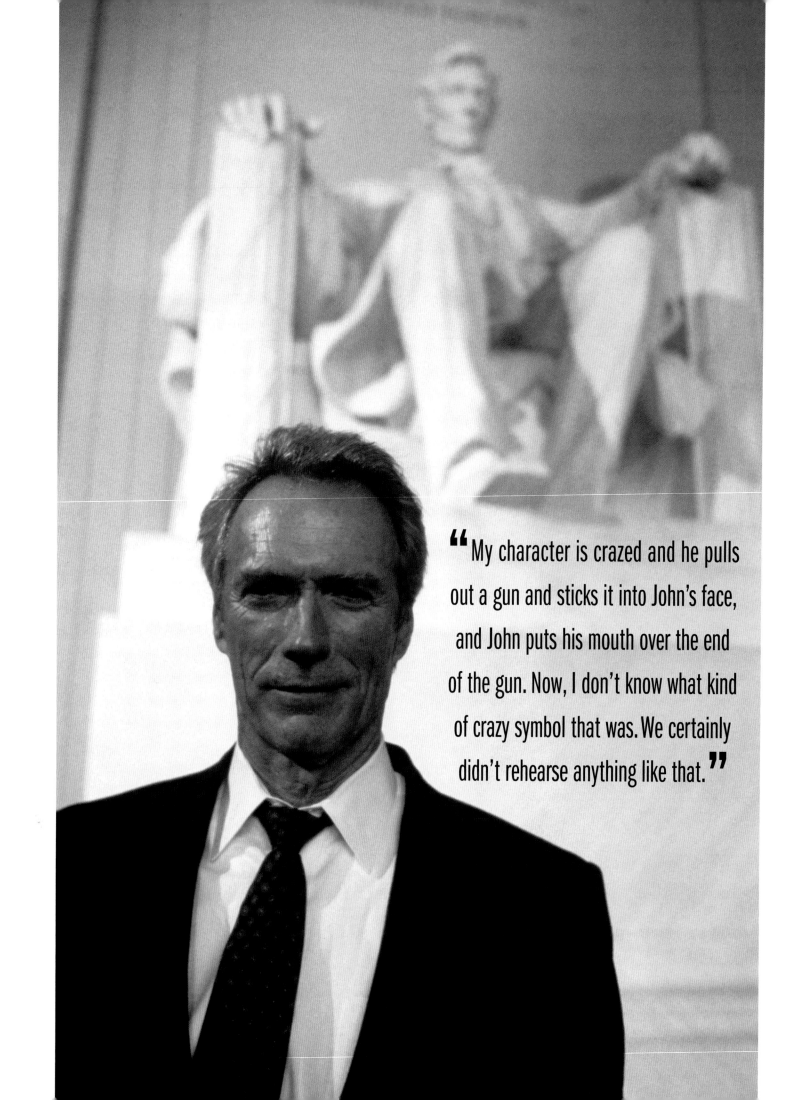

"My character is crazed and he pulls out a gun and sticks it into John's face, and John puts his mouth over the end of the gun. Now, I don't know what kind of crazy symbol that was. We certainly didn't rehearse anything like that."

It is that mystery of character that grants *In the Line of Fire* its best quality, the edge that Clint is always at least unconsciously looking for in his roles. There was some discussion of him directing the film, but he declined; he had for the moment wrung himself out doing double duty on *Unforgiven*. Wolfgang Petersen, whom Clint did not know but whose work he liked, got the job. It was, at a cost of $40 million, among the most expensive movies Clint had ever been involved in, but it didn't feel that way when it opened. There is no frenzy about the film, no sense of people trying to expand its spectacle into the realms of implausibility, which so often happens with action films. Without sacrifice of suspense, it is content to tell a rather intimate story while at the same time giving us a realistic sense of what it is like to protect the president of the United States, who is democratically committed to public appearance, an activity that is always fraught with danger.

In other words, this is a very balanced and rational movie, and it was received with relief and enthusiasm by critics and public alike. I suppose you could say that, taken together with *Unforgiven*, it completed Clint's "comeback" from his flirtation with the fringes. People had more or less failed to identify him as a serious actor and director in his younger incarnations; from here on out few would fail to see him as a not-so-old master. From being an actor and director from whom most people had expected very little, he was now largely transformed into someone from whom much was expected. Which sometimes had the paradoxical effect of limiting his freedom. Now he had the capacity to "disappoint" people when he felt like relaxing, making some nice little movie of no great consequence.

OPPOSITE A relaxed moment in Washington in front of the Lincoln Memorial and sharing some of the physical attributes of the great president. TOP Poster art for *In the Line of Fire*. LEFT Clint with Rene Russo on set. RIGHT John Malkovich as Leary, the would-be presidential assassin. The on-screen interaction between the two actors in character electrify the movie.

215

"It should've probably been released a lot differently, but who knows? It may have never done anything. But it's a picture that I was proud of. And I thought Kevin Costner gave kind of a brilliant performance in it. And the kid, and all of them, they were terrific."

A PERFECT WORLD 1993

John Lee Hancock's script—an original—was owned by Warner Bros. and was shown to Clint as, once again, a writing sample. He, of course, thought it the basis for an immediately makeable movie. Hmm, the studio thought—awfully good role for Kevin Costner, maybe even something for which he could snare an Oscar nomination. So, in April 1993, cast and crew repaired to the country around Austin, Texas, to shoot *A Perfect World*.

Clint and Costner were not a natural pairing. The latter likes to work slowly—painfully so, as Clint saw it—and there was a certain tension between them on the set. On the other hand, Clint has come to believe that Costner did the best acting of his life in the film, which takes up that favorite Eastwoodian theme, the creation and, in this case, the violent sundering of a surrogate family. Costner's Butch Haynes is an occasionally violent criminal, escaping from a Texas prison in 1963, and soon enough taking as a hostage a seven-year-old boy named Phillip Perry, played with an adorable sobriety by a kid named T.J. Lowther. He is the child of a single mother who is also a fundamentalist religious fanatic, which means, for Phillip, no trick or treating on Halloween, no trips to the county fair, none of the fun of childhood. Butch identifies with the boy's deprivation; he had a nasty father who prevented him from enjoying similar pleasures. So they bucket along the back roads, eating fast food, gulping RC Cola, with Phillip wearing a Halloween costume

(Casper the Friendly Ghost) he has filched from a store, and enjoying, in a matter of days, all the previously forbidden pleasures of childhood.

The state is in a swivit about the case. The child must be in danger—of his life, of abuse, of something. Clint's Red Garnett, the Texas Ranger in charge of the pursuit, is not so sure (Clint hadn't wanted to play the role, but Costner talked him into it). He knew Butch when he was not much older than Phillip, and thinks he was turned into a criminal not merely by his violent father, but by the state's inept welfare and criminal justice systems. Riding around in a trailer (or "mobile crime investigation unit"), he is the soul of good ol' boy patience, swigging Geritol, and expressing his partiality for Tater Tots, while his superiors bay for Butch's blood.

All along, though, we suspect that this film cannot come to a good end. There is, as in so many Eastwood movies, something destined, fated, in these lives. The crisis comes when they seek

217

KEVIN
COSTNER
CLINT
EASTWOOD
a Perfect
world

WARNER BROS. Presents

A MALPASO Production KEVIN COSTNER CLINT EASTWOOD LAURA DERN "A PERFECT WORLD" Music by LENNIE NIEHAUS
Film Editor JOEL COX Production designed by HENRY BUMSTEAD Director of photography JACK N. GREEN Written by JOHN LEE HANCOCK
DOLBY STEREO Produced by MARK JOHNSON and DAVID VALDES Directed by CLINT EASTWOOD

shelter with a black farm family—nice people with a fatal flaw. The mild-mannered father turns out to be abusive of his son—just as Butch's father was. He comes near to killing the man—and a terrified Phillip gut-shoots Butch. They go to ground in an open field, where the law, excessively majestic in its assembled firepower, has them trapped. Red goes forth unarmed to parley with Butch. And, misunderstanding an innocent move the latter makes, a hot-shot FBI sharpshooter kills him.

It is not quite a tragic story, but it is a deeply sad tale of mixed motive and misunderstood actions. It is one of Clint's best films and one that was not at all underappreciated by the critics, who greeted it with some of the best reviews an Eastwood film ever had. But the release was mishandled—it was thrown into the Christmas season, partly because the studio wanted to avoid a spring competition with an even riskier Costner film, *Wyatt Earp*, partly because they'd had good luck with the early winter release of Costner's *The Bodyguard*. "They spend millions on research, and then they release it on superstition," Clint was heard to grouse.

A particularly goofy reason for the film's failure was adduced by a couple of right-wing reviewers, who thought Clint had sold out what they (mis)understood to be his formerly conservative principles to embrace a new identity as a lefty wuss. How about that? In a matter of three decades, he had transformed himself from Crypto-fascist to liberal elitist. Calm down, guys. Have a Tater Tot.

Clint, of course, has no regrets whatsoever. "It was just that domestically it wasn't as strong as it could've been or should have been. But I've long ago given up wanting to make a movie and worrying about what it does and where the audience is. I'd just rather have the fun and freedom of making my comment. On an international level, it worked very well. In France and Italy and places like that it's quite revered." This, indeed, is one of the paradoxes in the career of this most American of filmmakers; like Howard Hawks and Raoul Walsh and many of his predecessors, the "Yankee cowboy" gained his first serious attention among the cinephiles resident on distant shores.

OPPOSITE **Poster art for** *A Perfect World*. ABOVE LEFT Kevin Costner and T.J. Lowther. ABOVE RIGHT Clint in character as the Texas Ranger. The film proved a critical success on release, and maintains a growing respect retrospectively.

THE BRIDGES OF MADISON COUNTY 1995

It was, no question about it, a bad book—a slender, soppy romance, primitively felt and written. Yet Robert James Waller's novel about the brief encounter between a wandering photographer and a farmer's wife sunk in unacknowledged boredom struck a popular nerve; it unaccountably sold millions of copies and Steven Spielberg acquired the movie rights. After due deliberation—and a certain amount of script problems—he decided not to direct. Why he thought of Clint as just the man for the job is unrecorded. But we must remember that both of these moviemakers have very sound populist instincts.

When books or films enjoy wild, seemingly unaccountable popularity, you can always find in them, if you look hard enough, a kernel of truth, that reality beneath convention that accounts for their success. We can probably guess, in this instance, that there are more restless housewives in America than anyone imagines, and that *The Bridges of Madison County* represents for them one of the largest guilty pleasures in modern literary—better make that sub-literary—history.

Still, the thing needed a little work. In particular Clint felt that Francesca Johnson, the Italian war bride transported to the Iowa hinterlands, needed to be a less passive figure than she was in the book, given the opportunity she needed to express her long-buried needs. She also needed to be portrayed by an actress who could invest her with a fiery, humorous, yielding complexity. He thought immediately of Meryl Streep, unquestionably the movie star with the greatest emotional range of her generation. Miss Streep, however, had her own opinion about the book; she had literally tossed a copy into the trash after reading a few pages of it.

So Clint got on the phone with her, urged her to read the script he wanted to send to her, and a couple of days later she signed on. A couple of months later they found themselves in Madison County, the seat of which, Winterset, was John Wayne's birthplace, an irony not lost on Clint; hard to imagine Duke Wayne playing a gobsmacked loner like Robert Kincaid waltzing around the kitchen with Francesca Johnson.

The shoot turned into a kind of love-fest. We have perhaps insufficiently noted how many really fine actors—ranging from

RIGHT Meryl Steep invested Francesca Johnson with a fiery, humorous, yielding complexity. OPPOSITE Clint as Robert Kincaid and Meryl Streep in Clint's first full-out romance.

Geraldine Page to Sean Penn—Clint has costarred with and/or directed over the years. They challenge him, and they remind him of his acting-student ideals, while his minimalism, in turn, reminds them that good screen acting essentially entails the business of not seeming to act at all. Very often, a mutual admiration society develops on Clint's sets. Which is what happened in Madison County in the early summer of 1994.

Streep is sometimes described as a "technical" actress, a little too calculating in her effects, which may have been true when she was younger, but is no longer so. She is, in her nature, funny, giggly, even girlish, and she has in recent years allowed that side of herself to show through more and more. Clint's instinctual way of working allowed their best moments to "feel captured as opposed to set up and driven into the ground."

I think that, at least as much as Richard LaGravenese's rebalanced script, the naturalism Streep and Eastwood found in their playing, a combination of ease and passion, is what saved the movie from its source. And Streep came to believe that the movie was not primarily about belated rewards, sexual and otherwise, bestowed on the deserving middle-aged. It was, she said to me, about, "Regret. And lost chances. And how things come to you at the wrong time." I believe she's right, and that's why Clint's first full-out romance works far better than anyone predicted it would—or perhaps deserves to have worked, given its dubious source.

"When I was doing *The Bridges of Madison County*, I said to myself, 'This romantic stuff is really tough. I can't wait to get back to shooting and killing.'"

ABOVE The two stars with their iconic central location, the bridge of Madison County.
OPPOSITE Clint directs his bucolic romance.

"A lot of the people I've played have been lonely
for one reason or another, either by their own choice
or through fate. Like in *The Bridges of Madison County*.
He's a loner. I seek out that sort of character.
I guess I relate to those kinds of people.
In terms of a story, basically, when I look at a character
I want him to have something that's bothering him."

ABSOLUTE POWER 1997

For a few years in the late 1980s and early 1990s, Clint largely returned to pure genre filmmaking. Three of the four movies he made in that period were crime dramas (a fourth was a good-natured tale involving space flight and espionage, and a fifth was a misfired adaptation of a nonfiction bestseller). There was, however, a difference between his genre work in this moment and the likes of *Pink Cadillac* and *The Rookie*. For one thing, all the crime films were based on novels by prominent practitioners of the thriller form. For another, they had much less of a tossed-off air; the situations they explored had a high degree of originality, the writing was good and the production values were all first-class.

That was certainly true of the first film in this series, *Absolute Power*. It featured major actors (Gene Hackman, Ed Harris, Laura Linney, Judy Davis), had a very potent central conceit, and offered Clint a role that drew on a number of notions he enjoyed playing. He is Luther Whitney, a world-class jewel thief, pretending now to be retired and spending much of his time sketching in Washington's art museums. He may be a typical Eastwood loner, but he is far from

retired. He's planning a robbery as meticulous as his drawings. It involves penetrating a strong room located off the bedroom of a rich, elderly political power-broker (E.G. Marshall). He is coolly scooping up cash and jewelry when the man's young wife and her lover, both drunk, enter the bedroom—Luther can observe them through a one-way mirror—with sex obviously on their minds. This quickly turns rough, the woman resists and the ruckus attracts the

LEFT Gene Hackman as the US President crossing the line of acceptable behavior. RIGHT Clint directs in a return to pure genre filmmaking. OPPOSITE Acting as the master-thief Luther Whitney.

attention of two armed men, who shoot her, causing her attacker, wounded by the desperate woman, to retreat to the bed, blubbering.

The shooters are Secret Service and her sadistically inclined lover turns out to be—yes—the President of the United States, played by Gene Hackman with his typical blend of menace and false piety. Luther is observed escaping the premises, and though he is not identified he is, putting it mildly, "a person of interest"—and a vast inconvenience—to any number of people, mostly representing the "absolute power" of big government to impose its will on ordinary people (the cop who is most sympathetic to Luther is Ed Harris's local detective).

One can make what one will of that plotline, but I think what most attracted Clint to this project was Luther's skill as a master of disguise. How he loves will-o-the-wisp roles, ghostly and otherwise. This is a point that is well developed in his relationship with his estranged daughter (Linney), who is a lawyer. She believes he has deserted her, and it is only when she penetrates his modest home that

she realizes he has attended every significant occasion in her life—graduations, school plays, her first court appearance—disguised, of course, and snapping pictures. Here, of course, the film touches on that other favorite Eastwood theme—the troubled family whose relationships are in need of repair.

David Baldacci's novel was obviously intended to refer, indirectly, to the Bill Clinton-Monica Lewinski affair, but that's not a matter William Goldman's good script at all emphasizes. To him, this POTUS is just a creep. The stress here is all on intricately worked out suspense, leading to a wonderfully appropriate *denouement*.

This richly mounted film, dark and elegant in manner, is an extraordinary entertainment, offering Clint a role that stresses spryness, irony, and reassuring confidence. He was at the time sixty-seven years old and, without denying that fact, he offered gaffers everywhere hope for their own continuing relevance. They just needed to get more exercise. And perhaps do some more crossword puzzles to keep their minds sharp.

ABOVE Clint Eastwood with Ed Harris. OPPOSITE Recalling *film noir* lighting, the movie was richly mounted and was dark and elegant in manner.

"With *Absolute Power*, I liked the gimmick of the book—the guy is outside the law, so he can't go to the police when he sees a situation involving a high-up government official."

MIDNIGHT IN THE GARDEN OF GOOD AND EVIL 1997

John Berendt's novelistically told nonfiction book became one of the most mysterious bestsellers of recent times. It is an account of a swishy antiques dealer named Jim Williams (played in the movie by Kevin Spacey), living the good life in elegant Savannah, Georgia, who is accused of murdering his lower-class lover (Jude Law, in one of his earlier movie roles).

He's a nice, tricky character—definitely an anti-Clint sort—and it is probably the ambiguities of his nature that drew Clint to this project. Berendt—renamed Kelso in the movie, played by John Cusack, and given a love interest (Alison Eastwood)—spent some five years in Savannah, soaking up the atmosphere, which is the best thing about his book, but is also a hard thing to capture in a movie,

which touches on the Gothic and exotic, but not at all suspensefully. This may be especially difficult for a director like Clint, who is at his best with stories driven by strong narratives. The fact that this film was so far from his beaten path was probably another attraction.

OPPOSITE John Cusack played the writer John Berendt. BELOW Kevin Spacey as the antiques dealer Jim Williams, here with Clint Eastwood the director.

well, ambition is a fine thing. So is the attempt to reach out in new directions, especially when an older filmmaker might be expected to be content with a more predictable path. Indeed, that search for new approaches, new themes, would very shortly pay large dividends for Clint. But not this time.

Midnight is the most languid film Clint ever made, lacking the try-anything liveliness of even his least aspiring genre efforts. It feels, much of the time, conscientious but sprawling, with none of its characters achieving wayward life. They don't seem to grow naturally out of the Savannah scene; rather, they seem to be pasted into it.

Reviewing the picture, Roger Ebert thought that the inherent realism of moviemaking, its natural drive toward the quotidian, fatally harmed the film. Berendt, he said, left much more to the reader's imagination. There's probably some truth to that notion. But I'm not sure it is one worth exploring, except in a theoretical sort of way. I think it's just a misfire—to which the director was, of course, more than entitled.

"I liked the atmosphere of Savannah. The central character, the journalist, goes down there and takes us on a journey. It's a town with a tremendous history and an interesting social structure."

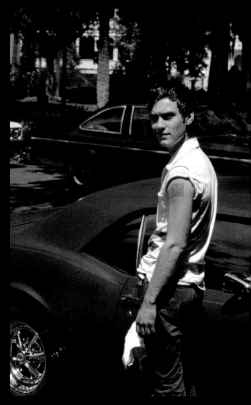

OPPOSITE Chablis Deveau entertains. ABOVE Irma P. Hall (*center*) with John Cusack (*left*) and Kevin Spacey (*right*). BOTTOM Kevin Spacey, the swishy antiques dealer (*left*), Irma P. Hall as Minerva (*center*), and Jude Law as the lower class lover (*right*).

TRUE CRIME 1999

Steve Everett is a drunk, a womanizer, and testy with his bosses. He is, in short, a familiar journalistic type, bouncing (and being bounced) from job to job. His redeeming characteristic is his "nose," constantly asniff for evidence of corruption and other forms of malfeasance. When we meet him he is employed at Clint's old hometown paper, the Oakland *Tribune*, where among other activities he's having an affair with the managing editor's wife. One morning he's handed a routine assignment—a human-interest story of the last day of a convicted murderer due to die by lethal injection at midnight in San Quentin, across the bay.

ABOVE Isaiah Washington as death row innocent Frank Beechum. OPPOSITE Clint as reporter Steve Everett, with his real daughter, Francesca, who played his daughter in the film.

Checking the files before going to interview Frank Beechum (Isaiah Washington), Steve's nose starts twitching. Something's not quite right about this case, in which Beechum was convicted for murder in a convenience store. Having met Beechum, we immediately begin to concur with Steve's suspicions. He is obviously a decent man, with a sympathetic wife (Lisa Gay Hamilton) and a lovely child. The prison staff are clearly on his side—they turn the place upside down to find the lost green crayon his daughter needs to complete the peaceful picture that is to be her last gift to him. Soon enough, Steve is engaged in a frantic chase for exculpatory evidence.

This race to the rescue is a story almost as old as the movies—something very similar occurs in the best of the several stories that comprise D.W. Griffith's *Intolerance* in 1916. It is very well done, and it provides the picture's melodramatic spine. But it is the portrayal of the desperate family that gives it true distinction. Washington plays the condemned man with great calmness, as one after the other his hopes for a reprieve are dashed. His main concern is to try to make his last day on earth as normal as possible for his child, who knows what's going on, yet desperately goes along with her father's charade. His wife, too, is doing the best she can to protect the little girl. But her despairing wail as she is led out of the visiting room for the last time is, I think, one of the most heartbreaking moments in all of Clint's films.

Need we say it? This is the Eastwoodian family most in need of heroic ministration. The very nature of the film—so much of it shot in the close confines of prison—forces us into intense intimacy with

233

them, intense sympathy with them. As for Clint, his playing of the screw-up reporter is terrific—comic, raffish, only reluctantly heroic as, finally, he races through the night in his decrepit car carrying a witness and the material evidence that will induce a pardon from the governor before the execution can be fully carried out. Nor does he get much for his pains. His wife is still going to divorce him, no matter how much he loves their child (played adorably by one of his own daughters, Francesca). He also loses his job. When last we see him it's Christmas Eve, and he's leaving a toy shop with a gift for his little girl—having, of course, flirted shamelessly with the store clerk. Across the plaza, he sees the Beechums, going about their peaceful business. They notice him as well. Shy waves are exchanged. These people truly have nothing in common, except what amounts to a chance encounter. "He's not going to go camping with him," Clint observes of his character. Nor does it appear that Steve Everett is likely to reform his manner. It is the perfect ending to what is, in its way, a perfect little movie, the kind of movie that everyone treats as routine—as if the expertise of its making were all that common, as if the way it tamps down emotions instead of forcing them up toward the frenzied, was all that usual.

ABOVE Clint Eastwood directs *True Crime*. OPPOSITE Clint as the deeply dysfunctional husband and father (with Diane Venora and daughter Francesca Fisher-Eastwood) in a rare moment of domestic harmony.

SPACE COWBOYS 2000

It's what's known in Hollywood as a "geezer" comedy—some beloved old-timers get together on some improbable mission or other and, before it is over, show the sneering youngsters a thing or two. They may be a few steps slower than they used to be, but they still have all their marbles. And they have the accumulated wisdom of their years to help see them through the tight spots.

So it is with *Space Cowboys*, which is a more than agreeable action comedy. The premise is that several decades ago NASA shot a communications satellite into space. Now it is in need of repair, and an old NASA nemesis, Bob Gerson (James Cromwell), thinks chief designer, Clint's Frank Corvin, is just the man for the job. He, in turn, nurses a modest resentment in that he never got to penetrate outer space—he was replaced by a monkey. He agrees to do the task if he can reassemble his old team of buddies—hot pilot Hawk Hawkins (Tommy Lee Jones), wise-guy astrophysicist Jerry O'Neill (Donald Sutherland), and engineer Tank Sullivan (James Garner), who has become a preacher in the intervening years. There's a certain amount of old-guy comedy as they get into shape for their mission, a certain amount of action when they realize that the station, built cooperatively with the Russians, is corrupt in unexpected ways. That is to say, it carries atomic weaponry, which the nasty Gerson has long ago conspired to install. Their more human problem is that Hawk has been diagnosed with terminal cancer. In the end he has to sacrifice himself by taking off for the moon and a lonely death if the mission is to be successfully completed. The sentiments attached to this incident are handled in the typically understated Eastwood way, and the movie includes one of those dicey returns to Earth's atmosphere that appear to be *de rigeur* in space epics, and it concludes with a neat settling of scores.

Clint loved working with these actors, most of whom he had acted with before; he told one reporter that if any one of them had turned down his proffered role he probably would not have made the movie, which proceeds at the nice, easy, joshing pace that is typical of Clint when he's in a lightsome mood. The film was well-liked and well-attended—just before it was released, NASA sent the septuagenarian John Glenn into orbit, which not only lent it good publicity, but plausibility as well. If my remarks about this film seem not particularly warm, I hasten to say that the fault is mine, not the movie's. I have never been particularly moved by space odysseys. Maybe it's the weightlessness. Maybe it's the cold. Maybe it's all that high-tech equipment blinking at the camera. Maybe it's that I'm just a hopeless groundling. But, in any event, more power to Clint for overcoming what may be a generational prejudice and making so humane and genial a film about astronauts.

OPPOSITE Four old geezers: Tommy Lee Jones, Clint Eastwood, James Garner, and Donald Sutherland as the *Space Cowboys*.
RIGHT Tommy Lee Jones as pilot Hawk Hawkins.
OVERLEAF With *Space Cowboys* Eastwood set himself the task of addressing Hollywood ageism, but turned in a warm, good-natured picture about second chances.

"You get a little older and they want you to play roles twenty years younger, which is ridiculous. They want you to play a forty-year-old guy. You don't want to play a forty-year-old guy anymore."

BLOOD WORK 2002

In hot pursuit of a serial killer, FBI agent Terry McCaleb is stricken by a massive heart attack. He requires a heart transplant to save his life. And that requires retirement from government service. When we meet him, he's living the quiet life—and moving very tentatively—on his boat, moored in the Los Angeles harbor. That's when Graciella Rivers (Wanda De Jesus) contacts him. Her sister has been murdered and no perpetrator has been apprehended. She's hoping for his help on the case. No thanks, says Terry. But, she says, it is her transplanted heart that is keeping him alive. That, of course, changes everything. And, once again, Clint is attempting to repair a family riven by tragic circumstances.

Blood Work, based on a novel by the highly regarded Michael Connelly, has perhaps the best premise—or gimmick, if you like—of any Eastwood movie. And his involvement in the identification and pursuit of the killer gets Terry moving in ways that endanger his health. He's both internally and externally threatened by this case. And he's soon shyly, sweetly involved romantically with Graciella and with her sister's son, of whom she's the guardian.

The viewer is advised to keep his eye on Clint's buddy, Jasper "Buddy" Noone, a rich slacker living on a nearby boat. He's played by Jeff Daniels, in his expertly good-natured way, though we come to suspect that he may have a darker agenda. Terry has his allies—a female detective with whom he may once have been romantically linked, an always-worried heart surgeon—and his enemies, notably a pair of local cops defending their investigative turf. He also does a lot of high-energy running about, which occasionally leaves him breathless—as it does us, watching his exertions.

Blood Work is undoubtedly a minor film, but it is also a highly entertaining one—thanks in large measure to the unique conceit that powers its story. And to Clint's willingness not just to play his age, but his willingness to play a seriously damaged man. We live in an age of heroic heart surgery, but not many movies are willing to show us older men attempting to come back from the operating rooms and not spend the rest of their lives taking huge quantities of drugs and shuffling along on life's fringes. OK, normalcy for Clint's

characters is a little more venturesome than it is for most men. But it's fun to see him setting an example for damaged old gaffers. He observed at the time that there's not enough shoe polish in the world to cover his graying hair, not a belt sander strong enough to plane off all his wrinkles, but that's not really the point. In this instance, he means to be the poster boy for active retirement, and he pulls that off with irony and with heartening *élan*.

OPPOSITE Impressive poster imagery from *Blood Work*. THIS PAGE Clint orchestrates the action. OVERLEAF Recently recovered from heart transplant surgery, FBI agent Terry McCaleb was Clint's most vulnerable hero, with Anjelica Huston (*center*) and Wanda De Jesus (*below*).

"I especially like McCaleb's vulnerability, both physically and psychologically."

MYSTIC RIVER 2003

Three boys are idling in the street, scratching their names in wet concrete. Along comes a man who pretends to be a cop. He abducts one of them—and with his partner subjects him to cruel sexual abuse. Eventually the boy escapes—but as a ruined figure.

When next we meet Dave (now played by Tim Robbins), he is a soft, inarticulate man, tenderly, protectively loving his son, but otherwise leading a sad and inconsequential life. His companions on that long-ago day are now played by Sean Penn as Jimmy, an ex-con, now gone straight and running a grocery store in the same working-class neighborhood where they grew up, and by Kevin Bacon, playing Sean, a police detective involved in a mysteriously sundered marriage. When Jimmy's daughter is senselessly murdered, the man goes berserk—this is probably Penn's most powerfully rageful performance—and he gradually convinces himself that Dave is the murderer, an opinion that is not shared by Sean, who is the lead investigator in the case.

Clint loved *Mystic River* the minute he read Dennis Lehane's novel, for obvious reasons. Here were three troubled families—all of whose unhappy lives are laid out for us to see—involved in highly fated circumstances. Here was an urban setting of a kind Clint had not previously explored. Here was a story that does not end neatly (the wrong man is punished for the murder). Here were roles that appealed to all kinds of wonderful actors. People were calling him up, proposing themselves for the roles. "Who would you like to play?" Clint would ask. "Oh, any of them," would come the reply. Brian Helgeland provided an adaptation in record time and, though this was undoubtedly the most complicated narrative Clint had ever taken, the shoot was, he says, one of the easiest he had ever undertaken—just because the film was so well laid out.

It even contained a bonus for him. In recent years he had begun contributing musical themes and songs to his pictures—with the faithful Lennie Niehaus contributing orchestrations. *Mystic River*'s score would be entirely credited to him. And the Boston Symphony

OPPOSITE Tim Robbins and Sean Penn head the impressive cast of *Mystic River*, filmed entirely on location in Boston.

245

Orchestra would play it, much to Clint's delight. Musically, there is always, to my ears anyway, something wistful about Clint's music, something that hints at a desire for happier endings than he sometimes supplies.

Be that as it may, the film was received with appropriate seriousness by the critics and the public alike and, in due course, Penn and Robbins received Academy Awards for their performances. But Clint and the film ran into the *Lord of the Rings* buzz saw. This was the third film in Peter Jackson's trilogy—subtitled *The Return of the King*—the first two installments of which had not been adequately acknowledged by the Academy, though all three films—expensive, expansively popular, huge-grossing—represented the kind of work the modern Academy enjoys honoring. This was the last opportunity for so doing and the film walked off with eleven Oscars. One imagines the trilogy continuing to command the nostalgic affection of the mass audience through all eternity. At the same time, one imagines *Mystic River* retaining its hold on people for whom spectacular fantasies have small appeal for a similar span. It is a demanding film that comes to an ending that is both hard to accept and yet truthful to life as many among us experience it. Another way of putting that is that it is a complex work of art that repays our repeated attention.

ABOVE With Malpaso branding, Clint oversees the movie that, up against *The Lord of the Rings: The Return of the King*, nonetheless secured Academy Awards for Sean Penn and Tim Robbins. OPPOSITE Sean Penn in a most powerfully rageful performance.

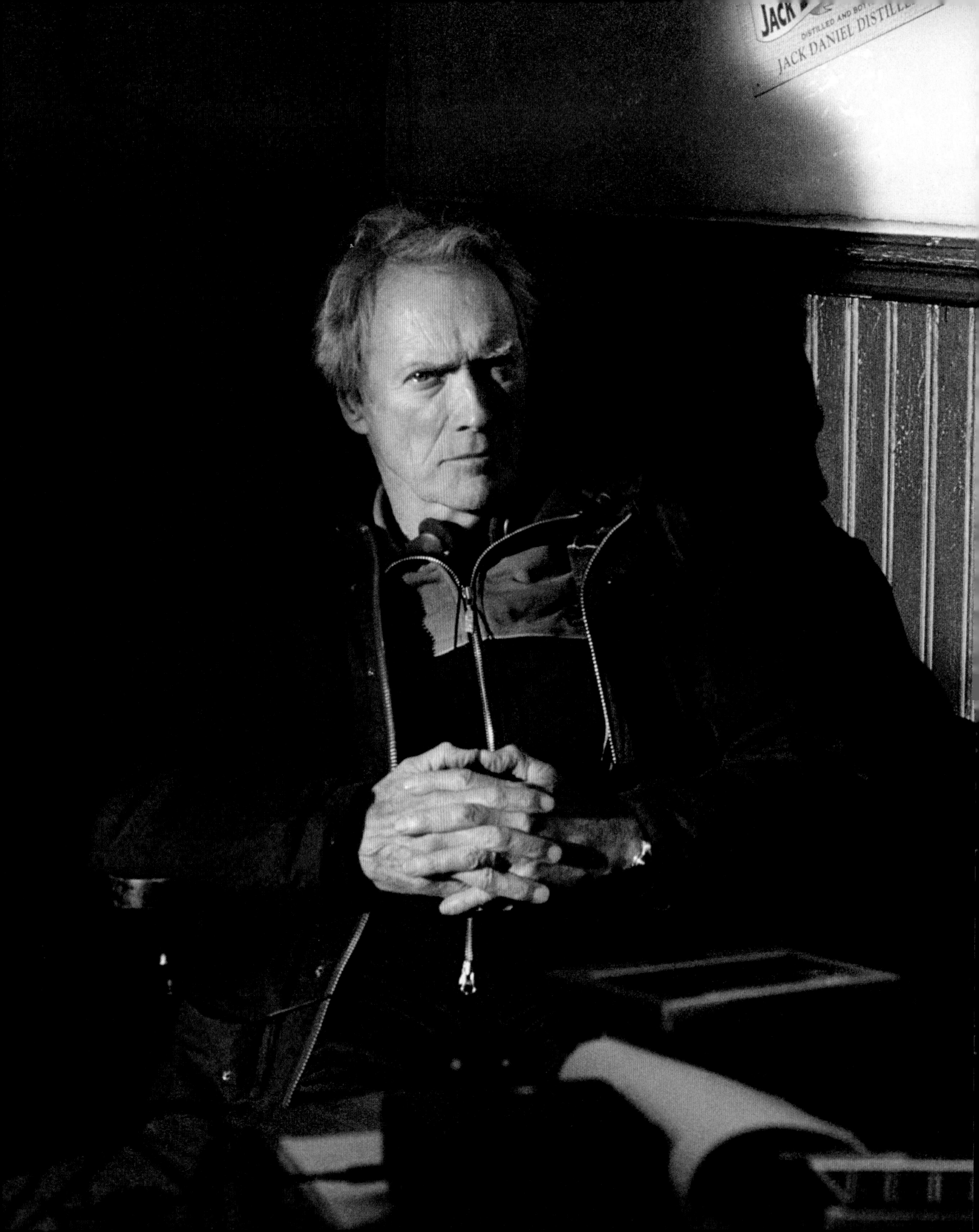
JACK DANIEL DISTILL

"I've always been fascinated with the stealing of innocence. It's the most heinous crime, and certainly a capital crime if there ever was one. I think anything to do with crimes against children is something that's very strong in my mind. So, that's what attracted me to this story—the fact that it comes back in adulthood, and things keep coming around. I just liked the story and figured I had to do it."

OPPOSITE Clint directs; "it was a great drama, and a challenge to do it."
TOP LEFT The three young boys. TOP RIGHT Kevin Bacon as Sean, the police detective.
BOTTOM LEFT Tim Robbins as Dave. BOTTOM RIGHT Sean Penn as Jimmy.

MILLION DOLLAR BABY 2004

This was a story in a well-received collection entitled *Rope Burns*, by Jerry Boyd, writing under the name F.X. Toole. The stories, primarily about boxing, reeked with authenticity, in that Boyd had worked much of his life in that world. That, naturally, appealed to Clint, as did the fact that the book was suggested to him by Paul Haggis, just beginning the great run of scripts he would write (and sometimes direct) in the first decade of the new century.

Clint also liked the theme of Boyd's story—the unlikely bonding of a craggy old trainer, operating a broken-down gym (Clint's Frankie Dunn) and an ill-used female boxer, Hilary Swank's Maggie Fitzgerald, both of whom were based on people Boyd had worked with in life.

It looked to Clint like a slam dunk. It was a low-budget proposition (about $30 million) and it was the kind of small-scale, emotionally intense film that he had mostly done well with over the years. But Warner Bros. had, for whatever bad reasons, been only a half-hearted supporter of *Mystic River*, a decision that had cost them quite a bit of money. Now here they were again in reluctant mood. Well—er— boxing pictures don't do very well, they said. But, Clint persisted, boxing is only the setting. It's really about a man estranged from his daughter, finding a surrogate on whom to lavish his bottled-up affection, and a woman equally estranged from her trailer-park family, too old, really, for the sport, but having nothing else she likes to do as much as boxing, finding a surrogate father in Frankie.

Yes, well still, said the studio, which relented only when Clint found another entity to put up half the budget. Here was art imitating life. Maggie was as persistent in getting Frankie to train her as Clint was in getting the picture a green light. Watched over by Morgan Freeman's wise and patient "Scrap-Iron" Dupris, who narrates the film, the

OPPOSITE **Clint as the craggy old trainer, Frankie Dunn, and Hilary Swank as the ill-used female boxer, Maggie Fitzgerald.**

unlikely pair prospers, until an evil opponent delivers an illegal blow to Maggie, putting her into a permanent coma. In the end, Frankie has no choice but to euthanize her.

Which, of course, touched off one of those feckless controversies that are such a tiresome aspect of American public life these days. High horses are ever available for moralists to climb aboard, the better to grab op-ed columns and cable TV appearances, but out there in common-sense America—the America Clint has represented since the beginning of his career—it is next to impossible to find anyone actually opposed to "mercy killing" when the situation is genuinely hopeless. Which the huge popular success of the movie proved.

It helped, of course, that the picture was so modestly mounted. This was clearly not a bunch of Hollywood swells spending fortunes to make an "important" point. A low budget in this case proved to be the best earnest of high intentions. But as important, I think,

is the trust Clint has built up with his audiences over the decades. No American filmmaker has more consistently challenged them to accept unhappy or ambiguous outcomes in his films. He may not always get them to come out to the theaters to see his work, but they never seem to lose faith in him—especially in his maturity—as a man entirely without cynicism, doing his best to present films that represent an honest, never overtly ideological view of life as he sees it.

This time, just a year after Oscar night visited disappointment on *Mystic River*, the Academy rewarded *Million Dollar Baby* and Clint with its Best Picture and Best Director prizes, Swank with Best Actress, and Freeman with his long-overdue Best Supporting Actor Oscar. Warner Bros. executives handsomely apologized to Clint for doubting him; they seem now to be once again trusting his instincts, which remain, as ever, among the best in the business. One thinks back to John Calley—"If he told me to date a monkey…"

OPPOSITE AND ABOVE Setting the scene for the movie that was to receive Academy Awards for Best
Picture and Best Director in 2004. Hilary Swank and Morgan Freeman also walked away with
the Best Actress and Best Supporting Actor Oscars for their respective roles in the film.

"I'm the same age this guy would be; I'm playing the same age. When you've lived so many years you understand people's family problems, and you can draw in your imagination why he had a deteriorating relationship with his daughter. Maybe it's a bad divorce, maybe in his younger days he was too involved in boxing and never spent any time with her. You've seen a lot of relationships come and go—in your family and other families. You have a lot of things to draw on. You use your imagination. And the dilemma of finally reaching a revival in his life and then having to lose it is a tragic situation."

THIS PAGE The movie was narrated by Morgan Freeman, who also played "Scrap-Iron" Dupris. Eventually, an illegal blow to Maggie halts her career in the ring and her decline sparked off the inevitable controversy about euthanasia.
OPPOSITE Poster art for *Million Dollar Baby*.
OVERLEAF A reflective moment in the changing room between the two much-loved actor heavyweights.

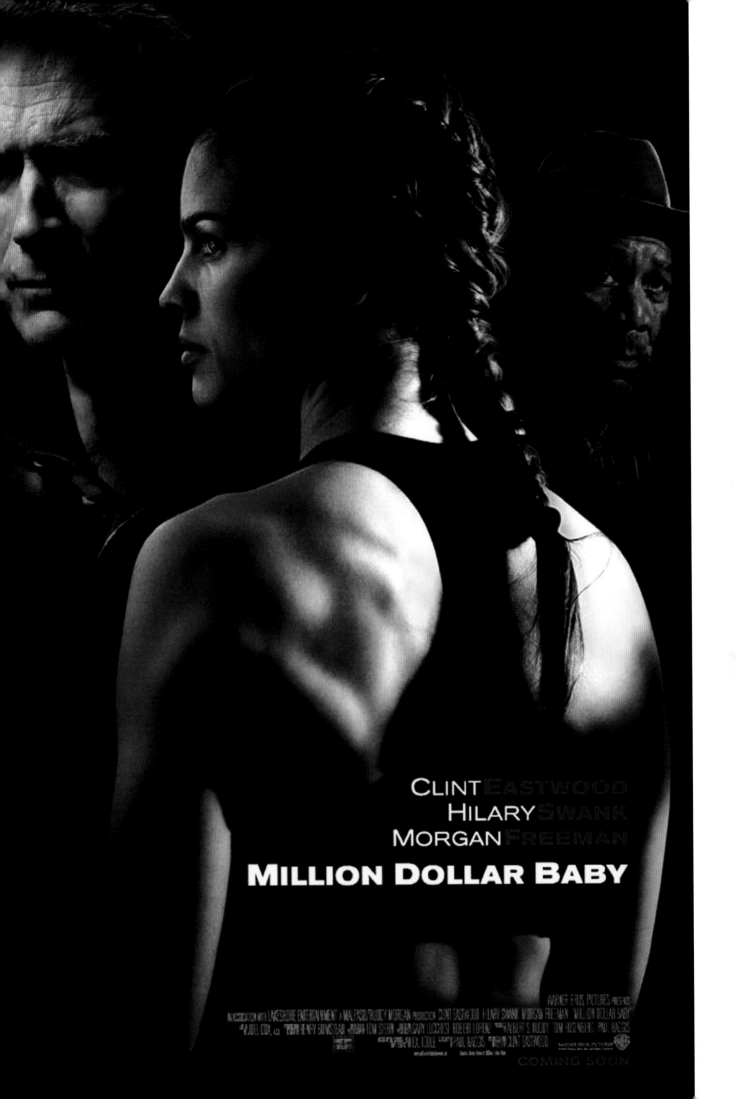

FLAGS OF OUR FATHERS 2006

The book, written by James Bradley and Ron Powers, recounts the wartime service of the former's father, one of the men who, thanks to Joe Rosenthal's immortal photo, became famous—pretty much for five minutes—for raising the American flag on Iwo Jima's Mount Suribachi. That is to say, the image abides, although very few know the names of the men in it. *Flags of Our Fathers*, to some degree profiting from "The Greatest Generation" hype, was a massive bestseller, acquired by Steven Spielberg, because of its story-behind-the-icon appeal. He decided, probably because he did not want to do another war movie, to ask Clint, whose interest in the property was well-known, to do the film.

Which turned out to be, in its most significant aspects, not so much a war story after all. For one thing, the flag-raisers did not feel like heroes. Without being in any great danger, they raised their flag largely because a first flag on the site was deemed too small, disappointingly invisible to the Army and Navy brass in the vast armada riding at anchor off shore. None of them imagined that Rosenthal or anyone else would create so powerful an image, or

that the fight for this tiny volcanic island would grind on for over a month, by which time Rosenthal's picture was appearing everywhere in America.

By this time there would only be three survivors of the incident available for exploitation. But that did nothing to deter the military publicists, and these young men found themselves touring the country selling war bonds. Their efforts culminated at Chicago's

OPPOSITE The simple yet effective poster based upon Joe Rosenthal's immortal photo at Mount Suribachi.
ABOVE The dramatic special effects of the vast armada in the Bay of Iwo Jima.

Soldier Field, where they clambered up a papier mâché replica of Suribachi, to the cheers of the multitude and to their own self-loathing. This was an emotion particularly felt by Ira Hayes, an American Indian who entered upon a lifetime of drunken self-disgust, which came to a premature end. They all felt that the real heroes of Iwo Jima were either still fighting anonymously or were buried in their battlefield graves. This was a feeling Clint, having spent a lifetime impersonating heroes without ever feeling like one, fully shared. So his movie, written by Paul Haggis and featuring actors who were not major stars, while sympathetic to the ordinary virtues of its characters, constituted a contemptuous assault on the false claims and false pieties with which the so-called "heroes of Iwo Jima" were presented to the home-front public by the managers of the nascent celebrity culture, which, in the years since the war, has become virtually the only culture to which anyone pays any substantial heed.

The film was mounted on an epic scale; Clint had never done a film of this scope before. But much to everyone's surprise, it became quite a large flop, though directorially and in every other way it was a handsome effort, which makes it hard to determine why it failed. Maybe by the time it went into release, "The Greatest Generation" notion—which was more an exercise in false nostalgia than a defen-sible historical idea—had run its course. Maybe people were still not ready to accept an iconoclastic view of an iconic event.

There is, however, a footnote to this story. In 2008, the motor-mouthed black director, Spike Lee, in effect accused Clint of racism for his failure to show black soldiers in his film, even though they had been present on Iwo. Clint allowed that that was true, but that they had not been present in the part of the battle that concerned him. Lee persisted, until Clint finally advised him "to shut his face." What he didn't do, though I wish that he had, was point to his record as the most color-blind of all directors.

Whether he was casting Scatman Crothers in a role that could easily have been played by a white actor, or using Morgan Freeman in *Unforgiven*, thus acknowledging the large presence of black people during the opening of the West, or making *Bird*, with its insistence on the genius of a black musician, or placing a black family at the center of *True Crime*, or casting blacks on an equal-opportunity basis, in all kinds of supporting roles (*Absolute Power*, *Mystic River*), his record on this issue is impeccable. All of which says nothing about *Invictus*, with its admiring portrayal of Nelson Mandela as its major character. On the question of race, Clint has nothing to apologize for. He simply feels, I believe, that his actions speak louder than words.

OPPOSITE Dramatic action in this movie, which was mounted on an epic scale.
ABOVE The director on location in Iwo Jima, although some shots were added in Iceland, where he was doubling its black sands for Iwo's when making *Flags of Our Fathers*.

LETTERS FROM IWO JIMA 2006

Clint recalls a meeting with Steven Spielberg and his line producer, Rob Lorenz, where the discussion centered on issues surrounding *Flags of Our Fathers*. In its course, the question of what the Japanese were thinking and feeling as they confronted the hopeless task of defending Iwo Jima arose. It was a difficult matter; most of them died on the island and there were few, if any, extant letters from them to their families at home. Nor was there any precedent for making a film sympathetic to the cause of an American enemy—particularly one that was as hated as the Japanese were in World War II.

Clint was particularly fascinated by the figure of General Nagaru Kuribayashi, the Japanese commandant on Iwo Jima, and wrote to a friend in Japan, asking if there were any books or other information available about him.

There was not much—except a slender volume of letters he had written home while he was a military attaché in the United States in the 1930s. These revealed him as a man impressed by the American character (and by its industrial capacity), and as someone convinced it would be a folly for Japan to wage war against the United States. He was, however, an honorable and dutiful man. He would, of course, fight for his country in such a conflict.

Clint decided to commission a script about this man and his hopeless fight for the island. Paul Haggis, writing the *Flags* script, recommended Iris Yamashita, a film scholar and would-be screenwriter, who had been helping him with research. She had written

OPPOSITE Ken Watanabe plays General Nagaru Kuribayashi, the Japanese commandant on Iwo Jima.

FROM THE DIRECTOR OF "FLAGS OF OUR FATHERS"
COMES THE COMPLETION OF THE IWO JIMA SAGA

硫黄島からの手紙

LETTERS FROM
IWO JIMA

A CLINT EASTWOOD FILM

DREAMWORKS PICTURES AND WARNER BROS. PICTURES PRESENT

A MALPASO/AMBLIN ENTERTAINMENT PRODUCTION KEN WATANABE KAZUNARI NINOMIYA TSUYOSHI IHARA RYO KASE SHIDOU NAKAMURA
"LETTERS FROM IWO JIMA" COSTUMES DESIGNED BY DEBORAH HOPPER EDITED BY JOEL COX, A.C.E. GARY D. ROACH PRODUCTION DESIGN HENRY BUMSTEAD JAMES J. MURAKAMI DIRECTOR OF PHOTOGRAPHY TOM STERN
CO-PRODUCER TIM MOORE EXECUTIVE PRODUCER PAUL HAGGIS STORY IRIS YAMASHITA & PAUL HAGGIS SCREENPLAY BY IRIS YAMASHITA BASED ON THE BOOK "PICTURE LETTERS FROM COMMANDER IN CHIEF"
BY TADAMICHI KURIBAYASHI EDITED BY TSUYUKO YOSHIDA, SHOGAKUKAN-BUNKO PRODUCED BY CLINT EASTWOOD STEVEN SPIELBERG AND ROBERT LORENZ DIRECTED BY CLINT EASTWOOD

DREAMWORKS PICTURES

www.iwojimathemovie.com

WARNER BROS. PICTURES

an unproduced screenplay about Japan in its immediate prewar days, and, bringing that research to her writing, produced an excellent script in a relatively short period of time. While he was shooting *Flags*, Clint grabbed a few shots for *Letters*, and while the former film was in post-production—a more than usually lengthy process because of its large number of special-effects shots—he went off to shoot the second film on a short schedule and a relatively small budget.

It turned out to be a masterly character study. There is reason to believe that Kuribayashi was assigned his command because he was on the outs with the Imperial General Staff, perhaps because he was suspected of being too sympathetic toward the enemy. It is certainly true that he did not know, until he arrived on Iwo, that he would have no support from the Japanese Navy and Air Force, which had been decimated in earlier engagements with the Americans. Nor did he know that many on his own staff would object to his strategy, which was to meet the Americans not on the beaches, but in a war of attrition fought from the caves and tunnels (which he ordered dug) further inland. He knew he could not win this battle against superior forces, but he knew he could impose devastating losses on the invaders—more Congressional Medals of Honor were awarded at Iwo than in any other battle in American history.

Perhaps as important in Clint's account of this battle was his portrayal of Kurabayashi as a humane officer, caring as best he could for the welfare of his troops in a situation where food and even water were scarce. This was a comparative rarity in the Japanese military, where the common soldier was generally treated with cruelty and contempt by his officers. The largest fiction of the film involves the general's relationship with an ordinary soldier, whom he keeps encountering by chance and who represents a humorous but touching humanity. This guy just wants to live and return home to his peaceful life as a baker (and husband and father).

Austerely yet gracefully portrayed by Ken Watanabe, Kuribayashi emerges as one of the great Eastwoodian heroes, a man doing his duty, knowing that he must die in so doing and accepting that fact without the slightest hint of self pity. I have in this book identified Clint as, most significantly, a dutiful man, so there is perhaps an irony in the fact that this most American of directors would find the avatar of the virtue that most significantly defines him in a man formed by traditions entirely the opposite of those that formed Clint. There is perhaps a further irony in the fact that it was *Letters from Iwo Jima*, not the much grander *Flags of Our Fathers*, that dominated the Ten Best lists and contended for the significant awards in the winter of 2006.

OPPOSITE The eloquent poster art for *Letters from Iwo Jima*.
THIS PAGE Scenes from the film which, at the heart, was a typical Eastwoodian character study: a man who puts his duty ahead of personal contentment.
OVERLEAF Clint directs Ken Watanabe in the austere landscape of Iwo Jima.

265

"Every movie I make teaches me something, and that's why I keep making them. I'm at that stage of life when I could probably stop and just hit golf balls. But in filming these two movies about Iwo Jima, I learned about war and about character. I also learned a lot about myself."

CHANGELING 2008

A mother's grief, police corruption, bold-faced duplicity—all of it true, all of it well-documented in the public records of the day, with all of them the subjects of this richly melodramatic, touchingly told tale that represents Clint Eastwood's most tragic statement of his obsessive interest in deeply afflicted families. The difference is that this time there is no stranger, mysterious or otherwise, to set the situation right.

It is 1928, and Christine Collins (played with a kind of restrained passion by Angelina Jolie, in an Academy Award-nominated performance) is a single mother working as a supervisor at the telephone company. One Saturday she is unexpectedly called in to work, obliging her to leave her son, Walter, unattended at home. He is under stern orders not to leave the house. But when Christine returns he is missing. In due course, the endemically corrupt Los Angeles police find a boy in Indiana that it claims is the missing child. Christine almost immediately recognizes that the child is an imposter. Now, aided by John Malkovich's Gustav Briegleb, a radio preacher and longstanding foe of the LAPD, she mounts a public crusade against the cops. She is rewarded by incarceration in a mental hospital.

Now, however, an honest cop discovers a farm in which a spectacularly perverted criminal imprisons (and ultimately murders) young boys. We are virtually certain that young Walter is one of his victims, though his body is never discovered. Meantime, the murderer takes to tormenting Christine, promising a confession but never delivering it. There is an extremely thin hope that the boy may have escaped and as the movie ends, she continues to hope for his recovery, which never occurs.

Truth is, as we know, very often inconvenient—especially to filmmakers who must always hope for satisfying endings. Yet Clint didn't care much about that. In interviews he kept insisting that crimes

"Eighty years ago, Los Angeles was out on the West Coast by itself. It became a world of its own. There were many bizarre incidents back then; inspiring a whole generation of *film noir* movies, and it's hardly changed. It's still corrupt."

against children are the most heinous ones, and that is what he wanted audiences to concentrate upon. He was also not averse to criticizing yet another inept and crooked police force.

The film is a beautifully made period piece, and J. Michael Straczynski's screenplay was interleaved with copies of antique newspaper clippings attesting to the accuracy of his research. Yet, somehow, it was dissatisfying to many viewers. The shift in gears from the lost-child story to the investigation of the perverse mass murder was jarring. And the failure to find an ending that satisfied people's need for closure was equally disappointing to the mass audience.

That said, the movie is, in many ways, an admirable effort, proof of Clint's uncompromising insistence on continuing to do what he wanted and needed to do at a time in his life when he could easily have relaxed into ease or silence. *Changeling* is a knotty movie, avoiding a conventional three-act structure, leaving most of the questions it raises deliberately unanswered. More than any of Clint's movies, it embraces his preference for ambiguity. I suspect that it, like *The Beguiled* or *Honkytonk Man*, among others of his less well-remembered films, may someday become the subject of revisionary study. There is something too haunting about it to be forgotten.

OPPOSITE Angelina Jolie played the character Christine Collins with a kind of restrained passion. ABOVE On the same set as *Dirty Harry,* Clint directs Angelina Jolie in this beautifully made period piece.

271

GRAN TORINO 2008

Yes, by the end of the movie we come to love Walt Kowalski. But the deepest pleasure we derive from Clint Eastwood's performance is how hard he makes it for us to do so. This is not just another grumpy old man failing to hide the "just kidding" twinkle in his eye. Walt's a retired assembly-line worker in Detroit who did not derive a lot of pleasure from his lifetime of hard labor. Probably his highest moments came during the Korean War, in which he won medals and—we learn—did some terrible things.

Now he is a new widower, consoled by his faithful dog, by his lovingly tended 1972 Gran Torino parked spiffily in his garage (it doesn't bother him, apparently, that it is regarded by car aficionados as a fake muscle car), and disgusted by his bourgeois children, the easy pieties of his priest, and, worst of all, upset by the Hmong families infesting his neighborhood—they're just "gooks" to him.

But they are gooks threatened by neighborhood gangs, and Walt is their only logical ally. The shy and socially inept son of Walt's immediate neighbors is their particular victim and, ultimately, his spunky and charming sister, the person most persistently trying to pry Walt out of his shell, is brutally beaten and raped by one of the gangs.

Can this mean old man be rallied to the side of these sweet and peaceable people? Well, sure. If you think otherwise, you haven't gone to the movies very often in recent decades. Walt puts the boy to work as an all-purpose handyman (with special responsibilities for the Gran Torino) and grudgingly responds to the girl's overtures. Next thing you know, Walt's sharing meals with his neighbors and defending them against their enemies. At the end of the movie, knowing that he's dying of lung cancer, he sacrifices his life for them.

In a lot of ways, this is a typical, indeed old-fashioned, Eastwood movie—small in scale and setting, easy to shoot on a short schedule, dependent on his own presence to carry the film commercially. What's

OPPOSITE Clint, as Walt Kowalski, and his new surrogate family. "To be seventy-eight years old and in a successful picture, that's nice."

best about the film is that it makes no overt, sentimental plea for Walt. He's as tough as any Eastwood hero has ever been—only a lot older. Like his predecessors he does the right thing—because, instinctively, he knows what the right thing is without necessarily being able to articulate it. As an actor, Clint has never sued his audiences for their favors, and he was not about to begin doing so late in life.

That's why he was mildly annoyed, first by the rumor that this was a return to Dirty Harry mode, then by a few critical interpretations of the film as such. Over the years people had come to love Harry for his cheekiness, for his insouciance. But those were not qualities Walt Kowalski shared with him. He really wasn't as hip as Harry had become. He was just a freak dinosaur, who turns out to be, somewhat to his own surprise, educable. And—pretty much hidden sub-theme here—in a mood to atone for some hateful acts in Korea. These were not, mind you, war crimes, but they were also not actions a man could be proud of as he prepared to confront his own life's end.

Good as it turned out to be, it was not a movie I expected to be a great success, and I'm not sure Clint did, either. But perhaps because it was released in the midst of a recession that engendered widespread sympathy for the working class, perhaps because it reminded audiences of how much Clint's "taciturnity" had meant to them over the years—he hadn't played a character like Walt in a couple of decades—perhaps because he was playing an old man which, chronologically, he surely was, without really looking or acting the part, the film was a huge hit. In fact, it has been said that dollar in, dollar out, it is the most successful movie he has ever made.

One must finally say it: there is something inspiring about Clint's latter-day career. It's inspiring to people of his own age. It's inspiring to people who know—if they're lucky, of course—that they will inevitably arrive at that age. The American Dream is, in fact, composed of many dreams—of which, surely, the dream of an old age rich in competency and usefulness is the last, largest, and most difficult to achieve.

ABOVE Clint, with Steve Campanelli and Bill Coe, directs Bee Vang in *Gran Torino*.
OPPOSITE The powerful poster art in which the chiselled star dominates.

CLINT EASTWOOD

GRAN TORINO

WARNER BROS. PICTURES PRESENTS

IN ASSOCIATION WITH VILLAGE ROADSHOW PICTURES A DOUBLE NICKEL ENTERTAINMENT

A MALPASO PRODUCTION "GRAN TORINO" EDITED BY JOEL COX, A.C.E. GARY D. ROACH

PRODUCTION DESIGNED BY JAMES J. MURAKAMI DIRECTOR OF PHOTOGRAPHY TOM STERN, AFC, ASC

EXECUTIVE PRODUCERS JENETTE KAHN TIM MOORE AND BRUCE BERMAN

STORY BY DAVE JOHANNSON & NICK SCHENK SCREENPLAY BY NICK SCHENK

PRODUCED BY ROBERT LORENZ BILL GERBER PRODUCED AND DIRECTED BY CLINT EASTWOOD

VILLAGE ROADSHOW PICTURES   WARNER BROS. PICTURES

COMING SOON
WWW.GRANTORINOMOVIE.CO.UK

INVICTUS 2009

It was Morgan Freeman calling. He said he had a good script he'd like Clint to read. He smiles recollecting: "Whenever anyone says that, you always sort of say to yourself, 'Well, we'll be the judge of that.'" But a few days later he was calling Freeman back to say that it *was* a good script and that he would like to direct it.

It was easy to see what Clint liked about the film that would eventually be called *Invictus*, the title of the inspirational poem by William Ernst Henley ("I thank whatever god may be for my unconquerable soul"), which had often lifted the spirits of Nelson Mandela during the twenty-seven years he spent in captivity in apartheid South Africa. Freed at last, and president of the country, he was in search of symbolic acts that would serve to unite his nation. Curiously, he settled upon rugby as one instrument of that desire.

It was a white man's game; blacks tended to play, and support, soccer in South Africa. This actually seemed to stir Mandela: the harder the case, the sweeter the solution to it. Besides, South Africa had a decent, if not necessarily great, team in the Springboks, headquartered in Cape Town, which could be at least a respectable competitor in the 1995 World Cup competition. Nelson Mandela, played, of course, by Freeman, summoned the Springbok's captain, Francois Pienaar (Matt Damon) to his office and, in effect, ordered him to win the cup. Which, eventually, the Springboks did.

It is a well-told story. Mandela is not presented as a completely saintly figure, though in Freeman's canny performance he is a very likable one. The several games covered in the movie—leading to their championship encounter with the All Blacks (named for their uniforms—there's a certain irony in that—and representing New Zealand) are hard-hitting and suspensefully realized. You don't have to understand all the exotic ins and outs of rugby to understand the progress of the games. The emotional high point of the film is Mandela's appearance in the stadium at the final game, wearing a replica of Pienaar's jersey, with its number 6 emblazoned on it.

It is a remarkably good-natured film. There are no villains in it—even the white presidential bodyguards, reluctantly serving with their black counterparts, are eventually caught up in the excitement of the quest for a symbolic triumph. You can see why Clint was drawn to the picture. For one thing, in his later years he seems to

like true stories—his last three movies had been inspired by actual events. For another, the film had a certain epic scope, which was something else—in the war films particularly—that has lately appealed to him. Most significantly, it had a moral he thoroughly approved of. "Forgiveness is his strength," he says of Mandela. "There's a certain morality he has that most politicians don't have. If we watch political events happening today and in past years, we all could have used somebody like him."

"It's a very inspirational story and everybody knows pretty much the history of Nelson Mandela. But this element of his history I don't think people are that familiar with. The fact that he took a sport that was being played by one segment of the population in South Africa and made it a unifying factor for his presidency... He was a great unifier."

OPPOSITE Clint and Morgan Freeman, who plays Nelson Mandela in *Invictus*, confer on location in South Africa.

277

In that idealistic thought lies the originality of *Invictus* as we look at it in purely Eastwoodian terms; it is his first film directly to engage a more or less contemporary political issue, to make the kind of "statement" that moviemakers are always yearning to put forth and generally do rather clumsily. That the issue it takes up—racism—has been central to Clint's own morality all his life doubtless makes the project particularly satisfying to him. That it does so without making any big, to-the-camera speeches or other openly moralizing acts is one reason it pleases us. For it to go into release just a few months before Clint's eightieth birthday bespeaks the best qualities of a career that has taken him from the fringe of our moviegoing consciousness to the center of it. People speak of him now as a "legend"—an identification he shrugs off, of course. That's a matter that is of supreme indifference to him. If people want to think of him as a legend there's nothing he can do about it. He has movies still to make. And he's not looking backward. The next one, perhaps appropriately, is called *Hereafter*.

ABOVE Matt Damon, who plays Francois Pienaar, meets the president in his office (*below*) and (*right*) upon the triumph of winning the 1995 Rugby World Cup competition—idealism, inspiration, stoicism, and duty: Mandela reflects the classic Eastwoodian virtues in *Invictus*.

MATT DAMON

HEREAFTER

A FILM BY CLINT EASTWOOD

WARNER BROS. PICTURES PRESENTS

A KENNEDY/MARSHALL PRODUCTION A MALPASO PRODUCTION MATT DAMON CÉCILE DE FRANCE "HEREAFTER" COSTUMES DESIGNED BY DEBORAH HOPPER EDITED BY JOEL COX, A.C.E. GARY D. ROACH
PRODUCTION DESIGN BY JAMES J. MURAKAMI DIRECTOR OF PHOTOGRAPHY TOM STERN, AFC, ASC EXECUTIVE PRODUCERS STEVEN SPIELBERG FRANK MARSHALL TIM MOORE PETER MORGAN WRITTEN BY PETER MORGAN
PRODUCED BY KATHLEEN KENNEDY ROBERT LORENZ **OCTOBER** PRODUCED AND DIRECTED BY CLINT EASTWOOD

WARNER BROS. PICTURES

PG-13 PARENTS STRONGLY CAUTIONED
MATURE THEMATIC ELEMENTS INCLUDING DISTURBING DISASTER AND ACCIDENT IMAGES, AND FOR BRIEF STRONG LANGUAGE

www.hereafter-themovie.com

HEREAFTER 2010

*H*ereafter is one of those anomalous Eastwood movies—not at all the sort of thing his core audience, both critics and regular moviegoers, expect from him. At this point they are more than willing to permit him to plunge more deeply and thoughtfully into genre conventions, taking them to unexpected and curiously rewarding places. But the afterlife?! The question of what we can expect—if anything—after we die? Who knew he was interested in that? Especially in the form of this movie, which refuses to give us any idea about what we might encounter when we inevitably confront the void—or the non-void—that awaits us when we pass over to the next world.

When it opened in the United States in the fall of 2010, *Hereafter* received mixed reviews, but most were largely tolerant of Clint's ambitions and of his well-earned right to take us somewhat by surprise—particularly given the film's pleasantly romantic air. The narrative braids three stories: that of Marie (the charming French actress Cécile De France), a journalist who dies in a tsunami and returns to life questioning what exactly happened to her when she briefly crossed over; Matt Damon's George Lonegan, a San Francisco psychic whose gift has become a burden to him; and Marcus, a little English boy winningly played by Frankie McLaren, whose brother, with whom he is very close, dies in an accident and who is desperate to stay in touch with him. These disparate lives are finally brought into close connection in London, where Peter Morgan's script maneuvers them in a plausible, if not necessarily probable, way.

"I've always been a romantic," Clint commented to a group of friends he invited to a screening a couple of weeks before the picture opened and, come to think of it, that's true enough. Think of the doomed romance with Tyne Daly in *The Enforcer*. Or *The Bridges of Madison County*. Or, more recently, the tender surrogate daughter-father relationship explored in *Million Dollar Baby*. There is still, I think, a reluctance to concede this side of Clint's nature among his traditional fan base—the working class guys who found him in pictures like *Where Eagles Dare* and rally around films like *Gran Torino* with particular passion. You can teach these loyalists new tricks, but you often can't make them really like the experience.

OPPOSITE The haunting poster art for *Hereafter*.
THIS PAGE Matt Damon plays a psychic whose gift has become a burden to him.

"It [Hereafter] raises a lot of questions, but that's where it ends. The questions are there. You pose them, and then it's up to the audience to meet you halfway and think about it in terms of their own lives."

You can see this in the way *Hereafter* performed at the American box office. It played well in the cities and upscale suburbs along the east and west coasts, but pretty much died in the middle of the country, where, as we have already had occasion to observe, the male population still wistfully awaits one last *Dirty Harry* sequel. And the female audience has no reason to expect a "woman's picture" from him—though in some respects (particularly in its gentle manner) that is what the movie is.

One rather imagines the film doing better, commercially speaking, overseas, where the cinephiles have long-since conceded *auteur* status to Clint, granting him the right to do what he feels like doing, no questions asked. In a perceptive review, Roger Ebert identified *Hereafter* as "the film of a man at peace." By this he means, I think, that Clint, having turned eighty, has reached a point where he feels free to explore themes and ideas as they find him or he finds them. This curiosity may be casually expressed but it is relentless, and often surprising. (Consider that his next film is a highly critical biography of the unlamented head of the American FBI, J. Edgar Hoover.)

Naturally, Clint hopes that his films find favor with his audience. But at some level I think he doesn't care all that much anymore about their performance at the box office. What he cares much more profoundly about is his own satisfaction—and entering into a dialogue with his viewers about topics he thinks are important. The film has no spiritual axe to grind. Clint is not a religious believer and he has said that he does not think we are likely to enjoy an afterlife. Yet it is a question, particularly at his age, that is bound to occur to him. Indeed, it may be the only really interesting topic for men and women of his age. So it is natural for him to pose questions about it. This, however, he does in a very cool and objective—even slightly ironic—way. Which means that the picture plays a little dryly perhaps, which seems to me a good thing. It relies for its appeal on its characters—on the earnestness of their quests for understanding, on their manifest good natures, particularly on the tenderness with one another and with everyone else they encounter.

I don't know if good nature can carry a non-comedic movie any more. We are used to higher dramatic intensity in films exploring "serious" topics. But I think the effort is worthwhile, in that, at the very least, room is left for leisurely and intelligent rumination on the topic at hand. I don't believe that *Hereafter* will be one of the films on which Clint's reputation will significantly rest in time to come. But that's all right; there are plenty of others to do that job. In the meantime, we have this agreeable, handsomely mounted, and rather intricate film to savor in our own good time.

OPPOSITE Clint directs Frankie McLaren on set (*top*) and Matt Damon's George Lonegan embarks on a fleeting romance with Bryce Dallas Howard's vulnerable Melanie (*below*).
ABOVE In the movie's most harrowing moment, French journalist Marie Lelay flees the devastating tsunami.

J. EDGAR 2011

Even by Clint Eastwood's austere standards, *J. Edgar* is a very plain movie. And all the more powerful being so. It simply tells the story of J. Edgar Hoover, head of the Federal Bureau of Investigation—or America's "top cop" as the headlines styled him—from the time he took charge of a predecessor organization in 1924 until his death in 1972.

In that period he was a revered figure. Or maybe just a feared figure. Whether he was chasing down gangsters in the middle west or trying to find the Lindbergh baby's kidnapper or, perhaps most important to him, keeping tabs on "subversives" he was a master of public relations. With his bulldog countenance and his take-no-prisoners attitude, he personified modern law enforcement and, to give the devil his due, he transformed the FBI into the model of a scientifically based law enforcement agency.

The true secret of his success, however, was his files. No one except Hoover, and perhaps his assistant, Helen Gandy (beautifully portrayed by Naomi Watts), knew what they contained. And no one wanted to find out. A succession of presidents were tempted to challenge him but, in the end, none of them did. After his death, Gandy destroyed all of the files; a few scraps of paper are the only evidence that they existed at all.

But they did, of course. And Hoover grew weirder and weirder as the years wore on. It is tempting to see him as the ultimate bureaucrat, fiercely defensive of his institution and his position within it, vicious with any challenges to his power (there weren't many). And he is played by Leonardo DiCaprio in a performance that is nothing short of towering—in a very quiet way. This is far more than a matter of expert age makeup. He speaks quietly, insinuatingly, reasonably. He had a forgivable eccentricity—he liked to play the horses—but under his leadership the FBI rolled out movies, radio programs, comic books, anything that kept his organization at the forefront of public consciousness for decades. His "special agents," always polite and clad in dark suits and ties, were a somewhat refreshing contrast to the more bumptious representatives of law and order at the height of his reign.

There were, of course, oddities about him, notably his sexuality. He was undoubtedly lucky that he lived in an era when "perpetual bachelorhood" was not an automatic signal of incipient homosexuality. It was put about that The Director, preoccupied with the fight against crime, simply didn't have the time and energy for sexual hanky-panky. He was frequently seen dancing with Ginger Rogers' mother and sometime after his death, the actress Dorothy Lamour claimed to have had a brief affair with him (not mentioned in the movie). That was enough to keep the gossips at bay. If Americans thought about this matter at all, they probably guessed that at some time Hoover would probably settle down into a comfortable, old-shoe relationship with some anonymous somebody or other. These were, after all, simpler times. The idea that a highly placed public figure might be gay was simply not thought about.

Which rather leaves out of the picture one Clyde Tolson. He was a Mormon, an FBI agent, and he is beautifully played in the picture by Armie Hammer as an obliging, good-natured fellow. Tolson lived with Hoover, took virtually every meal with him and every vacation, too. Were they just "pals?" Or was there something darker, deeper in their relationship? The movie, very sensibly in my

OPPOSITE The compelling poster art for *J. Edgar*.
THIS PAGE Leonardo DiCaprio's J. Edgar Hoover in dialogue with his loyal assistant, Helen Gandy, portrayed in the movie by Naomi Watts.

285

view, does not venture an opinion on this point. Again, there was something in the spirit of the times that protected them. Male "bonding," as we've since learned to call it, was considered a rare, but not unknown, alternative life style. (So was female bonding, and Hoover had the evidence on Eleanor Roosevelt's lesbianism to prove it.) This was especially true in the case of Hoover and Tolson. There was nothing furtive in their paring, rather the opposite, as the movie would have it. There is something almost tender in it. One would not call it redemptive, but it does render Hoover almost likable—for a few minutes at least. The tales of cross-dressing surfaced only after Hoover's death, and then only from a witness who was not entirely reliable.

This is a brave film. There was a time when J. Edgar Hoover was among the most prominent of living Americans and there was no way to make a reasonably honest film about him. Now there is a tendency to ask "J. Edgar Who?" and to wonder how so much secretive power came to reside in one man of rather limited, if dogged (and creepy) skills. And it is somewhat odd that Clint Eastwood, not a man known for publicly espousing his political interests, has chosen to make this film at this time. And to make of it such a devastating portrayal of a rather ordinary man caught in the grips of paranoia and hubris.

Does he intend it as a warning shot, a reminder that men like Hoover are an ever-present danger to democracy, which is always looking for simplified images of muscular virtue to celebrate? It would be hard to think anything else—especially since Dustin Lance Black's script is a model for enterprises of this kind, tracing Hoover's rise from Momma's Boy (she is unimprovably played by Judi Dench) to a posturing machismo figure, without ever raising its voice or pointing to the dangers he poses. The hollowness of the man is suggested merely by the odd lilt in DiCaprio's voice at certain tense or uncertain moments. Most of the time he is just calmly going about his business—which is the subversion of the republic, about whose best values he has not a clue.

The danger, of course, is that Hoover is too distant a figure, too much a man of another time and place for today's audience to forge an appalled relationship with. Clint obviously has bet the other way. With this handsomely crafted, impeccably acted movie he is saying that it can happen here—again and again. In making this point, distance (Hoover died almost 40 years ago) lends an eerie enchantment to this tale. It helps us to objectify the man, to see that he is far from being a rare bird in our political life—just a very busy and a very dangerous one. I don't think there has ever been a calmer, and therefore more potent, portrait of the demagogue of a serene bureaucrat than *J. Edgar*. It speaks softly, but it carries a very big stick.

"One thing about acting and directing is you're a constant student and I think that's the reason I'm still doing it at this stage in my life, as with every film you learn something, every project you learn something new—you learn something new about people, you learn something new about actors, acting, about directing, and that's what makes it exciting, that's why I'm still doing it. And a great part of being an actor is that it's a never-ending process. You can be ninety or twenty and you're still learning and naturally, at ninety, you've probably, unfortunately, forgotten a lot of things but it's great, that's the fun of it all, it's great fun and you're real lucky and you can make a living, manage to exist, in a profession that's fun."

JERSEY BOYS 2014

A while ago, Clint put it about that he might retire from acting. It was not definite, but it sounded as if he might only direct in the years ahead, and no one would have blamed him. He was in his early 80s, eager to continue directing but less and less inclined to "suit up" as he often put it.

In 2012 he had starred in *Trouble With the Curve*, a nice little baseball picture that also starred Amy Adams. It was directed and produced by his long-time associate, Rob Lorenz. It didn't do a lot of business, and agreeable as it was (he played an ageing baseball scout) it had a rather relaxed air—nobody trying too hard.

At the time, he was toying with the idea of doing a musical, perhaps starring Beyoncé, mostly (or so I thought) because he had never done one of those. But the thing kept being postponed until finally it dropped out of his calculations; no hard feelings, so far as I could tell. And the bug had clearly bitten him. In the spring of 2013, he began talking about directing *Jersey Boys*, the popular musical (or maybe it was a play with music), which had been a long-running Broadway hit. It was the story of Frankie Valli and his group The Four Seasons and, in addition to its other attractions, had a certain toughness of spirit that I think appealed to Clint. It was not a cream puff piece, it had its ups and downs, and it could be done for a comparatively modest price, using performers who were good, but not exactly established stars. One thought: this was a picture very much in Clint's wheelhouse.

Released in June, 2014, it is, I think, a good film. At the screening I attended I noted some sniffles from the impressionable, which I was not expecting. People seemed to identify with the struggles of this group. And though it has a substantial running time it has a briskness about it. *Jersey Boys* does not dither. In that sense it is very much a Clint Eastwood movie.

It was made at a time when Clint was under more pressure than is usual in his smoothly ordered life. He was, for one thing, finishing a new, and considerably delayed, house in Carmel, which was occasioning some grumble fits in his life. Far worse, there was trouble in the Eastwood marriage. His wife Dina decided to produce some documentaries about life in the Eastwood ménage, in which Clint indulged her. By all accounts they were not very good and they

Taking a brief hiatus from directing, Clint took on his first acting role since *Gran Torino* playing ageing baseball scout Gus Lobel in the 2012 film *Trouble with the Curve*.

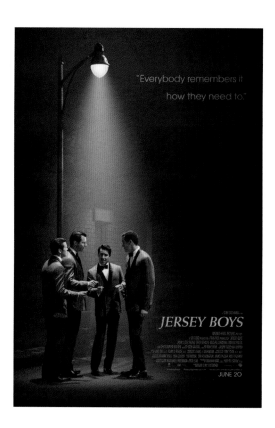

probably produced a certain strain in the marriage, which had attained a certain, inevitable age. By the summer of 2013, rumors of a separation were circulating and, indeed, a separation occurred—followed by a divorce. It was not, so far as an outsider could see, an acrimonious one. Clint did not speak of it for a time, and then his comments were mild, and tinged, I thought, more by sadness than anger. He once mentioned that perhaps Dina had a little "buyer's remorse," or maybe that was just a passing moment of regret. Mostly since that summer he has busied himself with filmmaking.

There was *Jersey Boys* to finish, of course. And, suddenly, there was another picture in the offing. This was contrary to Clint's usual practice. He has always been prolific, of course, but generally he takes a few months off between films. This time, however, he started the new film before he had fully wrapped *Jersey Boys*, and it represents a return to something like his previous form, in that the title sums it up. *American Sniper* is a very hard, tough film, like nothing he has done for something like a decade, and stars Bradley Cooper and Sienna Miller. I half-suspect that the old lion wanted to show everyone that he can still growl and paw the air when the spirit so moves him. Or maybe, moved as ever by instinct, he judges it just time to stop being a pussycat. What we can say is that, judging by Jason Hall's taut script, it's a picture that is perhaps going to irritate people who thought Clint was at last tamed.

Perish the thought, or the thought of retirement. He's fit. He's ready for action, world without end, it seems. And the truth is I wouldn't have him any other way. And you wouldn't either.

OPPOSITE **Poster art for** *Jersey Boys.*
THIS PAGE In a scene from the film, John Lloyd Young (Frankie), Erich Bergen,
Vincent Piazza and Michael Lomenda perform as Frankie Valli and the Four Seasons.

Author's note

There is, of course, no such thing as "objective" criticism or biography or history or whatever this book is. Everyone who practices these crafts brings to them their personal biases, the prejudices, and the enthusiasms, that the study of their subjects suggests to them. Even so, my relationship with Clint Eastwood is a rather special case, though I know there are others like it in the long history of artists and their writing friends. When I was practicing film criticism on a regular basis I had to recuse myself from writing about Clint's work some twenty years ago. Later, I wrote a lengthy biography about him, which was criticized here and there for my failure to forthrightly acknowledge the fact of our friendship. I have no desire to repeat that mistake.

So ... to state the obvious, this is an admiring account of a good friend's career. It seems obvious to me that no one would enter into such a friendship if one loathed that friend's work. Or merely wanted the dubious pleasure of being part of an entourage (which, in any case, Clint does not have). More than that, in the years since *Unforgiven*, I've been pleased to see that my feelings about Clint's work have more and more been mirrored in reviews and in other writing about him. He's always had, of course, a vast populist fan base, but now he has a following among knowledgeable and sophisticated moviegoers as well. I'm sure that pleases him. I'm equally sure that his choice of projects is unaffected by their admiration. He continues to operate out of the instincts that have served him well for so many decades. My instincts tell me to thank him publicly for the pleasure of his company over much of that time and to hope that this book pleases him as well as you, its reader.

RICHARD SCHICKEL

Richard Schickel and Palazzo Editions would like to thank the following for their invaluable assistance and support on this project. On management and creative liaison: Jeffrey Baker and Thomas Lucas at Warner Home Video; Jeff Briggs and Jeff Stevens at Warner Digital Archive; Julie S. Heath at Warner Still and Clip Licensing (and the many talented stills photographers); Rob Lorenz at Warner Bros. Entertainment Inc; Doug Freeman and Faith Ginsberg at Lorac Productions Inc.

Sources

With the exception of the sources listed below, all quotes by Clint Eastwood are taken from interviews with Richard Schickel.

47 Interview with Meriel McCooey, *Sunday Times Magazine*, 1969; 50 In *Clint Eastwood* by Alan Frank, Optimum, 1982, p. 26; 70 In *Clint Eastwood* by Robert Tanitch, Studio Vista, 1995, p. 51; 75 In *Clint Eastwood—Film-Maker* by Daniel O'Brien, Batsford, 1996, p. 11; 78-79 In *Clint Eastwood* by Alan Frank, Optimum, 1982, p. 36; 82 In *Clint Eastwood* by Robert Tanitch, Studio Vista, 1995, p.66; 90 Interview with Derek Malcolm in *The Guardian*, August 28, 1990; 99 In *Clint Eastwood* by Robert Tanitch, Studio Vista, 1995, p.77; 107 In *Clint Eastwood* by Robert Tanitch, Studio Vista, 1995, p. 88; 108 Interview with Michael Parkinson in *The Guardian,* October 7, 2003; 127 In *Clint Eastwood* by Alan Frank, Optimum, 1982, p. 63; 138 Interview on brightlightsfilm.com; 159 In *Eastwood* by Paul Duncan and Douglas Keesey, Taschen, 2006, p. 128; 198 In *Eastwood* by Paul Duncan and Douglas Keesey, Taschen, 2006, p. 143; 200 Interview with Derek Malcolm in *The Guardian*, August 28, 1990; 202 Interview with Derek Malcolm in *The Guardian*, August 28, 1990; 214 Interview in *Esquire* magazine, December 2008; 223 Interview in *Playboy* magazine, 1997; 227 Interview in *Playboy* magazine, 1997; 230 Interview in *Playboy* magazine, 1997; 239 Interview in *The Times*, August 30, 2000; 242 In *Eastwood* by Paul Duncan and Douglas Keesey, Taschen, 2006, p. 164; 249 Interview with Stella Papamichael, bbc.co.uk/films; 254 Interview with brightlightsfilm.com; 270 Interview on www.blockbuster.co.uk; 286 Interview for *Inside the Actor's Studio.*

Filmography

Revenge of the Creature (Universal-International)
82 minutes
Director: Jack Arnold
Screenplay: Martin Berkeley
Cinematographer: Charles S. Welbourne
Cast: John Agar (Clete Ferguson); Lori Nelson
(Helen Dobson); John Bromfield (Joe Hayes); Nestor
Paiva (Capt. Lucas); Grandon Rhodes (Jackson Foster);
Clint Eastwood (Jennings, a lab technician)
Opened May 13, 1955 see page 39

Francis in the Navy (Universal-International)
80 minutes
Director: Arthur Lubin
Screenplay: Devery Freeman
Cinematographer: Carl Guthrie
Cast: Donald O'Connor (Lt. Peter Stirling); Martha Hyer
(Betsy Donevan); Richard Erdman (Murph); Jim Backus
(Cmdr. E. T. Hutch); Clint Eastwood (Jonesy);
David Janssen (Lt. Anders); Leigh Snowden
(Nurse Appleby); Martin Milner (W. T. Rickson)
Opened August 5, 1955 see page 39

Lady Godiva (Universal-International) 89 minutes
Director: Arthur Lubin
Screenplay: Oscar Brodney, Harry Ruskin
Cinematographer: Carl Guthrie
Cast: Maureen O'Hara (Lady Godiva); George Nader
(Lord Leofric); Victor McLagen (Grimald); Rex Reason
(Harold); Clint Eastwood (First Saxon)
Opened November 2, 1955 see page 39

Tarantula (Universal-International) 80 minutes
Director: Jack Arnold
Screenplay: Robert Fresco, Martin Berkeley
Cinematographer: George Robinson
Cast: John Agar (Dr. Matt Hastings); Mara Corday
(Stephanie Clayton); Leo G. Carroll (Gerald Deemer);
Clint Eastwood (First Pilot)
Opened December 14, 1955 see page 39

Never Say Goodbye (Universal-International)
96 minutes
Director: Jerry Hopper
Screenplay: Charles Hoffman
Cinematographer: Maury Gertsman
Cast: Rock Hudson (Dr. Michael Parker);
Cornell Borchers (Lisa Gosting); George Sanders (Victor);
Ray Collins (Dr. Bailey); David Janssen (Dave Heller);
Shelley Fabares (Suzy Parker); Clint Eastwood
(Will, a lab assistant)
Opened March 10, 1956 see page 39

Star in the Dust (Universal-International) 80 minutes
Director: Charles Haas
Screenplay: Oscar Brodney
Cinematographer: John L. Russell Jr.
Cast: John Agar (Bill Jorden); Mamie Van Doren
(Ellen Ballard); Richard Boone (Sam Hall); Leif Erickson
(George Ballard); Coleen Gray (Nellie Mason);
James Gleason (Orval Jones); Clint Eastwood
(Tom, a ranch hand)
Opened June 13, 1956 see page 39

Away All Boats (Universal-International)
114 minutes
Director: Joseph Pevney
Screenplay: Ted Sherdeman
Cinematographer: Willam Daniels
Cast: Jeff Chandler (Jebediah S. Hawks);
George Nader (Lt. Dave MacDougall); Julie Adams
(Nadine MacDougall); Lex Barker (Commander Quigley);
Keith Andes (Doctor Bell); Richard Boone (Lt. Fraser);
Clint Eastwood (Sailor)
Opened August 16, 1956 see page 39

The First Traveling Saleslady (RKO) 92 minutes
Director: Arthur Lubin
Screenplay: Devery Freeman, Stephen Longstreet
Cinematographer: William Snyder
Cast: Ginger Rogers (Rose Gillray); Barry Nelson
(Charles Masters); Carol Channing (Molly Wade);
David Brian (James Carter); James Arness
(Joel Kingdom); Clint Eastwood (Jack Rice)
Opened August 1956 see page 40

Escapade in Japan (RKO/Universal-International)
93 minutes
Director: Arthur Lubin
Screenplay: Winston Miller
Cinematographer: William Snyder
Cast: Teresa Wright (Mary Saunders); Cameron Mitchell
(Dick Saunders); Jon Provost (Tony Saunders);
Roger Nakagawa (Hiko); Clint Eastwood (Dumbo,
a pilot)
Opened October 17, 1957 see page 40

Lafayette Escadrille (Warner Bros.) 93 minutes
Director: William A. Wellman
Screenplay: A. S. Fleischman
Cinematographer: William Clothier
Cast: Tab Hunter (Thad Walker); Etchika Choureau
(Renée Beaulieu); Marcel Dalio (Drill Sergeant);
David Janssen (Duke Sinclair); Paul Fix (General);
Clint Eastwood (George Moseley)
Opened November 1957 see page 40

Ambush at Cimarron Pass
(Regal/20th Century Fox) 73 minutes
Director: Jodie Copelan
Screenplay: Richard G. Taylor, John K. Butler
Cinematographer: John M. Nickolaus, Jr.
Cast: Scott Brady (Matt Blake); Margia Dean
(Teresa Santos); Clint Eastwood (Keith Williams);
Baynes Barron (Corbin); William Vaughan (Henry the Scout)
Opened March, 1958 see page 40

Rawhide (Columbia Broadcasting System)
60 minutes for television
Cast: Eric Fleming (Gil Favor); Clint Eastwood
(Rowdy Yates); Paul Brinegar (Wishbone); Steve Raines
(Jim Quince); James Murdock (Mushy); Rocky Shahan
(Joe Scarlet)
*Released January 9, 1959, leading to 217 epsiodes
see page 41*

A Fistful of Dollars (Jolly Film/Constantin/Ocean/
United Artists) 99 minutes
Director: Sergio Leone
Screenplay: Sergio Leone, Duccio Tessari,
Victor A. Catena, G. Schock
Cinematographer: Jack Dalmas (Massimo Dallamano)
Cast: Clint Eastwood (The Stranger); Marianne Koch
(Marisol); Gian Maria Volontè (Ramón Rojo);
Wolfgang Lukschy (John Baxter); Sieghardt Rupp
(Esteban Rojo); Joseph Egger (Piripero); Antonio Prieto
(Don Benito Rojo); José Calvo (Silvanito)
Opened October 16, 1964 see page 44

For a Few Dollars More (Produzioni Europee
Associati/Constantin/Arturo Gonzáles) 132 minutes
Director: Sergio Leone
Screenplay: Luciano Vincenzoni, Sergio Leone
Cinematographer: Massimo Dallamano
Cast: Clint Eastwood (The Stranger); Lee Van Cleef
(Col. Douglas Mortimer); Gian Maria Volontè (El Indio);
Mara Krup (Mary); Luigi Pistilli (Groggy); Klaus Kinski
(Wild); Josef Egger (Old Prophet); Panos Papadopoulos
(Sancho Perez); Benito Stefanelli (Luke)
Opened November 18, 1965 see page 48

The Witches (Dino de Laurentiis/Les Productions
Artistes Associés) 105 minutes
Director: (Part Five, *A Night Like Any Other*):
Vittorio De Sica
Screenplay: Cesare Zavattini, Fabio Carpi, Enzo Muzii
Cinematographer: Guisseppe Rotunno
Cast: Silvana Mangano (Giovanna); Clint Eastwood
(Charlie); Gianni Gori (Diabolik); Paolo Gozlino
(Mandrake); Angelo Santi (Flash Gordon);
Piero Torrisi (Batman)
Produced 1965 see page 52

The Good, the Bad and the Ugly
(Produzioni Europee Associates/United Artists)
161 minutes
Director: Sergio Leone
Screenplay: Luciano Vincenzoni, Sergio Leone
Cinematographer: Tonino Delli Colli
Cast: Clint Eastwood (Blondie); Eli Wallach (Tuco);
Lee Van Cleef (Sentenza/Angel Eyes); Aldo Giuffrè
(Union Captain); Luigi Pistilli (Father Pablo Ramirez);
Rada Rassimov (Maria)
Opened December 15, 1966 see page 56

Hang 'Em High (United Artists/Malpaso)
114 minutes
Director: Ted Post
Screenplay: Leonard Freeman, Mel Goldberg
Cinematographers: Richard Kline, Leonard Sough
Cast: Clint Eastwood (Marshal Jed Cooper);
Inger Stevens (Rachel Warren); Ed Begley
(Captain Wilson); Pat Hingle (Judge Adam Fenton);
Ben Johnson (Marshal Dave Bliss); Charles McGraw
(Sheriff Ray Calhoun); Ruth White (Madame "Peaches"
Sophie)
Opened August 3, 1968 see page 60

Coogan's Bluff (Universal/Malpaso) 93 minutes
Director: Don Siegel
Screenplay: Herman Miller, Dean Riesner,
Howard Rodman
Cinematographer: Bud Thackery
Cast: Clint Eastwood (Walt Coogan); Lee J. Cobb
(Det. Lt. McElroy); Susan Clark (Julie Roth);
Tisha Sterling (Linny Raven); Don Stroud
(James Ringerman); Betty Field (Ellen Ringerman);
Tom Tully (Sheriff McCrea); Melodie Johnson (Millie)
Opened October 2, 1968 see page 64

Where Eagles Dare (Metro-Goldwyn-Mayer)
158 minutes
Director: Brian G. Hutton
Screenplay: Alistair MacLean
Cinematographer: Arthur Ibbetson
Cast: Richard Burton (Maj. Jonathan Smith);
Clint Eastwood (Lt. Morris Schaffer); Mary Ure
(Mary Elison); Patrick Wymark (Col. Wyatt Turner);
Michael Hordern (Adm. Rolland)
Opened December 4, 1968 see page 68

Paint Your Wagon (Paramount/Malpaso)
158 minutes
Director: Joshua Logan
Screenplay: Alan Jay Lerner
Cinematographers: William Fraker, Loyal Griggs,
Nelson Tyler
Cast: Lee Marvin (Ben Rumson); Clint Eastwood
(Pardner); Jean Seberg (Elizabeth); Harve Presnell
(Rotten Luck Willie); Ray Walston (Mad Jack Duncan);
Tom Ligon (Horton Fenty); Alan Dexter (Parson);
William O'Connell (Horace Tabor)
Opened October 15, 1969 see page 72

Two Mules for Sister Sara (Universal/Malpaso)
116 minutes
Director: Don Siegel
Screenplay: Albert Maltz
Cinematographer: Gabriel Figueroa
Cast: Shirley MacLaine (Sara); Clint Eastwood (Hogan);
Manuel Fábregas (Col. Beltran); Alberto Morin (Gen.
LeClaire); David Estuardo (Juan); José Chávez (Horatio)
Opened February 12, 1970 see page 76

Kelly's Heroes (Metro-Goldwyn-Mayer) 144 minutes
Director: Brian G. Hutton
Screenplay: Troy Kennedy-Martin
Cinematographer: Gabriel Figueroa
Cast: Clint Eastwood (Pvt. Kelly); Telly Savalas
(MSgt. Big Joe); Don Rickles (SSgt. Crapgame);
Carroll O'Connor (Maj. Gen. Colt); Donald Sutherland
(Sgt. Oddball); Gavin MacLeod (Moriarty); Hal Buckley
(Capt. Maitland)
Opened June 23, 1970 see page 80

The Beguiled (Universal/Malpaso) 105 minutes
Director: Don Siegel
Screenplay: John B. Sherry, Grimes Grice
Cinematographer: Bruce Surtees
Cast: Clint Eastwood (Cpl. John McBurney); Geraldine
Page (Martha Farnsworth); Elizabeth Hartman (Edwina
Dabney); Jo Ann Harris (Carol); Darleen Carr (Doris);
Mae Mercer (Hallie); Pamelyn Ferdin (Amelia); Melody Thomas
Scott (Abigail); Peggy Drier (Lizzie); Patricia Mattick (Janie)
Opened March 31, 1971 see page 84

Play Misty for Me (Universal/Malpaso) 102 minutes
Director: Clint Eastwood
Screenplay: Jo Heims, Dean Riesner
Cinematographer: Bruce Surtees
Cast: Clint Eastwood (Dave Garver); Jessica Walter
(Evelyn Draper); Donna Mills (Tobie Williams);
John Larch (Sgt. McCallum); Jack Ging (Frank);
Irene Hervey (Madge); James McEachin (Al Monte);
Clarice Taylor (Birdie); Don Siegel (Murphy)
Opened November 12, 1971 see page 88

Dirty Harry (Warner Bros./Seven Arts/Malpaso)
102 minutes
Director: Don Siegel
Screenplay: Harry Julian Fink, Rita M. Fink, Dean Riesner
Cinematographer: Bruce Surtees
Cast: Clint Eastwood (Insp. Harry Callahan);
Harry Guardino (Lt. Al Bressler); Reni Santoni
(Insp. Chico Gonzalez); John Vernon (The Mayor);
Andrew Robinson (Scorpio Killer); John Larch (The Chief);
John Mitchum (Insp. Frank DiGiorgio)
Opened December 23, 1971 see page 92

Joe Kidd (Universal/Malpaso) 88 minutes
Director: John Sturges
Screenplay: Elmore Leonard
Cinematographer: Bruce Surtees
Cast: Clint Eastwood (Joe Kidd); Robert Duvall
(Frank Harlan); John Saxon (Luis Chama); Don Stroud
(Lamarr Simms); Stella Garcia (Helen Sanchez);
James Wainwright (Olin Mingo); Paul Koslo (Roy Gannon)
Opened July 14, 1972 see page 100

High Plains Drifter (Universal/Malpaso) 105 minutes
Director: Clint Eastwood
Screenplay: Ernest Tidyman
Cinematographer: Bruce Surtees
Cast: Clint Eastwood (The Stranger); Verna Bloom
(Sarah Belding); Marianna Hill (Callie Travers);
Mitch Ryan (Dave Drake); Jack Ging (Morgan Allen);
Stefan Gierasch (Mayor Jason Hobart); Ted Hartley
(Lewis Belding)
Opened August 22, 1973 see page 104

Breezy (Universal/Malpaso) 108 minutes
Director: Clint Eastwood
Screenplay: Jo Heims
Cinematographer: Frank Stanley
Cast: William Holden (Frank Harmon); Kay Lenz (Breezy);
Roger C. Carmel (Bob Henderson); Marj Dusay
(Betty Tobin); Joan Hotchkis (Paula Harmon);
Jamie Smith-Jackson (Marcy)
Opened November 18, 1973 see page 108

Magnum Force (Warner Bros./Malpaso)
124 minutes
Director: Ted Post
Screenplay: John Milius, Michael Cimino
Cinematographer: Frank Stanley
Cast: Clint Eastwood (Insp. "Dirty" Harry Callahan);
Hal Holbrook (Lt. Neil Briggs); Mitch Ryan (Officer
Charlie McCoy); David Soul (Officer John Davis);
Tim Matheson (Officer Phil Sweet); Kip Niven
(Officer Red Astrachan); Robert Urich
(Officer Mike Grimes)
Opened December 25, 1973 see page 112

Thunderbolt and Lightfoot (United Artists/
Malpaso) 115 minutes
Director: Michael Cimino
Screenplay: Michael Cimino
Cinematographer: Frank Stanley
Cast: Clint Eastwood (John "Thunderbolt" Doherty);
Jeff Bridges (Lightfoot); Geoffrey Lewis (Eddie Goody);
Catherine Bach (Melody); Gary Busey (Curly)
Opened May 23, 1974 see page 116

The Eiger Sanction (Universal/Malpaso)
123 minutes
Director: Clint Eastwood
Screenplay: Warren B. Murphy, Hal Dresner,
Rod Whitaker
Cinematographer: Frank Stanley
Cast: Clint Eastwood (Dr. Jonathan Hemlock);
George Kennedy (Ben Bowman); Vonetta McGee
(Jemima Brown); Jack Cassidy (Miles Mellough);
Heidi Brühl (Mrs. Anna Montaigne); Thayer David
(Dragon); Reiner Schöne (Karl Freytag)
Opened May 21, 1975 see page 120

The Outlaw Josey Wales (Warner Bros./Malpaso)
135 minutes
Director: Clint Eastwood
Screenplay: Philip Kaufman, Sonia Chernus
Cinematographer: Bruce Surtees
Cast: Clint Eastwood (Josey Wales); Chief Dan George
(Lone Watie); Sondra Locke (Laura Lee); Bill McKinney
(Terrill); John Vernon (Fletcher); Paula Trueman
(Grandma Sarah); Sam Bottoms (Jamie)
Opened June 30, 1976 see page 124

The Enforcer (Warner Bros./Malpaso) 96 minutes
Director: James Fargo
Screenplay: Stirling Silliphant, Dean Riesner
Cinematographer: Charles W. Short
Cast: Clint Eastwood (Insp. "Dirty" Harry Callahan);
Tyne Daly (Insp. Kate Moore); Harry Guardino
(Lt. Al Bressler); Bradford Dillman (Capt. McKay);
John Mitchum (Insp. Frank DiGiorgio); DeVeren Bookwalter
(Bobby Maxwell); John Crawford (The Mayor)
Opened December 22, 1976 see page 130

The Gauntlet (Warner Bros./Malpaso) 109 minutes
Director: Clint Eastwood
Screenplay: Michael Butler, Dennis Shryack
Cinematographer: Rexford Metz
Cast: Clint Eastwood (Ben Shockley); Sondra Locke
(Gus Mally); Pat Hingle (Josephson); William Prince
(Blakelock); Bill McKinney (Constable);
Michael Cavanaugh (Feyderspiel)
Opened December 21, 1977 see page 134

Every Which Way But Loose (Warner Bros./
Malpaso) 110 minutes
Director: James Fargo
Screenplay: Jeremy Joe Kronsberg
Cinematographer: Rexford Metz
Cast: Clint Eastwood (Philo Beddoe); Sondra Locke
(Lynn Halsey-Taylor); Geoffrey Lewis (Orville Boggs);
Beverly D'Angelo (Echo); Walter Barnes (Tank Murdock);
William O'Connell (Elmo)
Opened December 20, 1978 see page 138

Escape from Alcatraz (Paramount/Malpaso) 112 minutes
Director: Don Siegel
Screenplay: Richard Tuggle
Cinematographer: Bruce Surtees
Cast: Clint Eastwood (Frank Morris); Patrick McGoohan (Warden); Roberts Blossom (Doc); Jack Thibeau (Clarence Anglin); Fred Ward (John Anglin); Paul Benjamin (English); Larry Hankin (Charley Butts)
Opened June 22, 1979 see page 142

Bronco Billy (Warner Bros.) 116 minutes
Director: Clint Eastwood
Screenplay: Dennis Hackin
Cinematographer: David Worth
Cast: Clint Eastwood (Bronco Billy); Sondra Locke (Antoinette Lily); Geoffrey Lewis (John Arlington); Scatman Crothers (Doc Lynch); Bill McKinney (Lefty LeBow); Sam Bottoms (Leonard James); Dan Vadis (Chief Big Eagle)
Opened June 11, 1980 see page 146

Any Which Way You Can (Warner Bros./Malpaso) 115 minutes
Director: Buddy Van Horn
Screenplay: Stanford Sherman
Cinematographer: David Worth
Cast: Clint Eastwood (Philo Beddoe); Sondra Locke (Lynn Halsey-Taylor); Geoffrey Lewis (Orville Boggs); William Smith (Jack Wilson); Harry Guardino (James Beekman); Ruth Gordon (Senovia "Ma" Boggs)
Opened December 17, 1980 see page 150

Firefox (Warner Bros./Malpaso) 136 minutes
Director: Clint Eastwood
Screenplay: Alex Lasker, Wendell Wellman, and Craig Thomas
Cinematographer: Bruce Surtees
Cast: Clint Eastwood (Mitchell Gant); Freddie Jones (Kenneth Aubrey); David Huffman (Captain Buckholz); Warren Clarke (Pavel Upenskoy); Ronald Lacey (Semelovsky); Kenneth Colley (Colonel Kontarsky)
Opened June 18, 1982 see page 154

Honkytonk Man (Warner Bros./Malpaso) 122 minutes
Director: Clint Eastwood
Screenplay: Clancy Carlile
Cinematographer: Bruce Surtees
Cast: Clint Eastwood (Red Stovall); Kyle Eastwood (Whit); John McIntire (Grandpa); Alexa Kenin (Marlene); Verna Bloom (Emmy); Matt Clark (Virgil); Barry Corbin (Arnspringer); Jerry Hardin (Snuffy)
Opened December 15, 1982 see page 158

Sudden Impact (Warner Bros./Malpaso) 117 minutes
Director: Clint Eastwood
Screenplay: Joseph C. Stinson
Cinematographer: Bruce Surtees
Cast: Clint Eastwood (Harry Callahan); Sondra Locke (Jennifer Spencer); Pat Hingle (Chief Jannings); Bradford Dillman (Captain Briggs); Paul Drake (Mick); Audrie J. Neenan (Ray Parkins); Jack Thibeau (Kruger); Michael Currie (Lt. Donnelly)
Opened December 9, 1983 see page 162

Tightrope (Warner Bros./Malpaso) 114 minutes
Director: Richard Tuggle
Screenplay: Richard Tuggle
Cinematographer: Bruce Surtees
Cast: Clint Eastwood (Capt. Wes Block); Geneviève Bujold (Beryl Thibodeaux); Dan Hedaya (Det. Molinari); Alison Eastwood (Amanda Block); Jenny Beck (Penny Block); Marco St. John (Leander Rolfe); Rebecca Perle (Becky Jacklin)
Opened August 17, 1984 see page 166

City Heat (Warner Bros./Malpaso/Deliverance) 93 minutes
Director: Richard Benjamin
Screenplay: Sam O. Brown (Blake Edwards), Joseph C. Stinson
Cinematographer: Nick McLean
Cast: Clint Eastwood (Lieutenant Speer); Burt Reynolds (Mike Murphy); Jane Alexander (Addy); Madeline Kahn (Caroline Howley); Rip Torn (Primo Pitt); Irene Cara (Ginny Lee); Richard Roundtree (Dehl Swift); Tony Lo Bianco (Leon Coll); William Sanderson (Lonnie Ash); Nicholas Worth (Troy Roker); Robert Davi (Nino); Jude Farese (Dub Slack); John Hancock (Fat Freddy); Jack Thibeau (Garage Soldier); Gerald S. O'Loughlin (Counterman Louie)
Opened December 7, 1984 see page 170

Pale Rider (Warner Bros./Malpaso) 115 minutes
Director: Clint Eastwood
Screenplay: Michael Butler, Dennis Shryack
Cinematographer: Bruce Surtees
Cast: Clint Eastwood (Preacher); Michael Moriarty (Hull Barret); Carrie Snodgress (Sarah Wheeler); Chris Penn (Josh LaHood); Richard Dysart (Coy LaHood); Sydney Penny (Megan Wheeler); Richard Kiel (Club); Doug McGrath (Spider Conway)
Opened June 28, 1985 see page 174

Heartbreak Ridge (Warner Bros./Malpaso) 130 minutes
Director: Clint Eastwood
Screenplay: James Carabatsos
Cinematographer: Jack N. Green
Cast: Clint Eastwood (Sergeant Thomas Highway); Marsha Mason (Aggie); Everett McGill (Major Malcolm A. Powers); Moses Gunn (Staff Sergeant Webster); Eileen Heckart (Little Mary Jackson); Mario Van Peebles (Corporal "Stitch" Jones)
Opened December 5, 1986 see page 178

Bird (Warner Bros./Malpaso) 161 minutes
Director: Clint Eastwood
Screenplay: Joel Oliansky
Cinematographer: Jack N. Green
Cast: Forest Whitaker (Charlie "Bird" Parker); Diane Venora (Chan Parker); Michael Zelniker (Red Rodney); Samuel E. Wright (Dizzy Gillespie); Keith David (Buster Franklin); Michael McGuire (Brewster); James Handy (Esteves); Damon Whitaker (Young Bird)
Opened June 1, 1988 see page 182

The Dead Pool (Warner Bros./Malpaso) 91 minutes
Director: Buddy Van Horn
Screenplay: Steve Sharon
Cinematographer: Jack N. Green
Cast: Clint Eastwood (Insp. "Dirty" Harry Callahan); Patricia Clarkson (Samantha Walker); Liam Neeson (Peter Swan); Evan C. Kim (Insp. Al Quan); David Hunt (Harlan Rook/Ed Butler); Michael Currie (Capt. Donnelly)
Opened July 13, 1988 see page 188

Pink Cadillac (Warner Bros./Malpaso) 122 minutes
Director: Buddy Van Horn
Screenplay: John Eskow
Cinematographer: Jack N. Green
Cast: Clint Eastwood (Tommy Nowak); Bernadette Peters (Lou Ann McGuinn); Timothy Carhart (Roy McGuinn); Tiffany Gail Robinson (McGuinn Baby); Angela Louise Robinson (McGuinn Baby); John Dennis Johnston (Waycross); Michael Des Barres (Alex)
Opened May 26, 1989 see page 192

White Hunter Black Heart (Warner Bros./Malpaso) 112 minutes
Director: Clint Eastwood
Screenplay: Peter Viertel, James Bridges, Burt Kennedy
Cinematographer: Jack N. Green
Cast: Clint Eastwood (John Wilson); Jeff Fahey (Pete Verrill); Charlotte Cornwell (Miss Wilding); Norman Lumsden (Butler George); George Dzundza (Paul Landers); Edward Tudor-Pole (Reissar)
Opened May 16, 1990 see page 196

The Rookie (Warner Bros./Malpaso) 120 minutes
Director: Clint Eastwood
Screenplay: Boaz Yakin, Scott Spiegel
Cinematographer: Jack N. Green
Cast: Clint Eastwood (Nick Pulovski); Charlie Sheen (David Ackerman); Raul Julia (Strom); Sonia Braga (Liesl); Tom Skerritt (Eugene Ackerman); Lara Flynn Boyle (Sarah); Pepe Serna (Lt. Ray Garcia)
Opened December 7, 1990 see page 200

Unforgiven (Warner Bros./Malpaso) 131 minutes
Director: Clint Eastwood
Screenplay: David Webb Peoples
Cinematographer: Jack N. Green
Cast: Clint Eastwood (William "Bill" Munny); Gene Hackman (Little Bill Daggett); Morgan Freeman (Ned Logan); Richard Harris (English Bob); Jaimz Woolvett (The Schofield Kid); Saul Rubinek (W.W. Beauchamp); Frances Fisher (Strawberry Alice); Anna Levine (Delilah Fitzgerald)
Opened August 7, 1992 see page 204

In the Line of Fire (Castle Rock/Columbia) 128 minutes
Director: Wolfgang Petersen
Screenplay: Jeff Maguire
Cinematographer: John Bailey
Cast: Clint Eastwood (Frank Horrigan); John Malkovich (Mitch Leary); Rene Russo (Lilly Raines); Dylan McDermott (Al D'Andrea); Gary Cole (Bill Watts); Fred Dalton Thompson (Harry Sargent); John Mahoney (Sam Campagna); Gregory Alan Williams (Matt Wilder); Jim Curley (President); Sally Hughes (First Lady)
Opened July 9, 1993 see page 212

A Perfect World (Warner Bros./Malpaso) 138 minutes
Director: Clint Eastwood
Screenplay: John Lee Hancock
Cinematographer: Jack N. Green
Cast: Kevin Costner (Robert "Butch" Haynes); Clint Eastwood (Chief Red Garnett); Laura Dern (Sally Gerber); T.J. Lowther (Phillip "Buzz" Perry); Keith Szarabajka (Terry Pugh); Leo Burmester (Tom Adler); Paul Hewitt (Dick Suttle); Bradley Whitford (Bobby Lee)
Opened November 24, 1993 see page 216

The Bridges of Madison Country
(Warner Bros./Malpaso) 134 minutes
Director: Clint Eastwood
Screenplay: Richard LaGravenese
Cinematographer: Jack N. Green
Cast: Clint Eastwood (Robert Kincaid); Meryl Streep (Francesca Johnson); Annie Corley (Carolyn Johnson); Victor Slezak (Michael Johnson); Jim Haynie (Richard Johnson); Sarah Kathryn Schmitt (Young Carolyn); Christopher Kroon (Young Michael)
Opened June 2, 1995 see page 220

Absolute Power (Castle Rock Entertainment/
Malpaso) 121 minutes
Director: Clint Eastwood
Screenplay: William Goldman
Cinematographer: Jack N. Green
Cast: Clint Eastwood (Luther Whitney); Gene Hackman (President Allen Richmond); Ed Harris (Seth Frank); Laura Linney (Kate Whitney); Scott Glenn (Bill Burton); Dennis Haysbert (Tim Collin); Judy Davis (Gloria Russell)
Opened February 14, 1997 see page 224

Midnight in the Garden of Good and Evil
(Warner Bros./Malpaso) 155 minutes
Director: Clint Eastwood
Screenplay: John Lee Hancock
Cinematographer: Jack N. Green
Cast: John Cusack (John Kelso); Kevin Spacey (Jim Williams); Jack Thompson (Sonny Seiler); Irma P. Hall (Minerva); Jude Law (Billy Hanson); Alison Eastwood (Mandy Nicholls); Paul Hipp (Joe Odom); Lady Chablis (Chablis Deveau)
Opened November 21, 1997 see page 228

True Crime (Warner Bros./Malpaso) 127 minutes
Director: Clint Eastwood
Screenplay: Larry Gross, Paul Brickman, Stephen Schiff
Cinematographer: Jack N. Green
Cast: Clint Eastwood (Steve Everett); Isaiah Washington (Frank Louis Beechum); Lisa Gay Hamilton (Bonnie Beechum); James Woods (Alan Mann); Denis Leary (Bob Findley); Bernard Hill (Warden Luther Plunkitt); Diane Venora (Barbara Everett)
Opened March 19, 1999 see page 232

Space Cowboys (Warner Bros./Malpaso)
130 minutes
Director: Clint Eastwood
Screenplay: Ken Kaufman, Howard Klausner
Cinematographer: Jack N. Green
Cast: Clint Eastwood (Frank Corvin); Tommy Lee Jones (Hawk Hawkins); Donald Sutherland (Jerry O'Neill); James Garner (Tank Sullivan); James Cromwell (Bob Gerson); Marcia Gay Harden (Sara Holland); William Devane (Eugene Davis)
Opened August 4, 2000 see page 236

Blood Work (Warner Bros./Malpaso) 110 minutes
Director: Clint Eastwood
Screenplay: Brian Helgeland
Cinematographer: Tom Stern
Cast: Clint Eastwood (Terry McCaleb); Jeff Daniels (Jasper "Buddy" Noone); Anjelica Huston (Dr. Bonnie Fox); Wanda De Jesus (Graciella Rivers); Tina Lifford (Detective Jaye Winston); Paul Rodriguez (Detective Ronaldo Arrango)
Opened August 9, 2002 see page 240

Mystic River (Warner Bros./Malpaso) 137 minutes
Director: Clint Eastwood
Screenplay: Brian Helgeland
Cinematographer: Tom Stern
Cast: Sean Penn (Jimmy Markum); Tim Robbins (Dave Boyle); Kevin Bacon (Sean Devine); Laurence Fishburne (Sgt. Whitey Powers); Marcia Gay Harden (Celeste Boyle); Laura Linney (Annabeth Markum); Kevin Chapman (Val Savage)
Opened October 15, 2003 see page 244

Million Dollar Baby (Warner Bros./Malpaso)
132 minutes
Director: Clint Eastwood
Screenplay: Paul Haggis
Cinematographer: Tom Stern
Cast: Clint Eastwood (Frankie Dunn); Hilary Swank (Maggie Fitzgerald); Morgan Freeman (Eddie Scrap-Iron Dupris); Jay Baruchel (Danger Barch); Mike Colter (Big Willie Little); Lucia Rijker (Billie "The Blue Bear"); Brian F. O'Byrne (Father Horvak)
Opened December 15, 2004 see page 250

Flags of Our Fathers (Warner Bros./Malpaso)
132 minutes
Director: Clint Eastwood
Screenplay: William Broyles Jr., Paul Haggis
Cinematographer: Tom Stern
Cast: Ryan Phillippe (John "Doc" Bradley); Jesse Bradford (Rene Gagnon); Adam Beach (Ira Hayes); John Benjamin Hickey (Keyes Beech); John Slattery (Bud Gerber); Barry Pepper (Mike Strank); Jamie Bell (Ralph "Iggy" Ignatowski); Paul Walker (Hank Hansen)
Opened October 20, 2006 see page 258

Letters from Iwo Jima (Warner Bros./Malpaso)
141 minutes
Director: Clint Eastwood
Screenplay: Iris Yamashita
Cinematographer: Tom Stern
Cast: Ken Watanabe (General Kuribayashi); Kazunari Ninomiya (Saigo); Tsuyoshi Ihara (Baron Nishi); Ryo Kase (Shimizu); Shido Nakamura (Lieutenant Ito); Hiroshi Watanabe (Lieutenant Fujita); Takumi Bando (Captain Tanida); Yuki Matsuzaki (Nozaki)
Opened December 9, 2006 see page 262

Changeling (Universal/Malpaso) 141 minutes
Director: Clint Eastwood
Screenplay: J. Michael Straczynski
Cinematographer: Tom Stern
Cast: Angelina Jolie (Christine Collins); Gattlin Griffith (Walter Collins); Michelle Gunn (Sandy); Frank Wood (Ben Harris); John Malkovich (Rev. Gustav Briegleb); Colm Feore (Chief James E. Davis); Devon Conti (Arthur Hutchins); Jeffrey Donovan (Captain J.J. Jones); John Harrington Bland (Dr. John Montgomery); Pamela Dunlap (Mrs. Fox)
Opened October 31, 2008 see page 268

Gran Torino (Warner Bros./Malpaso) 116 minutes
Director: Clint Eastwood
Screenplay: Nick Schenk
Cinematographer: Tom Stern
Cast: Clint Eastwood (Walt Kowalski); Christopher Carley (Father Janovich); Bee Vang (Thao Vang Lor); Ahney Her (Sue Lor); Brian Haley (Mitch Kowalski); Geraldine Hughes (Karen Kowalski); Dreama Walker (Ashley Kowalski); Brian Howe (Steve Kowalski); Scott Eastwood (Trey)
Opened January 9, 2009 see page 272

Invictus (Warner Bros./Malpaso) 134 minutes
Director: Clint Eastwood
Screenplay: Anthony Peckham
Cinematographer: Tom Stern
Cast: Matt Damon (Francois Pienaar); Morgan Freeman (Nelson Mandela); Langley Kirkwood (George); Grant Roberts (Ruben Kruger); Penny Downie (Mrs. Pinnear); Robert Hobbs (Willem)
Opened December 11, 2009 see page 276

Hereafter (Warner Bros./Malpaso) 129 minutes
Director: Clint Eastwood
Screenplay: Peter Morgan
Cinematographer: Tom Stern
Cast: Matt Damon (George Lonegan); Cécile De France (Marie LeLay); Bryce Dallas Howard (Melanie); Frankie McLaren (Marcus/Jason); George McLaren (Marcus/Jason); Thierry Neuvic (Didier)
Opened October 15, 2010 see page 280

J. Edgar (Warner Bros./Malpaso/Imagine
Entertainment) 137 minutes
Director: Clint Eastwood
Screenplay: Dustin Lance Black
Cinematographer: Tom Stern
Cast: Leonardo DiCaprio (J. Edgar Hoover); Naomi Watts (Helen Gandy); Josh Lucas (Charles Lindbergh); Armie Hammer (Clyde Tolson); Ed Westwick (Agent Smith); Judi Dench (Anne Marie Hoover); Dermot Mulroney (Colonel Schwarzkopf)
Opened November 9, 2011 see page 284

Trouble with the Curve (Warner Bros./Malpaso)
111 minutes
Director: Robert Lorenz
Screenplay: Randy Brown
Cinematographer: Tom Stern
Cast: Clint Eastwood (Gus); Justin Timberlake (Johnny); Amy Adams (Mickey); John Goodman (Pete Klein); Chelcie Ross (Smitty); Raymond Anthony Thomas (Lucious); Ed Lauter (Max); Clifton Guterman (Neil)
Opened September 21, 2012 see page 287

Jersey Boys (Warner Bros./GK Films/RatPac
Entertainment) 135 minutes
Director: Clint Eastwood
Screenplay: Marshall Brickman, Rick Elice, John Logan
Cinematographer: Tom Stern
Cast: John Lloyd Young (Frankie Valli); Vincent Piazza (Tommy DeVito); Erich Bergen (Bob Gaudio); Michael Lomenda (Nick Massi); Christopher Walken (Angelo 'Gyp' DeCarlo); Joseph Russo (Joe Pesci)
Opened June 20, 2014 see page 287

OPPOSITE The singular good looks of the budding young actor in profile, 1960.
OVERLEAF Clint as Walt Kowalski in *Gran Torino* – as tough as any Eastwood hero has ever been.

Picture credits